The Lyle
Price Guide
to
COLLECTIBLES

D1311220

The publishers wish to express their sincere thanks to the following for their kind
help and assistance in the production of this volume:

ANNETTE CURTIS
JANICE MONCRIEFF
MARGOT RUTHERFORD
JENNIFER KNOX
NICHOLA PARK
KAREN KILGOUR
JOSEPHINE McLAREN
TANYA FAIRBAIRN

While every care has been taken in the compiling of information contained in this
volume the publishers cannot accept any liability for loss, financial or otherwise,
incurred by reliance placed on the information herein.

SBN 0-86248-043-4

Printed and bound by R. J. Acford, Chichester, Sussex.

Price Guide to COLLECTIBLES

Time was when collectors were either elderly eccentrics or schoolkids practising to be elderly eccentrics.

Maybe it's the speed at which life is moving nowadays, with new technology creating new materials and totally new tastes every other week, maybe it's more people having more money to spend and more leisure time in which to spend it, maybe it's just a reaction against the feeling of impermanence fostered by our throwaway society, but it seems that the whole world is going on a collecting jag. And why not?

The collecting bug can bite at any time and there's just no telling what form the infection will take. I know of a retired colonel who has a large collection of Teddy Bears — and can talk for hours on the subject, and then there's the Sussex housewife whose obsession is model trains and steam engines.

The really nice thing is that, in most cases, the actual objects collected are only part of the story. As the collection grows, so does the knowledge of the subject. Who knows — you could be on the way to becoming a world's authority on the development of the mediaeval hourglass — and all because you were once given an egg-timer with 'Souvenir of Shanklin' pokerworked round the rim.

The other nice thing, of course, is that antiques in general, and collectibles in particular, are rising in value.

So how do you get onto this treasure trail?

First of all, you must look around for something you can relate to — and make sure you have room to accommodate a collection of your chosen objects. If carved oak makes you wince, for example, there would be little point in starting a collection of Jacobean four-poster beds. Particularly if you live in a small maisonette on the twenty-fourth floor.

Having found something to your taste — and you probably already own something which will make a good basis for a collection — go out and look around. Jumble sales, white elephant stalls, the barrows tucked away at the end of less trendy street markets, junk shops, Oxfam shops, 'box and contents' lots at auction sales, closing down sales of long-established shops, even your local municipal rubbish tip could well provide you with really first-class examples.

There are treasures all around, but there are no maps plastered with great big Xs, and, anyway, half the excitement of collecting lies in the random search being rewarded with a prize — even if it is someone else's junk.

Tony Curtis

CONTENTS

Advertising Signs. 11
American Indianware 16
Amusement Machines. 22
Animalia 26
Armour .28
Autograph Letters 30
Automatons 38
Automobilia 41
Badges. .44
Banknotes 47
Bayonets 51
Beer Bottle Labels 53
Belleek .58
Bells 59
Berlin Woolwork 60
Bible Boxes 61
Bicycles. 62
Birdcages 64
Birds. 65
Biscuit Tins 66
Blue & White China 67
Books 69
Bottles .76
Bronze Animals. 80
Buckles .82
Bus Tickets 84
Butter Stamps. 90
Buttons .91
Cameras. 92
Cane Handles 96
Car Mascots 97
Card Cases 98
Cards 99
Carnival Glass 102
Chamber Pots 103
Children's Books 104
Cigar Bands 110
Cigarette Cards 112
Cigarette Cases 120
Cigarette Packets 122
Clarice Cliff 130
Cloisonne. 131
Comics 132
Commemorative China 136
Copper & Brass 139

Corkscrews. 142
Costume 145
Costume Design 150
Crested China 154
Cups & Saucers 157
Decanters. 159
Decanter Labels 160
Decoys 161
De Morgan 167
Dinky Toys 168
Disneyana 171
Dolls. .175
Dolls' Houses 182
Doorstops 184
Doulton. 185
Egg Cups 187
Electric Light Bulbs 188
Enamel 189
Etuis. .190
Fairground Gallopers 191
Fairings 192
Fans 198
Firemarks 201
Fishing Reels 204
Flags. .205
Games. 206
Gloves. 209
Goldscheider 210
Goss 211
Gramophone Needle Tins 216
Gramophones & Phonographs 221
Hair Combs 224
Hat Pins. 225
Hats 226
Horn 227
Horse Brasses 228
Icons. .229
Inros 233
Irons. .236
Ivory. .237
Jewellery 239
Keys 241
Lace 242
Leach .243
Lead Soldiers 244

Liberty 246
Locks 247
Magic Catalogues 248
Maps 251
Masks 256
Martinware 257
Mary Gregory 258
Match Box Labels 259
Match Cases 265
Matchstrikers 266
Medals 270
Medical 273
Minerals 274
Miniature Furniture 275
Miniatures 276
Model Planes 278
Model Ships 279
Model Trains 282
Models 284
Mottoware 286
Money Banks 287
Moorcroft Pottery 289
Mulls 290
Musical Boxes 291
Musical Instruments 294
Mustard Pots 296
Nautical Items 297
Nazi Memorabilia 298
Netsuke 300
Nutmeg Graters 303
Paperweights 306
Parian 309
Patch Boxes 310
Photographs 311
Pictorial China 322
Pin Boxes 324
Pin-Up Magazines 326
Pipes 328
Pin Cushions 331
Pistols 332
Plates 334
Polyphones 336
Postcards 337
Posters 343
Pot Lids 347
Powder Flasks 349
Prams 350
Prattware 351

Pub Signs 352
Purses 354
Quilts 355
Radios 358
Railway Tickets 360
Railwayana 362
Rattles 364
Razors 365
Robertson's Golly Badges 366
Rock'n Roll 368
Royal Dux 377
Ruskin Pottery 378
Samplers 379
Scent Bottles 382
Scrimshaw 384
Seals 385
Shells 386
Shoes 387
Shop Signs 388
Signed Photographs 389
Slag Glass 392
Snuff Bottles 393
Snuff Boxes 398
Spoons 400
Sporting Memorabilia 402
Staffordshire Figures 404
Stevengraphs 406
Tea Caddies 410
Teapots 412
Telephones 414
Thimbles 415
Tiles 416
Tobacco Tins 417
Tools 418
Toys 420
Transport 423
Treen 425
Tsubas 426
Tunbridgeware 428
Typewriters 429
Valentine Cards 430
Vinaigrettes 432
Walking Sticks 434
Watchstands 435
Watches 436
Weathervanes 440
Whistles 441
Wood, Ralph 442

ACKNOWLEDGEMENTS

Abbots, *The Hill, Wickham Market, Suffolk.*
Aldridge's, *130-132 Walcot Street, Bath, Avon.*
Alfie's Antique Market, *13-15 Church Street, London.*
Allen & May, *18 Bridge Street, Andover.*
Anderson & Garland, *Anderson House, Market Street, Newcastle.*
Gilbert Baitson, *194 Anlaby Road, Hull, Yorks.*
Richard Baker & Thomson, *9 Hamilton Street, Birkenhead, Merseyside.*
T. Bannister & Co., *7 Calbourne, Haywards Heath, W. Sussex.*
Barber's, *Town Mill, Bagshot Road, Chobham, Surrey.*
Stan Beaumont, *13a Oakfield, Off Oakfield Road, Anfield, Liverpool. (Cigar Bands)*
Tessa Bennett, *Bennett Book Auctions, 72 Radcliffe Terrace, Edinburgh. (Cigarette Cards)*
Biddle & Webb, *Ladywood, Middleway, Birmingham.*
Boardman's, *Station Road Corner, Haverhill, Suffolk.*
Bonhams, *Montpelier Galleries, Montpelier Street, London.*
Bonsor Penningtons, *82 Eden Street, Kingston-on-Thames.*
John F. Bradshaw, *33 Shaw Crescent, Sanderstead, Surrey. (Railway Tickets)*
British Antique Exporters, *206 London Road, Burgess Hill, W. Sussex.*
Brogden & Co., *38 & 39 Silver Street, Lincoln.*
Wm. H. Brown, *31 St. Peter's Hill, Grantham, Lincs.*
Bruton, Knowles & Co., *Albion Chambers, 55 Barton Street, Gloucester.*
Buckell & Ballard, *49 Parsons Street, Banbury, Oxfordshire.*
Burrows & Day, *39/41 Bank Street, Ashford, Kent.*
Burtenshaw Walker, *66 High Street, Lewes, Suffolk.*
Butler & Hatch Waterman, *86 High Street, Hythe, Kent.*
Butterfield & Butterfield, *1244 Sutter Street, San Francisco.*
Button, Menhenitt & Mutton, *Belmont Auction Rooms, Wadebridge.*
Alan Cadwallender, *63 Green Street, Middleton, Manchester. (Comics)*
Capes, Dunn & Co., *The Auction Galleries, 38 Charles Street, Manchester.*
Chancellor's, *31 High Street, Ascot, Berks.*
H.C. Chapman & Son, *The Auction Mart, North Street, Scarborough.*
Christie's, *8 King Street, St. James's, London.*
Christie's & Edmiston's, *164-166 Bath Street, Glasgow.*
Christie's S. Kensington, *85 Old Brompton Road, London.*
Clarke Gammon, *45 High Street, Guildford, Surrey.*
Coles, Knapp & Kennedy, *Georgian Rooms, Ross-on-Wye.*
D.G. Cook, *275 Locking Road, Weston-super-Mare, Avon. (Tobacco Tins)*
Cooper Hirst, *Goldway House, Parkway, Chelmsford.*
Crystals Auctions, *Athol Street, Douglas, I.O.M.*
Dacre, Son & Hartley, *1-5 The Grove, Ilkley, Yorks.*
Dee & Atkinson, *The Exchange, Driffield, Yorks.*
Dickinson, Davy & Markham, *10 Wrawby Street, Brigg, S. Humberside.*
Wm. Doyle Galleries Inc., *175 East 87th Street, New York.*
Dreweatt, Watson & Barton, *Donnington Priory, Newbury, Berks.*
Hy. Duke & Son, *40 South Street, Dorchester, Dorset.*
Edwards, Bigwood & Bewlay, *The Old School, Tiddington, Stratford-on-Avon.*
Elliott & Green, *40 High Street, Lymington, Hants.*
R.H. Ellis & Sons, *44-46 High Street, Worthing, Sussex.*

H. Evans & Sons, *Hull, Yorks.*
Farrant & Wightman, *2/3 Newport Street, Old Town, Swindon.*
John Francis, Thomas Jones & Sons, *King Street, Carmarthen.*
Frank H. Fellows & Sons, *Bedford House, 88 Hagley Road, Birmingham.*
John D. Fleming & Co., *Melton House, High Street, Dulverton.*
Fox & Sons, *5 & 7 Salisbury Street, Fordingbridge, Hants.*
Garrod Turner, *50 St. Nicholas Street, Ipswich, Suffolk.*
Geering & Colyer, *Highgate, Hawkhurst, Kent.*
Goss & Crested China Ltd., *N. J. Pine, 62 Murray Road, Horndean, Hants. PO8 9JL.*
  Tel. No: 0705-597440
Andrew Grant, *59-60 Foregate Street, Worcester.*
Graves, Son & Pilcher, *38 Holland Road, Hove, Sussex.*
Gray's Antique Market, *58 Davies Street, London.*
Alistair Grey, *67 Braddon Road, Loughborough, Leics. (Bus Tickets)*
Gribble, Booth & Taylor, *West Street, Axminster, Devon.*
Arthur G. Griffiths & Sons, *57 Foregate Street, Worcester.*
Rowland Gorringe, *15 North Street, Lewes, Sussex.*
Hall Wateridge & Owen, *Welsh Bridge, Shrewsbury.*
James Harrison, *35 West End, Hebden Bridge, W. Yorks.*
Heathcote Ball & Co., *47 New Walk, Leicester.*
John Hogbin & Son, *53 High Street, Tenterden, Kent.*
Honiton Galleries, *High Street, Honiton, Devon.*
Edgar Horn, *47 Cornfield Road, Eastbourne, Sussex.*
Hilary Humphries, *15 Dullingham Road, Newmarket, Cambs. (Cigarette Packets)*
Jackson-Stops & Staff, *Fine Art Dept., 14 Curzon Street, London W1.*
Michael Jones, *27 Chinbrook Road, Grove Park, London, SE12 9TQ. (Beer Bottle Labels)*
G.A. Key, *Market Place, Aylesham.*
Lacy Scott & Sons, *3 Hatter Street, Bury St. Edmunds.*
Lalonde Bros. & Parham, *Station Road, Weston-super-Mare.*
Ruth Lambert, *Weston Favell, Northampton. (Gramophone Needle Tins)*
W.H. Lane & Son, *Morrab Road, Penzance, Cornwall.*
Langlois, *10 Waterloo Street, Jersey, C.I.*
Lawrence Fine Art, *South Street, Crewkerne.*
James & Lister Lea, *11 Newhall Street, Birmingham.*
Locke & England, *Walton House, 11 The Parade, Leamington Spa.*
Love's, *St. John's Place, Perth.*
Mallams, *24 St. Michael's Street, Oxford.*
S. Marshall, *23 Lock Laxford, East Kilbride. (Cigarette Cards)*
May, Whetter & Grose, *Cornubia Hall, Par, Cornwall.*
John Milne, *9-11 North Silver Street, Aberdeen.*
Moore, Allen & Innocent, *33 Castle Street, Cirencester.*
Morphets, *4-6 Albert Street, Harrogate, Yorks.*
Morris, Marshall & Poole, *2 Short Bridge Street, Newtown, Powys.*
Alfred Mossop & Co., *Kelsick Road, Ambleside, Cumbria.*
McCartney, Morris & Barker, *Corve Street, Ludlow, Salop.*
Neales, *192 Mansfield Road, Nottingham.*
D.M. Nesbit & Co., *7 Clarendon Road, Southsea, Hants.*
Northampton Auction Galleries, *33-39 Sheep Street, Northampton.*
Nostalgia, *13 Harleslade, Brandy Cove, Bishopston. (Advertising Signs)*
Olivers, *23-24 Market Hill, Sudbury, Suffolk.*
Osmond, Tricks, *Regent Street Auction Rooms, Clifton, Bristol.*
Outhwaite & Litherland, *Kingsway Galleries, Fontenoy Street, Liverpool.*
J.R. Parkinson, Son & Hamer, *14 Bolton Street, Bury, Lancs.*

Parsons, Welch & Cowell, *129 High Street, Sevenoaks, Kent.*
Pattison Partners & Scott, *Ryton.*
Pearsons, *Walcote Chambers, High Street, Winchester.*
Phillips, *7 Blenheim Street, New Bond Street, London.*
Phillips & Brooks, *39 Park End Street, Oxford.*
Phillips & Jolly's, *The Auction Rooms, Old King Street, Bath.*
John H. Raby & Son, *St. Mary's Road, Bradford.*
Samuel Rains & Son, *Trinity House, 114 Northenden Road, Sale, Manchester.*
S. Reeve & V. Gladwish, *17 Montague Road, Uxbridge, Middx. (Match Box Labels)*
Renton & Renton, *16 Albert Street, Harrogate, Yorks.*
Riddetts, *Richmond Hill, The Square, Bournemouth.*
Russell, Baldwin & Bright, *Ryelands Road, Leominster.*
Sandoe, Luce Panes, *Chipping Manor Salerooms, Wotton-under-Edge.*
M. Philip H. Scott, *East View, Bedale, Yorks.*
Shouler & Son, *43 Nottingham Street, Melton Mowbray.*
Robert W. Skinner Inc., *Bolton Gallery, Mass.*
Andrea.Smith, *Manderley, 27 Sutton Lane, Adlington, Lancs. (Robertson's Golly Badges)*
Smith-Woolley & Perry, *43 Castle Hill Avenue, Folkestone.*
Sotheby's, *34-35 New Bond Street, London.*
Sotheby Bearne, *Rainbow, Torquay, Devon.*
Sotheby's Belgravia, *19 Motcomb Street, London.*
Sotheby Beresford Adams, *Booth Mansion, Chester.*
Sotheby's Chester, *Watergate Street, Chester.*
Sotheby, King & Chasemore, *Station Road, Pulborough.*
Spear & Sons, *The Hill, Wickham Market, Suffolk.*
H. Spencer & Sons Ltd., *20 The Square, Retford, Notts.*
Stride & Son, *Southdown House, St. John's Street, Chichester.*
T.K. Suttie, *Riverside Cottage, 13 Bridge End, Billington, Nr. Blackburn. (Pictorial China)*
Christopher Sykes, *11 Market Place, Woburn, Milton Keynes.*
David Symonds, *High Street, Crediton, Devon.*
Taylor, Lane & Creber, *Western Auction Rooms, Plymouth.*
Laurence & Martin Taylor, *63 High Street, Honiton, Devon.*
Liz Taylor, *Ancrum, Jedburgh, Roxburghshire.*
Louis Taylor & Sons, *Percy Street, Hanley, Stoke-on-Trent.*
Terry Antiques, *175 Junction Road, London N19.*
Theriault, *P.O. Box 151, Annapolis, Maryland, 21404.*
Turner, Rudge & Turner, *29 High Street, East Grinstead.*
V. & V.'s, *The Memorial Hall, Shiplake-on-Thames.*
Vidler & Co., *Auction Offices, Cinque Ports St., Rye, Sussex.*
Wallis & Wallis, *Regency House, 1 Albion Street, Lewes, Sussex.*
Tom Walsh, *Capricorn Curios, 48 St. Annes Road, Blackpool. (Radios)*
Warren & Wignall, *113 Towngate, Leyland, Lancs.*
Thomas Watson, *27 North Street, Bishops Stortford.*
Way, Riddett & Co., *Town Hall Chambers, Lind Street, Ryde, I.O.W.*
Neil Wayne, *Old Chapel, Bridge Street, Belper, Derby. (Razors)*
J.M. Welsh & Son, *The Old Town Hall, Great Dunmow, Essex.*
Whitehead's, *111-113 Elm Grove, Southsea, Hants.*
Whitton & Laing, *32 Okehampton Street, Exeter.*
Richard Withington, *Hillsboro, New Hampshire 03244.*
Woolley & Wallis, *The Castle Auction Mart, Salisbury.*
Eldon E. Worrall & Co., *15 Seel Street, Liverpool.*
Wyatt & Son with Whiteheads, *59 East Street, Chichester, Sussex.*
Yesterday's Paper, *24 Fishergate York. (Pin-Up Magazines)*

ADVERTISING SIGNS

There was a time when enamel advertising signs could be found pinned to every available wall surface colourfully proclaiming the purity and authenticity of every imaginable product. Indeed this was such a common practice that companies employed men whose only job was to fix these signs on site.

Whatever your needs, be it a good shave or the best powder to use for dipping sheep, a persuasive slogan was but a glance away.

These signs have survived in fair quantities mainly as a result of the sturdy material used in their production while early examples of advertising material, being printed on paper and distributed as handbills were all too fragile and easily destroyed. This is a pity for they carried a great deal more interesting information on the product and its uses than the enamel signs did.

Double-sided enamel sign for Blue Bell tobacco, in three colours, 22 x 14in. (Nostalgia) £25

Double-sided enamel sign in two colours, for White May, 18in. wide. (Nostalgia) £25

Edwardian double-sided barber's shop item in three colours. (Nostalgia) £45

Single-sided three-colour design for Brooke Bond Tea. (Nostalgia) £15

Single-sided enamel sign for Spratt's Mixed Ovals, 12 x 30in. (Nostalgia) £25

Ogden's St. Julien Tobacco, enamel sign showing two blends of tobacco, 18 x 60in., circa 1900. (Sotheby's) £66

Sunlight Soap, enamel sign of boy holding bars of Sunlight soap, 33½ x 32½in., circa 1905. (Sotheby's) £176

Blue on yellow double-sided enamel sign for Lyons Cakes, 16 x 17½in. (Nostalgia) £15

Double-sided three-colour enamel sign for Will's Capstan cigarettes, 18in. diam. (Nostalgia) £40

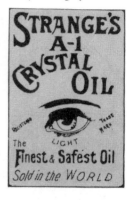

Enamelled sign of an elf in red costume, 30 x 24in. (Bonham's) £80

Enamelled sign for Fry's Chocolate by Chromo, Wolverhampton, 30 x 36in. (Bonham's) £340

Enamelled advertising sign for Strange's A-1 Crystal Oil by Chromo, Wolverhampton, 42 x 20in. (Bonham's) £190

Painted tin four-colour calendar sign, single-sided, for the Radio Times. (Nostalgia) £40

Enamelled sign advertising Nile Spinning & Doubling Co. Ltd., by Wildman & McGuyer Ltd., Birmingham, 24 x 36in. (Bonham's) £60

Enamelled sign advertising Robin Starch, 35½ x 29½in. (Bonham's) £160

Multi-coloured enamel sign, single-sided, for St. Bruno Flake tobacco. (Nostalgia) £75

Circular single-sided enamel sign in blue on yellow for Lyons Cakes, 17in. diam. (Nostalgia) £15

Rare advertising plaque by T. J. & J. Mayer for Huntley & Palmers. (Phillips) £850

Enamelled sign advertising Cooper's Sheep Dipping Powder, in the form of a playing card, 30 x 20in. (Bonham's) £260

Morse's Distemper enamel sign by Hassall, 60 x 40in. (Sotheby's) £385

'Selo Film' enamel sign in yellow, red and black, 14in. wide. (Sotheby's) £198

A decorative enamel sign for 'Pullars of Perth', Cleaners and Dyers, 24in. high, circa 1920. (Sotheby's) £44

Fry's Edwardian cabinet for chocolate, with two mirrored sliding doors, in ebonised wooded case. (Nostalgia) £125

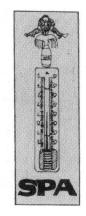

Enamelled advertising sign for Spa by Email Belg, 27 x 8½in. (Bonham's) £55

Single-sided four-colour enamel sign for Corona drinks, 10 x 30in. (Nostalgia) £20

Single-sided three-colour design enamel sign, 30in. wide, for Golden Shred marmalade. (Nostalgia)   £20

Single-sided enamel sign in black on white for Spratt's dog food, 12 x 12in. (Nostalgia) £25

Pub mirror with red and gilt lettering in original moulded plaster frame, 26½ x 35in. (Bonham's)   £200

Double-sided four-colour enamel sign for Park Drive cigarettes, 12 x 16in. (Nostalgia) £25

Single-sided sign in black on white for Spratt's budgerigar and canary mixture, 12 x 12in. (Nostalgia)   £35

Enamelled sign advertising Puritan Soap, on yellow ground, 24 x 36in. (Bonham's) £105

Shaped, printed and enamelled sign for Depot for Oceanic Footwear, 13 x 19in. (Bonham's)   £85

Double-sided four-colour sign for Castrol, 20in. wide. (Nostalgia) £30

Three-colour single-sided enamel sign for Spiller's Shapes for dogs, 30in. wide.(Nostalgia) £15

Single-sided two-colour enamel sign for Cadbury's chocolates, 14 x 24in. (Nostalgia) £20

Single-sided sign with coat-of-arms in top corner, for Rowntree's Cocoa, 19in. wide. (Nostalgia) £75

Single-sided three-colour enamel sign for Smith's Glasgow tobacco mixture, 30in. wide. (Nostalgia) £50

Three-colour illustrated enamel sign for Royal Daylight paraffin oil, double-sided, 18 x 22in. (Nostalgia) £35

Single-sided three-colour enamel sign for John Bull Tyre, 36in. wide. (Nostalgia) £35

Single-sided three-colour enamel sign for South Wales News, 18in. wide. (Nostalgia) £20

AMERICAN INDIANWARE

Interest in the material culture of the American Indians has led to a number of specialist sales being devoted to their crafts.

Working with tools of bone or ivory and using all available materials such as animal hides, quills, corn husks, willow and beads they produced artefacts of both great practical use and beauty. The buffalo provided the Indians with food, clothing and shelter. Hides were also painted and used in a decorative way.

Beadwork was introduced in the mid 16th century in the south, and in the north and east in the 18th and 19th century. The use of certain types and colours of beads helps the historian to determine the extent of 'white' contact with certain groups of Indians.

Haida Indian argillite pipe carved with totemic animals, 6¼in. long. (Sotheby's) £1,320

Kwakiuth wood ceremonial food bowl in the shape of a whale, 24¾in. long. (Sotheby's) £4,000

Haida argillite pipe of elongated shape, 8in. long. (Sotheby's) £462

Eastern Sioux inlaid catlinite pipe with carved wooden stem, 28½in. long. (Robert W. Skinner Inc.) £85

Woodlands pipe tomahawk with hardwood handle and iron blade, 20¼in. long. (Robert W. Skinner Inc.) £2,400

Haida horn ladle carved from black mountain goat horn with openwork handle, 12in. long. (Sotheby's) £880

Haida basketry rain hat with painted totemic design, 17in. diam. (Robert W. Skinner Inc.) £235

Pair of Woodlands moccasins in tanned deerskin with quillwork strips, 10in. long. (Robert W. Skinner Inc.) £1,535

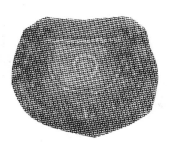

Apache strike-a-light pouch in leather with beaded designs, 5in. wide. (Robert W. Skinner Inc.) £165

One of a pair of Sioux beaded rawhide man's leggings, with beadwork strips, 34in. long. (Robert W. Skinner Inc.) £285

Haida argillite pipe of triangular form, 5¼in. long. (Sotheby's) £495

American Indian North-East Woodlands ball-headed club, 21½in. long. (Sotheby's) £11,550

Jivaro Indian shrunken head with long brown hair, 4in. high. (Sotheby's) £935

Early Woodlands finger woven garter or straps, interwoven with pony beads, 45in. long. (Robert W. Skinner Inc.) £865

Early Northern Plains gun case in tanned leather with wool applique panels, 56in. long. (Robert W. Skinner Inc.) £665

Woman's two-piece Navajo dress with red and blue ends, 50½in. long. (Robert W. Skinner Inc.) £2,600

Woodlands carved burl crooked knife with ball and claw handle, 9in. long. (Robert W. Skinner Inc.) £1,200

Tlingit basketry bowl with three design bands, 6in. diam. (Robert W. Skinner Inc.) £115

Haida argillite pipe carved in the form of a clam shell, 3¾in. diam. (Sotheby's) £1,210

Choctaw cane splint basket with square base, in brown, orange and natural, 15in. wide. (Robert W. Skinner Inc.) £200

Navajo rug with blanket style design, 5ft.4in. x 3ft. 8in. (Robert W. Skinner Inc.) £65

Sioux beaded leather vest with fringed bottom, 18½in. long. (Robert W. Skinner Inc.)£400

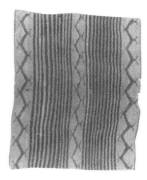

Navajo blanket with herringbone designs in blue, 5ft.3in. x 4ft.2in. (Robert W. Skinner Inc.) £385

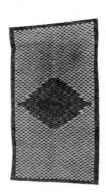

Saltios blanket with multicoloured geometric designs, 8ft.3in. x 4ft.4in. (Robert W. Skinner Inc.) £665

Apache basketry ola with star design on base, 12½in. high. (Robert W. Skinner Inc.) £435

Haida carved argillite group showing three men, 9in. high. (Robert W. Skinner Inc.) £2,065

Apache basketry bowl with radiating fretted design, 6in. diam. (Robert W. Skinner Inc.) £215

Tlingit covered rattle top basket, with banded key design, 5in. diam. (Robert W. Skinner Inc.) £315

Tlingit basketry bowl with false embroidered decoration, 8½in. diam. (Robert W. Skinner Inc.) £135

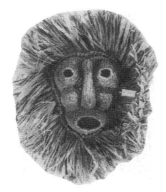

Apache basketry ola with triangular panels with motifs, 11¾in. high. (Robert W. Skinner Inc.) £565

Iroquois corn husk false face society mask with fringed edge, 15in. long. (Robert W. Skinner Inc.) £300

Navajo blanket in striped design with fretted centres, 6ft. x 3ft.7in. (Robert W. Skinner Inc.) £285

Iroquois moosehair embroidered birchbark cigar case, 3¼in. wide. (Robert W. Skinner Inc.) £365

Plains buffalo-hide painted ghost dance shield with bird design, 17in. diam. (Robert W. Skinner Inc.) £365

Woodlands beaded coat with double collar, fringed edge and silk applique. (Robert W. Skinner Inc.) £4,065

Chippewa loom beaded bandolier bag in multi-coloured geometric design, 14in. wide. (Robert W. Skinner Inc.) £500

Apache basketry tray with rattlesnake designs and figures, 17in. long. (Robert W. Skinner Inc.) £285

Haida argillite carved totem, with hawk at top, 14¼in. high. (Robert W. Skinner Inc.) £465

Chippewa beadwork bandolier bag with square pouch, 44½in. long. (Sotheby's) £352

Pair of Northern Plains woman's leggings in red wool flannel with beadwork, 18½in. long. (Robert W. Skinner Inc.) £265

Navajo child's blanket, bands with zig-zag designs, 60 x 41in. (Robert W. Skinner Inc.) £415

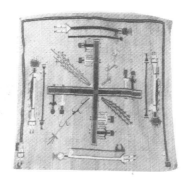

Early Woodlands beaded bandolier bag in blue wool flannel with red straps, 35in. long.(Robert W. Skinner Inc.) £2,000

Navajo sand painting rug on natural tan field, 5ft.8in. x 5ft.7in. (Robert W. Skinner Inc.) £1,735

Sioux beaded pipe bag with attached knife sheath, 33in. long. (Robert W. Skinner Inc.) £550

Early Woodlands beaded bandolier bag in red wool, 36in. long. (Robert W. Skinner Inc.) £2,265

Opaque watercolour by Harrison Begay of a Navajo man and woman on horseback, signed. (Robert W. Skinner Inc.) £515

Early Woodlands beaded bandolier bag in red flannel, 32in. long. (Robert W. Skinner Inc.) £1,535

Navajo child's blanket with horizontal striped centre panels, 49½ x 34½in. (Robert W. Skinner Inc.) £415

Portrait of an Indian by Edward S. Curtis, 1903, 12½ x 16½in. (Robert W. Skinner Inc.) £285

Plains painted parfleche, ties in front middle, 27in. long. (Robert W. Skinner Inc.) £185

Sioux beaded leather pipe bag with flag motifs and woven horsehair quirt, 19in. long. (Robert W. Skinner Inc.) £435

Pair of Cree embroidered mittens in tanned deer skin, 9½in. long. (Robert W. Skinner Inc.) £615

Northern Plains pipe bag in tanned hide with floral beaded panel, 28in. long. (Robert W. Skinner Inc.) £150

AMUSEMENT MACHINES

Now that highly sophisticated video games and complex electronically operated machines dominate the amusement arcades, attention is wistfully returning to the great mechanical devices of a bygone age.

Fast gaining in popularity with collectors, amusement machines form a fascinating collection and offer an excellent investment potential.

The promise of challenge and entertainment suggested by these evocatively named contraptions is almost irresistible. One may have one's fortune told, test one's grip, take part in a death dive and experience the delights of one pennyworth of the Gay Deceiver — all good clean fun.

'Haunted House' automaton in wooden case with glazed window, circa 1935, 70in. high. (Sotheby's) £264

'The Night Watchman', coin-operated automaton by The British Automatic Co. Ltd., circa 1935, 66½in. high. (Sotheby's) £528

'The Haunted House', coin-operated automaton, circa 1935, 70½in. high. (Sotheby's) £462

'The Drunkard's Dream', coin-operated automaton, 66½in. high, circa 1935. (Sotheby's) £528

Caille gambling machine with five coin slots, circa 1910, 25½in. high. (Sotheby's) £165

'The Burglar', coin-operated automaton, circa 1935, 67in. high. (Sotheby's) £385

AMUSEMENT MACHINES

Little 'Five-Win' Allwin gambling machine, 24½in. high, circa 1935. (Sotheby's)£150

Auto Stereoscope in oak casing with coin slot, circa 1930, 22½in. high. (Sotheby's) £165

'Playball' Allwin with seven winning chutes, in oak case, circa 1920, 27½in. high. (Sotheby's) £71

'Pussy' Shooter, amusement machine, circa 1935, 76in. high. (Sotheby's) £308

'Laughing Sailor', amusement machine, coin-operated bearing Ruffler & Walker plaque, 68½in. high, circa 1935. (Sotheby's) £528

White City 'Screen Stars' gambling machine in oak casing, circa 1940, 26½in. high. (Sotheby's) £71

Allwin 'Peerless de Luxe' with seven winning chutes, circa 1925, 29½in. high. (Sotheby's) £77

Green Ray 'Television' amusement machine, circa 1945, 75in. high. (Sotheby's) £209

'Zodiac' coin-operated fortune-teller, circa 1940, 24½in. high. (Sotheby's) £121

Early Genco pinball bagatelle table with glass top, circa 1935, 39in. long. (Sotheby's) £300

Gottlieb & Co. **'World Fair'** pinball table with glass top, 51in. long. (Sotheby's) £93

'Test Your Strength' amusement machine with iron grip handle, circa 1925, 50in. high. (Sotheby's) £385

'Pussy' Shooter, coin-operated amusement machine by British Automatic Co. Ltd., circa 1935. (Sotheby's) £330

American coin-operated muto-scope **'Death Dive'**, circa 1915, 50in. high. (Sotheby's) £352

'Haunted Churchyard' automaton in mahogany case, circa 1912, 72in. high. (Sotheby's) £440

AMUSEMENT MACHINES

Ahrens '22-Man Football' game, coin-operated, in oak casing, circa 1930, 43¾in. wide. (Sotheby's) £440

Ahrens stereoscopic viewer in oak cabinet, circa 1925, 68in. high. (Sotheby's) £495

'Great Race' game, coin-operated, in oak casing, 47in. wide, circa 1925. (Sotheby's) £440

Arhens 'Test Your Strength' amusement machine in painted wooden case, circa 1922, 79in. high. (Sotheby's) £528

Caillie Brothers grip-test amusement machine in green-painted case, circa 1910, 59in. high. (Sotheby's) £528

Mutoscope by the International Reel Co., circa 1905, 74in. high. (Sotheby's) £350

ANIMALIA

The Victorians' love of natural forms must have given some 19th century homes the appearance of a kind of nightmarish, petrified safari park. For, apart from static birds perpetually poised in attitudes of flight or feeding, carnivores cut off in mid roar and converted into carpeting, there came a multitude of specimens from small prickly-backed creatures to giant water-buffalo.

One has the uneasy feeling that if, in the second half of the 19th century, any creature stood still for more than five seconds, it was in danger of being seized by an itinerant taxidermist, rapidly stuffed and sold within minutes to a passing Victorian, anxious to be a little nearer to nature while sitting in his button-backed chair by the fire.
Nothing, it would appear, was immune from the process — with even the family dog occasionally getting the full treatment.

A mounted fox head inscribed 'Wexford Hounds 14th Oct 1904'. £10

Lion skin rug of a male African lion with snarling head, 120in. long. £350

Unusual Barbedienne gilt bronze mounted lacquered ostrich egg, 23cm. high, circa 1870. £200

A large stuffed moose head. £100

19th century specimen of a Russian brown bear. £400

A stuffed stag's head with eleven points. £20

ANIMALIA

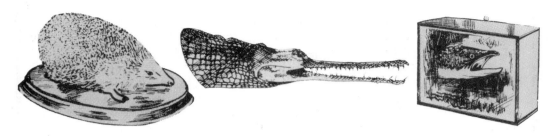

Victorian stuffed hedgehog.
£20

Unusual stuffed and mounted
cayman, 37in. long.   £90

Cased stuffed fish, labelled
'Thames Trout', dated
1883.   £35

Pair of squirrels beneath
a glass dome.   £15

Victorian stuffed otter in its natural
habitat.   £85

Huge mounted head
of an Indian water
buffalo.   £100

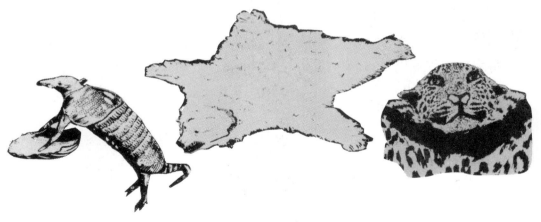

Animal ashtray in shell
work.   £10

Norwegian polar bear rug, 66in.
wide.   £460

Leopard skin rug, moun-
ted on felt backcloth,
72in. long, nose to tail
tip.   £400

ARMOUR

Although full suits of armour are a little bulky to contemplate collecting, quite apart from costing anything from a few hundred to many thousands of pounds, such articles as gauntlets, arm and shoulder defences and particularly breastplates can lead to an interesting and not too expensive collection.

Independent breastplates have been known since the 14th century, and examples of these can of course be on the dear side, but those from later centuries can be found from as little as £50 upwards.

Beware of reproductions, however, for they have been made for the last hundred years. All those I have seen come complete with a suitable hole or dent where the heart is, along with the story about how the ploughman turned it up where the battle of Culloden (or suitable local shindig) took place.

A mid 16th century German or Swiss puffed breastplate, chest embossed with three radial bands. (Wallis & Wallis) £155

A German articulated mitten gauntlet, circa 1525, 12in., roped, embossed studded border to cuff. (Wallis & Wallis) £140

A good pair of 19th century French cuirassier's breast and back plates, brass studs to borders. (Wallis & Wallis)£190

A heavy mid 18th century German Cavalry trooper's breastplate, deep musket ball proof mark. (Wallis & Wallis) £90

A German breastplate of bulbous form, circa 1540, distinct medial ridge, slender waist. (Wallis & Wallis) £165

An early 19th century German Cavalry trooper's breastplate, brass studded decoration to borders. (Wallis & Wallis) £150

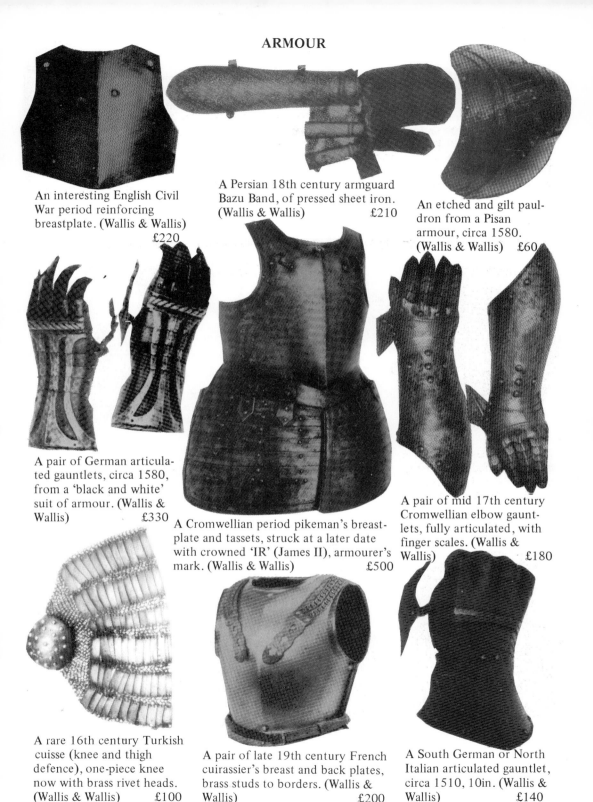

An interesting English Civil War period reinforcing breastplate. (Wallis & Wallis) £220

A Persian 18th century armguard Bazu Band, of pressed sheet iron. (Wallis & Wallis) £210

An etched and gilt pauldron from a Pisan armour, circa 1580. (Wallis & Wallis) £60

A pair of German articulated gauntlets, circa 1580, from a 'black and white' suit of armour. (Wallis & Wallis) £330

A Cromwellian period pikeman's breastplate and tassets, struck at a later date with crowned 'IR' (James II), armourer's mark. (Wallis & Wallis) £500

A pair of mid 17th century Cromwellian elbow gauntlets, fully articulated, with finger scales. (Wallis & Wallis) £180

A rare 16th century Turkish cuisse (knee and thigh defence), one-piece knee now with brass rivet heads. (Wallis & Wallis) £100

A pair of late 19th century French cuirassier's breast and back plates, brass studs to borders. (Wallis & Wallis) £200

A South German or North Italian articulated gauntlet, circa 1510, 10in. (Wallis & Wallis) £140

AUTOGRAPH LETTERS

A survey of the trade in autograph letters, manuscripts and documents makes entertaining reading because of the number of curiosities that turn up. Among those singled out for notice is an autograph poem by Arthur Conan Doyle written in 1922. This uninspired offering of only 22 words sold at Phillips for £55. A document signed by Henry VIII fetched £1,300 and a letter penned from the Victory by Nelson just before his death sold at Phillips for £440.

When Marc Chagall used a felt tipped pen to scrawl a drawing on the title page of his 'poems' published in 1975 he made the book worth £420 to a buyer in Sotheby's. Thomas Chippendale's marriage certificate of 1748 sold for £620 to the Chippendale Society at Phillips and Bernard Shaw signed a cheque in 1940 that was sold for £160. Lord Byron dashed off a satirical poem about Angerstein, the man whose picture collection formed the basis of the National Gallery, and Sotheby's sold the 14 line effort for £3,500.

John Winthrop, America's first astronomer, Hollis Professor of Mathematics at Harvard, fine autograph letter signed, 3 pages, quarto, to Jonathan Belcher, Chief Justice of Nova Scotia. (Sotheby's)   £400

H. Walpole, fine autographed letter signed, to Captain Waldegrave, 2 pages, quarto, Strawberry Hill, 22 October 1789. (Sotheby's)   £480

William III and the Order of the Garter, document signed William R at head and counter-signed by Gilbert Burnet, 2 pages, folio, 3 May 1694.(Sotheby's)
£190

Leon Trotsky, highly important autograph letter signed, written a month before his deportation to Mexico, 4 pages, quarto, 22 November 1936. (Sotheby's)
£1,650

Jean-Francois Millet, autograph letter signed,
to the critic Theophile Silvestre, 4 pages,
octavo, Barbizon, 17 August 1867. (Sotheby's)
£275

Charles Stewart Parnell, autograph letter signed,
to Thomas W. Johnson, 3 pages, framed, octavo,
House of Commons, 17 August 1877.
(Sotheby's)   £150

J. R. R. Tolkien, autograph statement signed
'In all my works I take the part of the trees
as against all their enemies', on an oblong slip
of paper. (Sotheby's)   £155

Prince Eugene of Savoy, letter signed in Italian, one page, folio, to Marchese Ficino
Pepoli of Bologna congratulating him on
wife's delivery of first child, Vienna 1731.
(Sotheby's)   £80

Edward Lear, illustrated autograph letter
signed, one page, to Mrs Digby Watts asking
not to be asked to dine on Thursday and
with a charming drawing of a giant parrot,
diminutive cat and even smaller dog, Sept.
1863. (Sotheby's)   £160

Camille Pissarro, autograph letter signed, 3
pages quarto, to his wife Julie describing
the progress of his work, London, June 1892.
(Sotheby's)   £380

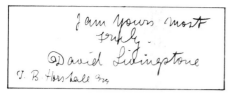

David Livingstone, autograph letters arranging to procure beads for next visit to Africa, 4 pages, 8vo, to J. B. Horsfall MP, Kensington Palace Gardens, January 1858. (Sotheby's) £440

Lancelot Brown, 'Capability', autograph letter signed, one page, quarto, to an unnamed peer asking him to repay a bond, 16 December 1779. (Sotheby's)   £110

Charles V, Document with stamped signature, being a grant of arms to Michael Schmidt, on vellum, c. 40 x 70cm., countersigned, engrossed majuscules in first line, Brussels, 6 October 1553. (Sotheby's) £198

Campbell Roy, illustrated autograph letter signed, with drawings on each page and on a full page at the end, to Mrs. Facey of Faber's criticising the artwork for one of his books, 4 pages, quarto. (Sotheby's)£130

James Francis Edward Stuart, autograph letter unsigned, one page octavo, informing correspondent that bearer of letter will provide details of his circumstances, integral leaf with small seal, Sept. 1706. (Sotheby's) £220

Lady Emma Hamilton, three autograph letters signed Emma and E. H., 3 pages, quarto and octavo, from 12 Temple Place to Sir Richard Puleston. (Sotheby's) £280

Autograph letter signed 'J Reynolds', to 'Offy', his favourite niece, Theophila Gwatkin, 1 page, London, 'Saturday' 1781.(Sotheby's) £350

W. H. Auden, autograph manuscript of his 'Ode to the George Washington Hotel' comprising 60 lines with 2 revisions signed and inscribed to the Manager and all staff, 5 pages, octavo and small quarto. (Sotheby's) £550

Katherine Manners, Duchess of Buckingham, autograph letter to her husband George Villiers asking leave to go 'with the wenches' to Oatlands, one page, folio. (Sotheby's) £60

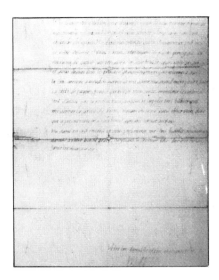

Mary Queen of Scots, remarkable autograph letter written at the age of 11 to her mother Mary of Guise announcing her intention to make her first communion, one page, folio, Meudon Easter 1554. (Sotheby's) £5,200

Prince Napoleon Bonaparte, 1822-91, son of Jerome Bonaparte, known as 'Plon Plon', collection of about 85 autograph letters, signed and letters signed 'Napoleon Bonaparte' etc., May 1843 to January 1891 to a variety of correspondents. (Sotheby's) £250

William IV, series of eleven autograph letters signed 'William', 17 pages, 4to, St. James's, Bushy House, and the Admiralty, 28th April 1817 to 1828 to Sir Richard Puleston, announcing his marriage, discussing his health and his tours abroad, etc. (Sotheby's)   £250

Ludwig Van Beethoven, example of his handwriting removed from a letter, 29 words, on a slip of paper 1 x 4½in. (Sotheby's)   £320

Horatio Nelson, fine autograph letter signed Nelson and Bronte to Emma Hamilton, 4 pages, quarto, sending a watch for their child and mentions that a comb is on its way to Emma etc., Victory, 20 January 1804. (Sotheby's)   £2,500

Charles II, King of England, letter relating to plantations in America, counter signed by Earl of Arlington, 1672. (Robert W. Skinner Inc.)   £1,000

Ralph Waldo Emerson, autograph letters to George Eliot (Mrs G H Lewes), 3 pages introducing a visitor to her, Concord, Nov. 1873. (Sotheby's)   £140

Cardinal Bentivoglio, a collection of letters written during the time he was Nuncio in France and Flanders, with Sir Arthur Conan Doyle's bookplate, his signature on title and a long autograph note about the author, 8vo, G. Steidel, 1753. (Sotheby's)   £121

Elizabeth I, important letter signed Elizabeth R at head, to Sir Nicholas Throckmorton, her ambassador to Scotland, containing a major statement about Elizabeth's policy towards the fate of Mary Queen of Scots, July 1567. (Sotheby's)   £16,500

Albert Einstein, autograph letter signed about relevance of Lanczos' work to Einstein's theories on relativity, 1 page, Princeton 1949. (Sotheby's)   £1,050

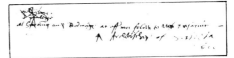

Alexander Stewart, 1493-1513, natural son of James IV and Archbishop of St. Andrews, letter signed with autograph p.s., one page, oblong octavo. (Sotheby's)   £180

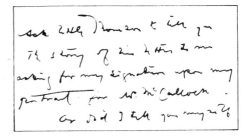

James McNeill Whistler, autograph invitation, signed with his stylised butterfly, to breakfast at 12 o'clock on Sunday 22 July at Tite Street, on stiff card. (Sotheby's)   £80

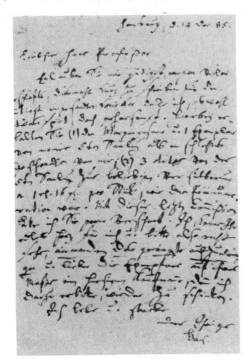

Carl Philipp Emanuel Bach, fine autograph letter signed, 1 page, octavo, Hamburg, 14 December 1785. (Sotheby's)   £5,500

Silius Titus, 1623?-1704, autograph letters to Alban Coxe, written from the Siege of Donnington Castle, one page, integral address leaf, folio, Donnington, 2 October 1644. (Christie's)   £132

[handwritten letter in French]

Donathien Sade, autograph letter, unsigned, to his lawyer Gaufridy, relating to the scandal caused by Sade's keeping a number of young girls at his chateaux for his pleasures, 4 pages, quarto, Provence, June 1775. (Sotheby's)   £550

Napoleon I, letter signed Bonaparte, one page, folio to Archbishop of Milan, attractive vignette heading showing female figure, Milan 13 December 1796. (Sotheby's)   £280

Virginia Woolf, fine series of 25 autograph or typed letters signed and 16 postcards, 50 pages, quarto and octavo, 52 Tavistock Sq. and Monks House, 1927-36, to Julian Bell. (Sotheby's)   £3,500

AUTOMATONS

The genius of the 18th and 19th century craftsmen is perhaps best exhibited in his ability to construct the most ingenious and delicate of automatons. Developed by the Swiss Jacquet-Droz family, and later by the French, mechanical toys grew in complexity until the mid-Victorian era, by which time most occupations, from shoe cleaning to piano playing, had been interpreted with mechanical ingenuity to make delightful adult playthings.

Most depend solely on the driving power of a spring, but many inventors propelled their machines by compressed air, water, sand, mercury and steam. The best examples, worth hundreds or even thousands, are by Vaucanson, Robertson and Rechsteiner, particularly writing and drawing automatons, and talking dolls developed by Von Kempelen.

Mass production of mechanical toys reared its head about 1870 with the rising German tin plate industry and, craftsmanship inevitably suffering, they became simply playthings for children.

A thriving trade developed in importing these toys from Germany to England mainly as a result of their popularity with adults buying for young people for it is a matter of record that they held only a limited appeal for children their subject matter being considered somewhat sophisticated and their independence of movement thought to be 'off putting'.

Adults, however, continued to buy most enthusiastically and to preserve these fascinating pieces and it is thanks to them that we have so many good examples to wonder at and enjoy today.

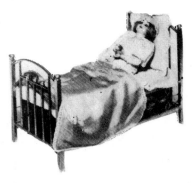

A sleeping doll automaton, the doll lying in a brass bedstead, probably French, circa 1910, 14in. (Sotheby's)   £462

A hand-operated automaton of a garden tea party, German late 19th century, approx. 12½in. high by 11½in. wide. (Sotheby's)   £1,540

An automaton of a young girl seated at an upright piano, the French bisque head marked 4, 41cm. high, (restored). (Phillips)   £1,500

38

A musical conjuror automaton, probably Decamps, French 1880, overall height 17in. (Sotheby's) £2,530

Dancing negress automaton with key wound mechanism, in good condition, 10½in. high. (Sotheby's) £120

A crying Jumeau musical automaton by Lambert, the bisque head impressed 211 and (Depose Tete Jumeau 4) French, circa 1890, height 20½in. (Sotheby's) £330

A lady conjuror automaton, lavishly dressed in pink silk, mounted on square plinth, probably French, circa 1905, 26in. high.(Sotheby's) £990

A musical conjuror automaton by Lambert, the bisque head impressed (Depose Tete Jumeau 4), overall height 19½in., French, circa 1880. (Sotheby's) £198

An S.F.B.J. bisque doll and ball automaton, circa 1910, French, height 13in. (Sotheby's) £186

A Bontems singing bird automaton with three birds under a cage, French, mid 19th century, 21½in. high. (Sotheby's) £5,500

A coin-operated monkey pianist automaton, with the mechanism contained in the oak base, probably French, late 19th century, 16in. high. (Sotheby's) £1,200

A musical monkey harpist automaton, probably by Vichy, French, circa 1870, 19in. high. (Sotheby's) £2,000

AUTOMATONS

A musical automaton, the bisque head impressed (Depose Tete Jumeau Bte. S.G.D.G. 4), French, late 19th century, height 20in. (Sotheby's) £1,210

A cane birdcage automaton with bisque doll, German, circa 1915, overall size 13in. (Sotheby's) £506

A French Bebe automaton in original silk dress and underclothes, early 20th century. (Sotheby's) £1,000

A musical automaton by Lambert, in pale green silk dress and shoes, French, 1885, height 19½in. (Sotheby's) £1,870

Automaton magician, 52½in. high, 36½in. wide. (Robert W. Skinner Inc.) £240

French bisque automaton doll, in original blue taffeta gown, circa 1880, height 19in. (Sotheby's) £4,260

French ballerina automaton with bisque head impressed S.F.B.J. 801, Paris, circa 1900. (Sotheby's) £1,045

A musical conjuror automaton standing at her magic box, French, circa 1880, 18in. high by 12in. wide. (Sotheby's) £2,090

Two Schoenau & Hoffmeister automaton dolls dressed as Pulchinelles, German, late 19th century, 21in. high by 12½in. (Sotheby's) £660

AUTOMOBILIA

It all started in Britain around the 1890's. In those days cars were bought by the wealthy and driven by chauffeurs. Then 'sporty types' adopted the new hobby of motoring and, becoming owner-drivers, created a demand and a market for new and improved 'extras'.

Of the wide range of accessories including, radiator caps, oil cans, hub caps, steering wheels, mascots, speedometers, fascia panels and other related gadgets, the massive head-lamps once fixed to fast cars such as Lagondas and Alvis are most enthusiastically collected.

Evidence of the increasing nostalgia for the early days before road tax, insurance or speed limits, is clearly demonstrated by the hordes of visitors and traders attending autojumbles, specialised sales and special events such as those held at Beaulieu.

Powell & Hamner side lamp with oil illuminant, circa 1905, 11in. high.(Sotheby's) £60

Smith's tachometer calibrated from 1000 to 2500 rpm, 6½in. diam., plaque inscribed and dated 1933. (Christie's) £200

Early 20th century Bleriot brass head lamp, 12in. high. (Sotheby's) £44

Car head lamp with 4in. diam. reflector, 10in. high, circa 1910. (Sotheby's) £50

Speedometer from a 30's Morris complete with clock. (Vernon's) £20

Lucas 'King of the Road' head lamp, 13½in. high, circa 1905. (Sotheby's) £60

Lucas 'King of the Road' head lamp with red-painted reservoir, 13½in. high, circa 1905.(Sotheby's)£66

Poster for Bosch Zundung, circa 1908. (Vernon's)   £50

S. Smith side lamp with oil illuminant and brass fittings, circa 1905, 13¼in. high. (Sotheby's)   £55

Enamel Automobile Association badge. (Sotheby's) £22

Mahogany showcase made from a brass Rolls Royce Silver Ghost radiator shell with Spirit of Ecstasy mascot, 35in. high. (Christie's)   £200

Royal Automobile Club Associates car badge in enamel. (Sotheby's) £22

Lucas 'King of the Road' side lamp with oil illuminant, circa 1905, 10in. high. (Sotheby's)   £60

French poster 'Diort' for the 'Societe de Construction de l'Ouest', circa 1905. (Vernon's)   £150

Mid 19th century Piper hand lamp with glass window and brass casing, Canadian, 10in. high. (Sotheby's)   £38

42

Lucas 'King of the Road' side lamp with brass reservoir, 12in. high, circa 1905. (Sotheby's) £52

De Dion Bouton poster, circa 1903. (Vernon's) £100

Late 19th century English hand lamp in brass casing, with two hinged doors at front, 8¼in. high. (Sotheby's) £44

Montreal Motorists League car badge. (Sotheby's) £20

Radiator from a pre war M.G.T.- Type. (Vernon's) £70

Enamel car badge for KNILM. (Sotheby's) £25

Lucas 'King of the Road' car head lamp, with 4in. diam. reflector, circa 1910, 12½in. high. (Sotheby's) £55

Peugeot poster 'Le Petit Pouget Montait Une Peugeot'. (Vernon's) £65

Early 19th century Merrywether & Sons fire engine lamp with candle illuminant, 14in. high. (Sotheby's) £80

BADGES

There are many interesting aspects to a collection of badges. Through a study of their regimental motifs, numerals, materials and design, one may follow the changes and reforms of the system as well as the history of particular regiments.

A start can often be made on a domestic level. Most families have, at one time or another had a serving soldier in the family and for sentimental reasons soldiers tend to keep their badges.

A cap badge may be identified as such by the fastening. Usually this consists of a prong, a slide or two metal loops designed to be fastened by a split pin. A cap badge is normally larger than those designed to be worn on a uniform collar.

It is a good idea to consult an old Army List for information on who wore what and when. Specialist sales embracing all aspects of military history and interest are held at Wallis & Wallis of Lewes, Sussex.

A pre-1881 other rank's brass Glengarry badge of The 49th (Hertfordshire) Regt. (Wallis & Wallis)£18

A pre-1881 other rank's brass Glengarry badge of The 37th (North Hampshire) Regt. (Wallis & Wallis)   £22

A Victorian officer's silver pouch belt badge of a Volunteer Bn. The Rifle Brigade, hallmark Birmingham 1897. (Wallis & Wallis) £40

A white metal cap badge of The 4th Volunteer Bn. The Queen's Regt. (Wallis & Wallis)   £46

An officer's silvered pouch belt badge of The North York Rifles. (Wallis & Wallis)   £50

A pre-1881 other rank's Glengarry badge of Thd 39th (Dorsetshire) Regt. (Wallis & Wallis)   £50

A pre-1881 officer's gilt and silvered Glengarry badge of The 25th (The King's Own Borderers) Regt. (Wallis & Wallis) £60

A post-1902 officer's silvered helmet plate of The 1st Volunteer Bn. The Royal West Kent Regt. (Wallis & Wallis) £65

The centre device from a bell-topped shako badge of The 2nd (Queen's Royal) Regt., silvered star with battle honours. (Wallis & Wallis) £80

A Victorian darkened brass Maltese Cross helmet plate of The Harrow Rifles (18th Middlesex), white metal centre of crossed arrows and wreath. (Wallis & Wallis) £90

An officer's silvered skull and crossbones shako badge of The 17th Light Dragoons. (Wallis & Wallis) £90

An officer's gilt and silvered 1847 (Albert) pattern helmet plate of The 7th (Princess Royal's) Dragoon Guards. (Wallis & Wallis) £90

A pre-1881 officer's gilt bear-skin grenade badge of The 101st (Royal Bengal Fusiliers) Regt. (Wallis & Wallis) £100

A silver World War II Free Czech Air Force pilot's badge, by Spink, with pricker numbering on the reverse '309', 3 lug attachment. (Wallis & Wallis) £100

A late Victorian officer's gilt helmet plate of The Derbyshire Regt. (Sherwood Foresters). (Wallis & Wallis) £100

BADGES

A universal pattern officer's copper gilt badge for the Waterloo shako. (Wallis & Wallis)   £110

A late Victorian officer's blackened helmet plate of The 2nd Volunteer Bn. The East Surrey Regt. (Wallis & Wallis)   £110

A late Victorian officer's gilt helmet plate of The York & Lancaster Regt. (Wallis & Wallis)   £115

An officer's gilt, silvered and enamel 1844 (Albert) pattern shako badge of The Nottinghamshire Militia. (Wallis & Wallis)   £150

An other rank's brass 1816 (Regency) pattern shako badge of The 2nd (Queen's Royal) Regt. (Wallis & Wallis)   £180

An early Victorian officer's gilt bell-topped shako badge of The Hartford Militia. (Wallis & Wallis)   £185

A Regency officer's shako badge of The 31st (Huntingdonshire) Regt. of Foot, circa 1822. (Wallis & Wallis)   £200

An officer's gilt and silvered 1844 (Albert) pattern shako badge of The 25th (King's Own Borderers) Regt. (Wallis & Wallis)   £290

An officer's shako badge of The 13th Light Dragoons, 1830 pattern. (Wallis & Wallis)   £350

BANK NOTES

Banknotes have been used as currency in England since 1665, and most early examples are worth many times their face value.

18th century banknotes are valuable and in particular the many different issues of each of the banks of Scotland. These are so many and varied that a separate and specialist field of collecting has been established. A Scottish £1 of the mid 18th century fetched over £1,000.

Imperfectly manufactured notes also have their devotees, but they obtain far less in percentage terms compared with misprinted stamps. Other areas of interest include the money issued to the troops during the Second World War which is of greater value than the regular issue.

Condition is an important factor and a fragile note should be stored in a plastic envelope so that it can be seen and handled while protected from damage.

Bank of Poyais, unissued One Dollar at St. Joseph 182-, by W. H. Lizars, rare, some foxing. (Christie's) £60

Bank of England 2/6, signed K. O. Peppiatt 1941, very rare. (Christie's) £500

The States of Guernsey Five Shillings or Six Francs, 5th August 1914, rare. (Christie's) £850

Union Bank £5 proof on card by Perkins, Bacon & Petch. (Christie's) £100

John McAdam & Company 5/- note issued in 1763, bearing portrait of George III, damaged, extremely rare. (Christie's) £720

The Caledonian Banking Company £20 proof on card circa 1838. (Christie's) £200

Thistle Bank £1 1770, on unwatermarked paper. (Christie's) £820

Greenock Bank Company £1 issued 15th May 1830. (Christie's) £140

Government of India, One Thousand Rupees, 2nd June 1913, Bombay, scarce. (Christie's) £180

City of Glasgow £100 printed by Perkins, Bacon & Petch, very rare. (Christie's) £400

Bank of Scotland proof of £1 on card, engraved by W. H. Lizars on copper. (Christie's) £180

Paisley Banking Co. One Guinea dated 2nd May 1826. (Christie's) £210

National Bank £1 proof on card, some staining. (Christie's) £220

British Linen Company £100 issued 1905, issue lasted only 2 years, very rare. (Christie's) £720

Dundee Banking Company £1 of 1824, torn on right side. (Christie's) £320

Bank of Scotland proof £100 note in black and white, by Bradbury & Evans. (Christie's) £150

Union Bank £1 in green and blue on unwatermarked paper, dated 1864. (Christie's) £140

National Bank £20 proof on paper dated 1889. (Christie's) £100

Ship Bank £1 proof by Joseph Swan, cracked in two places. (Christie's) £150

Royal Bank of Scotland £1 dated 9th Feb. 1750, on watermarked paper, rare. (Christie's) £1,350

Banking Company of Aberdeen 5/- issued in 1799, very rare. (Christie's) £700

Union Bank £100 dated August 1877 but unissued, in black with red. (Christie's)£100

Montrose Bank One Guinea dated 16th December 1814, very rare. (Christie's)   £750

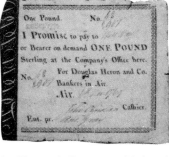

Douglas Heron & Company £1 dated 6th November 1769. (Christie's)   £650

Perth Banking Co. £1 proof by W. H. Lizars, (Christie's)   £240

Sir William Forbes, James Hunter & Company £1, 181-. (Christie's)   £100

Bank of Scotland proofs of the One Guinea of 1825. (Christie's)   £200

North of Scotland Bank Ltd. £1 overprinted with the Town and Country Bank.(Christie's)   £160

Western Bank £10 proof on card by W. H. Lizars, engraved. (Christie's)   £150

Bank of England 5/-, signed K. O. Peppiatt 1941, very rare. (Christie's)   £620

BAYONETS

The earlier bayonets were of the "plug" type; that is, they had hilts which fitted tightly into the barrel of muzzle loaders so that, having fired off his gun at the onrushing attackers, a soldier without time to reload could plug the bayonet in and convert his gun into a kind of pike. He could, too, if he was kept standing around in the rain for a long time waiting for his officers to decide to begin the battle, plug the bayonet in and keep his charge dry. Only, since the hilts were usually made of wood which swelled when wet, he sometimes couldn't get the bayonet out again in time and was left struggling while the opposing army took pot shots at him from a safe distance. Embarrassing, to say the least.

So, eager not to lose every possible chance of killing someone, the military mind came up with the idea of a bayonet with a socket handle which fitted round the outside of the gun barrel, with the blade bent out of the way of discharging bullets.

An unusual plug bayonet from a sporting gun, circa 1700, tapered blade 12¼in., brass ferrule, turned fruitwood swollen grip, with small bulbous top and brass tang button washer. (Wallis & Wallis)   £55

A late 17th century plug bayonet, shallow diamond section double edged blade 9in., with square section forte. Steel collar with short ribbed steel crosspiece. Turned swollen fruitwood hilt, with ribbed brass pommel. (Wallis & Wallis)   £60

A scarce brass hilted Italian M. 1856 bayonet for the Bersaglieri carbine, double edged blade 18in., ribbed hilt, spring button lug, in its brass mounted leather scabbard. (Wallis & Wallis)   £60

A scarce Volunteer sword socket bayonet, flat single edged blade 24in., with double edged tip, integral steel socket and knucklebow. (Wallis & Wallis)   £65

BAYONETS

A good Spanish plug bayonet, tapering, spear-shaped blade 9¾in., etched with floral and foliate patterns and at forte with Spanish Royal Arms and 'Fabricad Toledo 1860', brass crosspiece with acorn terminals. (Wallis & Wallis)   £70

A Nazi Police Parade bayonet, plated blade 12½in., by 'A.C.S.', plated hilt with staghorn grips with Police emblem, in its black leather scabbard with plated mounts with leather frog and dress knot. (Wallis & Wallis)   £70

A rare 1838 brass hilted Brunswick sword bayonet, double edged, spatulate blade 22in., with short fuller, also stamped with crown, 'VR', 'Enfield'. (Wallis & Wallis)   £95

An 1859 Enfield Naval cutlass bayonet, plain single edged slightly curved blade, 26½in., with long clipped back point, maker (German) 'A. & E. H.', steel guard, diced black leather grips, in its steel mounted leather scabbard. (Wallis & Wallis)   £175

A rare sword bayonet for the Jacobs double-barrelled rifle, double edged blade 30in., with double central fuller, steel half-basket guard with double muzzle ring in quillon, diced leather grip, in its steel mounted leather covered wooden scabbard with frog stud. (Wallis & Wallis)   £260

BEER BOTTLE LABELS

Labelled beer bottles were probably in general use from around 1850 and it is true to say that these printed paper labels have been collected ever since. Victorian and Edwardian collections still turn up from time to time and are highly prized.

The first labels were used on beer bottles to identify the brewer and type of beer and only latterly were they used on soft drink and wine bottles.

Whilst all types of bottle labels are collected, the most popular category deals with beer bottles and this has been extended to include barrel labels. The hobby is especially popular in Eastern Europe and in Germany where some collectors have in excess of 300,000 different labels in their possession. This may seem an impressive figure but it represents only a fraction of the multitude of labels which have been issued over the years.

Labels are collected both for their design — and some are delightful — and for their historical and social context; in many instances they are the only known relics of once substantial businesses. The disappearance of so many breweries over the span of the last 100 years has resulted in a mass of obsolete labels. These are very popular with collectors. It is also possible from a study of labels to follow the changing tastes in beers over a period of time.

Societies exist in Germany, America, New Zealand and Australia as well as in the U.K. Here, the society has some 400 members, and numbers have increased steadily as a result of the many special beers produced to mark the Queen's Silver Jubilee.

One of the earliest commemorative labels. Issued for a 21st birthday. Red and black on buff.
£2

Issued to celebrate victory in the 1914-18 War by a brewery which is now part of Bass. Red and black on buff. £1.50—£2

Issued to celebrate victory in the 2nd World War. Red and black on white. £1

A popular occasion for brewers — this marks the Coronation of George VI. Red, white and blue. £2—£3

An attractive label of the 1950's. Blue and black on white.
30p

Another George VI Coronation label. This one is blue, red, white and gold.
£2

BEER BOTTLE LABELS

A popular event with many labels known. This multi-coloured label is very attractive. £1—£1.50

Such special beers proved popular and were kept on as here for George V Jubilee. Blue, red, white and fawn. £1

Issued in the 1920's by a brewery which is now part of Whitbread. Red and black on buff paper. £1.50

Very many beers were issued for this recent event. Label is blue, red and white. 30p

A 1930's label from a brewery which is part of Allied. Multi-coloured. £2—£3

A 1950's label issued by a still existing family owned brewery. Red, buff and black on white. 25p

Simple label issued c. 1940. Dark orange on white. 60p

For a beer popular in the North East issued in 1950's. Yellow, red and blue. 30p

An early Charrington label c. 1930. Browns and blue on buff. 60p

BEER BOTTLE LABELS

A 1940's label with the ever popular brewer's trademark. Red and black on white. 50p

An own-label Guinness c. 1950. Black on buff. 30p

To mark the 50th anniversary of the then company which is now part of Allied. Red and black on white.
£1.50

A beautiful label printed in 1897. Yellow, red, gold and black. £1

Many brewers boasted of their Letters Patent. This 1930's label is brown on buff. £1—£1.50

The only label known from a tiny brewery dated c.1915. Ornate and multi-coloured.
£20—£30

A tradition recently being revived. This 1920's label is green, red, black and blue.
£1.50

A Victorian label from a company founded in 1673. Red and buff on white. 75p

An Irish label of the 1920's. Printed black on green. £2

Issued c. 1940 by a brewery which was taken over in 1944. Blue, red and brown on white. 75p

A war time label — small in view of paper shortages. Red and black on white. 50p

A handful of labels were issued for the Festival in 1951. Red and black on buff. 50p—75p

A very strong beer first brewed for the trade with Tsarist Russia. Multi-coloured and in use in the 1940's. 30p

Not all labels were issued by breweries. Very many bottlers existed and used their own. This 1940's label is blue, black and red on white. 30p

Many brewers issued their own Guinness labels — this one dates from c. 1950 and is black on buff. 25p

BEER BOTTLE LABELS

An unusual label to be issued by a brewery in the heart of England. Blue, red and white.   30p

Very few commemorative items for this occasion. Brewery is now part of Courage. Gold, blue, red and white.   £2–£2.50

An unusual shape in use in the 1950's. Brown and black on buff.   60p

Circular label c. 1930. Green, blue, red and blue on white.   £1–£1.50

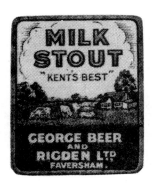

A once popular drink that contained little or no milk. Green, red and white.
£1

A 1940's label showing the brewery's trading area. Blue, yellow and brown on white.   40p

BELLEEK

One of the most distinctive form of porcelain is Belleek, produced in Co. Fermanagh since 1863.

It is made of a parian paste with an unusual iridescent pearly glaze, which is modelled into a variety of ornamental wares; particularly pieces featuring shells, marine forms and an open basketwork design.

The firm originally traded as David McBirney and Company, and some of the original designs are still in production to this day. Earlier works are often marked "Belleek Co. Fermanagh" with the printed trademark of an Irish wolfhound and harp, while later works, after 1891, usually bear the trademark together with "Co. Fermanagh, Ireland".

One of a pair of Belleek pitchers with scrolled handles and applied floral decoration. (Robert W. Skinner Inc.) £190

Belleek hexagonal basket with trelliswork body, 1891-1926, 28.4cm. wide. (Sotheby's)£286

Belleek croaking frog, circa 1900, 5½in. high. (Sotheby's Belgravia) £200

Late 19th century Belleek kettle on stand in the form of a dragon, 14in. high. (Robert W. Skinner Inc.) £1,570

Belleek honey pot in the form of a beehive, 6¼in. high. (Sotheby's Belgravia) £170

Belleek ice pail with decorative lid. (Stride & Son) £500

BELLS

Throughout the ages, bells have been made in all shapes and sizes ranging downwards from massive church bells, school bells, fire service bells, ships' bells, tradesmens' bells to small table bells. The latter is perhaps the most popular with collectors because of their size and delicacy.

Table bells are frequently made of silver, fine porcelain or glass. The glass examples include Cranberry, Nailsea, Bristol, Burmese or the very rare Tiffany.

An interesting collection can be gathered together from the wide range of reasonably priced brass hand bells currently on the market.

One of a pair of mid 19th century amber glass bells with white rims, 29.5cm. high. (Sotheby's) £93

Late 19th/early 20th century silver bell in the form of a lady, German, 4.4oz., 10.5cm. high. (Sotheby's) £319

George III silver table bell by Abraham Portal, London, 1764, 6oz.11dwt., 4¾in. high. (Sotheby's) £420

Late 19th century Meissen table bell, 10cm. high, with pierced angular handle. (Sotheby's) £340

Bronze bell with cast pierced crown, 1633, 12in. diam. (Sotheby's) £198

A 19th century muffin seller's hand bell, 10in. high, in perfect condition. (Vernon's) £45

Berlin woolwork is a simplified system of embroidery originating in Berlin in the early 19th century and similar in concept to the modern painting by numbers kit.

The designs, usually of exotic birds and flowers or copies of famous paintings, were first printed on squared paper. The needlewoman, working in wools, then transferred these patterns to a canvas most commonly using the tent or cross stitch, and often embellished the work with beads or cut pile areas. The finished product was generally applied to footstools, chairs and firescreens but, if the proud creator was particularly pleased, the work was often mounted in a rosewood or maple frame and hung on the wall of the living room to be admired by all. A popular subject for pictures was the sailing ship and a great number of these were worked by sailors during the long sea voyages.

By the 1830's, designs were being printed directly on to the canvas itself, and as the popularity of woolwork grew in both Europe and America so did the number of patterns available; reaching 14,000 designed for the British market alone around 1840. Early examples are often more subdued in colour than the later which, after the discovery of the purple analine dye became a little bit gaudy.

Berlin woolwork saw its decline in the 1870's, supposedly after criticism that it debased the art of embroidery, but I think its relative frivolity just did not gel with the more austere furniture which was beginning to dominate fashionable taste in the last quarter of the century.

Victorian lady's chair with original Berlin woolwork cover.   £250

Berlin woolwork and Italian firescreen showing Queen Victoria's pets, circa 1840, 51 x 31in.   £220

Plushwork and Berlin woolwork overmantel in rococo frame, 1840's, 56 x 44in.   £286

BIBLE BOXES

These chests are commonly referred to as bible boxes although they were also used for storing and transporting important documents, books and small items of value. They were of particularly sturdy construction so that they might withstand the rigors of a long journey by horse-drawn carriage.

Popular in the days when almost every family possessed a bible — sometimes the only reading material kept in a house, these boxes were constructed of oak, usually decorated with low relief carving frequently incorporating a date or initials and fitted with hinges and a strong lock. The bible, not only read for spiritual guidance, also provided a record of the family history and this valuable register of births, marriages and deaths could be kept safely under lock and key in a stout box such as this. The boxes, like the bibles, were passed on from generation to generation and remained popular in that form until around the time of William and Mary.

The earlier boxes with flat tops date from the 16th century and are usually about 61cm. wide and as much as 25.5cm. deep. Later examples often have a sloping lid which could be used as a lectern to rest a book upon whilst reading.

Writing boxes developed about the same time as bible boxes, are usually much shallower. As the style developed it became the custom to fit writing boxes with feet and later to place them on a stand until finally they became free standing pieces of furniture.

By the William and Mary period, demand had somewhat abated, possibly because every family possessing one had kept it in good order for succeeding generations.

17th century oak bible box.   £85

An oak bible box showing the Stuart Coat-of-Arms, retaining the original handblocked paper.   £200

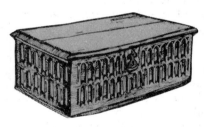

An oak bible box, its front and sides carved with two rows of flutings, with a reeded edge to the top, circa 1600.   £350

Commonwealth carved oak bible box, 1657, 2ft. wide.   £525

BICYCLES

The invention of the bicycle brought a new way of life to many Victorian men and women by making it possible for even the lowest paid workers in that society to experience independence and mobility for the first time and at a very low cost.

Nowadays, pre-1900 bicycles are very much in vogue and fairly expensive. In the seventies, when demand was restricted to a small group of enthusiasts, their value showed only a moderate improvement and it is not so long ago that £500 seemed like a lot to pay for a bicycle. Now we see that some fine examples will fetch thousands.

One does not have to pay that type of money to start a collection however, for there are many examples from early in the 20th century which can be bought for more modest sums.

Early 19th century velocipede. £800

Early 20th century French child's hippo tricycle with black painted chassis. £88

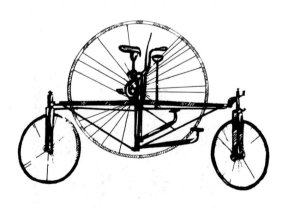

A James Starley Coventry lever tricycle built by Haynes & Jeffy's, 1877.   £2,000

Mid-Victorian velocipede with cast-iron frame and iron rimmed wooden wheels.   £620

Dursley-Pedersen pedal cycle, circa 1905, with three-speed gearing. £820

Rudge Whitworth tricycle with 5ft.5in. black frame, circa 1899. £110

Ipswich made 19th century boneshaker. £500

53in. ordinary bicycle, 5ft. high, circa 1880, English. £750

Beale's 'Facile' bicycle of 1874. £1,000

Swift pedal tricycle with steering by twin hand grips, 1880. £1,850

BIRDCAGES

During the Middle Ages, it was quite a common practice to keep birds such as jays and magpies as pets in cages, while doves, pigeon and quail were less fortunate, being kept mainly to provide extra meat for the table.

It had always been the fashion for members of the nobility to have birds in cages, sometimes made of gold and set with jewels and semi precious stones. It would seem, too, that the cages were far more important than their inhabitants, for these were frequently stuffed specimens which, of course, required less care and attention than their live brethern. Larks, goldfinches and other brightly coloured birds were popular, as were parrots whose exotic appearance, mimicry and scarcity value all contributed greatly to his Lordship's assets in the one-upmanship stakes.

Most early cages were of basket work with a turf set in the base for reasons of hygiene, but few of these have survived. Better examples from the 18th century were made in an architectural style, of mahogany, often in the shape of a house but, by the end of that century, the dome-shaped top became popular and remained the standard design feature throughout the 19th century, when brass was the most commonly used material.

One of the more interesting shapes to be found, are those modelled after the Crystal Palace, which dates it fairly conclusively at about 1851, the year of the Great Exhibition.

There is, of course, always a demand for parrot cages but those made of white metal should be valued at about half the price of a good brass cage.

19th century brass parrot cage. £120

Late Victorian brass birdcage with etched glass decoration. £35

Early 18th century Dutch tin-glazed birdcage, 39cm. high. £2,100

Late 19th century Italian painted wood birdcage, 122in. high. £1,500

19th century ormolu birdcage with ogee rop, 24in. high. £2,000

Mid 19th century 'Crystal Palace' brass birdcage. £75

BIRDS

Here we have further evidence of the Victorian mania for armchair rustication. They liked to surround themselves with natural specimens and, to keep them dust free, they placed them under glass. Wax fruit, specimens from the sea-shores but, above all, they loved their stuffed birds.

Birds were displayed in a variety of poses, frequently set in a mock up of their natural habitat: this was often a talking point as many exotic birds were imported from South America and the Far East.

The more common species are still collected and it is worth noting that certain unusual or rare examples can fetch an awful lot of money!

Very rare passenger pigeon, mounted on branch, 22in. high, in glass dome.   £500

A cased specimen of a cockerel 'Preserved by John Pear, All Saints Green, Norwich'.   £30

Stuffed barn owl.   £55

White-tailed sea eagle and chick in glass case, 36in. high.   £120

An extremely rare stuffed specimen of the Great Auk.   £10,000

Fine stuffed peregrine falcon in glass case, 20½in. high.   £225

BISCUIT TINS

One of the chief delights of Christmas between 1868 and the end of the 1930's was to buy the most delicious biscuits in a decorative tin. The tins, originally designed to keep the product in fresh condition, soon became an important sales feature and manufacturers vied with each other to produce the most inventive novelties.

The idea of printing on tin was pioneered in Britain around 1860 by Benjamin George who patented his many new processes, but it was not until after 1889 that the secrets of simple production methods became available to printed tin manufacturers in general.

Huntley & Palmers who produced some of the earliest decorated tins seem to have been the most prolific manufacturers of these delightful boxes, in a range so vast it became necessary to publish a catalogue informing their customers of available designs.

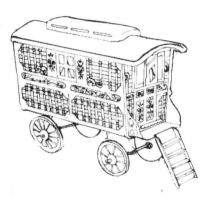

Huntley & Palmers pedestal biscuit tin decorated with classical figures.£15

Jacob's gypsy caravan biscuit tin, circa 1905.   £45

Huntley & Palmers book biscuit tin, circa 1903.
                £50

Rare Edwardian Macfarlane Lang tinplate biscuit tin, with hinged roof, 19.5cm. long.   £90

Huntley & Palmers laundry basket biscuit tin, circa 1904.   £26

Jacob & Co., Coronation coach biscuit tin, 1937.
                £40

BLUE & WHITE CHINA

Following the discovery, during the second half of the 18th century, of an inexpensive, successful method of transfer printing designs on to comparatively inexpensive earthenware, vast quantities of blue and white tableware were produced. Blue was found to be the most manageable colour to work with when using the new process.

The name associated with this development is that of John Brooks, whose new techniques seem to have been taken to the Worcester factory and taught to an apprentice, one, Thomas Turner who founded the Caughley factory in Shropshire in 1772. It was at this factory, one of the most prolific manufacturers of blue and white earthenware, that the ever popular 'Willow' pattern evolved. Marks of the factory are a crescent, C. S. or the word Salopian. The Caughley works continued until 1799 when they were taken over by John Rose, a former Caughley apprentice, who had left three years earlier to start the Coalport factory.

This method of transfer printing was taken up by the potteries of Staffordshire, Yorkshire and Lancashire, resulting in a mass market both at home and for export.

There are many hundreds of designs, most following a theme such as, famous houses, topographical subjects, American scenes (America was one of the main markets), floral subjects, romantic scenes and many more.

Early pieces, produced by famous potters, can be pricey but there are still many thousands of later and less expensive examples around.

Staffordshire covered vegetable dish with high domed cover, circa 1825, 12¼in. long. (Robert W. Skinner Inc.) £410

Dublin delftware meat dish, Delamain's factory, circa 1760, 43cm. high. (Sotheby, King & Chasemore) £140

Staffordshire washbowl and jug showing Lafayette at Franklin's tomb, circa 1825, 12in. diam. (Robert W. Skinner Inc.) £490

Caughley shell-shaped dish, circa 1778-82, 8in. diameter. (Sotheby's) £210

Worcester blue and white bough pot of bombe shape, circa 1765-70, 9in. diam. (Sotheby's) £374

One of a pair of Companie-des-Indes blue and white plates, painted with a tree peony. (Sotheby, King & Chasemore) £150

Adams silver mounted blue and white mug with angular handle, London, 1802, 12.5cm. high. (Christie's) £198

Staffordshire jug with pictorial decoration. (British Antique Exporters) £20

Charger from an English ironstone dinner service of fifty-three pieces, circa 1810. (Sotheby, King & Chasemore) £410

Caughley porcelain mask jug. (Russell, Baldwin & Bright) £230

Large Staffordshire platter with wide floral border, circa 1825, 19in. wide. (Robert W. Skinner Inc.) £205

Mid 19th century Chinese blue and white water filter, 37cm. high. (Sotheby's) £170

Liverpool blue and white meat dish, 14½in. (Vernon's) £200

BOOKS

Book Collecting is a growing market which every year attracts new devotees among people who have previously only looked on books as 'good reads' for whiling away long journeys. Now the collecting of books is becoming one of the new 'Commodity markets' and a safe resort for money against inflation. There is fierce bidding at specialised book auctions all over Britain and the days are sadly gone when a box of mixed books which might well contain a first edition could be picked up for pennies at a local junk shop.

For a book enthusiast to buy wisely it is essential to learn something about the subject and then to specialise for this is a huge world indeed.

Some categories are more popular than others — medicine has a dedicated but fairly small following as has war-like subjects and books about British regiments. Books dealing with travel, topography and wild life of every kind come near the top of the popularity poll especially if they contain fine plates and illustrations.

The snobbism that sometimes shows itself in more specialised books is refreshingly absent in the world of modern firsts. Most sought after are Penguin first editions in paperback — especially the first thirty and those brought out during the war when they were printed on thin paper and their fragility made it difficult for them to survive. Rarity is a quality which makes any book collectable.

There are enough books continually coming up for sale to keep the most avid collector busy for a lifetime just reading the catalogues. No matter what you want to study and no matter how much you wish to spend, you will be sure to find something to suit your taste and your purse.

The Holy Bible, containing the Old and New Testaments, with Apocripha, done into verse for the Benefit of Weak Memories, 78 x 54mm., B. Harris, Senoir, 1701. (Sotheby's) £1,210

Naturliches Zauber-Buch, oder Neuerofneter Spielplatz rare Kunste, 7th Edition, 2 volumes, 1798. (Sotheby's) £105

Passio Domini Nostri Jesu Christi, no. 231 of 250 copies, 6 wood engraved illustrations by Eric Gill, 4to, 1926. Golden Cockerel Press. (Sotheby's) £175

The National Sports of Great Britain, 1st Edition, first issue, title and text in English and French, additional coloured aquatint title and dated 1820. (Christie's) £4,950

T. Sturge Moore, A Brief Account of the Origin of the Eragny Press, limited to 241 copies, 15 woodcut illustrations by Lucian Pissarro, 1903. (Sotheby's) £260

Beatrix Potter, Changing Pictures, a Book of Transformation Pictures, 6 coloured illustrations, each composed of slats which slide away to reveal another picture when lever is pulled, inscription dated 1893.(Sotheby's) £748

Samuel Howitt, 'The British Sportsman', New Edition, 4to, 1834. (Sotheby's) £630

John Keats, 'Endrymion', no. 317 of 500 copies, wood engraved frontis, 2 initials and 53 illustrations by John Buckland-Wright, 11 full page, 1947. (Sotheby's)　　　£175

John Skinner Prout, Tasmania Illustrated, 18 lithographed plates, Hobart, 1844; bound with two tinted lithographs: Nicolas Chevalier: Victorian Scenery: Grampians and Gippsland, 10 chromolithographed plates, signed and dated 1864. (Christie's)　　　£3,850

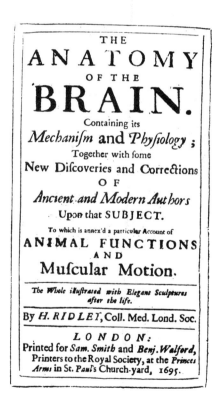

Humphrey Ridley, The Anatomy of the Brain Containing its Mechanism and Physiology, 1st Edition, 5 folding plates with explanatory text, 1695. (Sotheby's)　　　£1,100

Robert McAlmon, A Hasty Bunch, 1st Edition, 1922. (Sotheby's)　　　£90

The Common Carol Book, limited to 225 copies, 22 wood-engraved illustrations by Eric Gill, David Jones and others, 1926. (Sotheby's)   £70

John Gould and R. Bowdler Sharpe, The Birds of New Guinea and the Adjacent Papuan Islands, 5 volumes, 320 hand-finished coloured lithographed plates by John Gould and W. Hart, 1875-1888. (Christie's)£16,500

Andre Maurois, Ariel, 1935, first Penguin printed. (Phillips)   £70

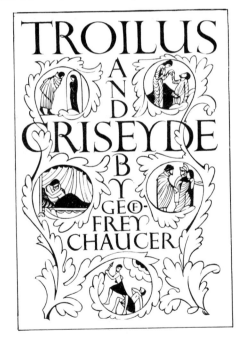

William Bligh, Voyage in the Resource From Coupang to Batavia, number 80 of 350 copies, 4 pages of facsimile, double page pictorial title and 3 wood-engraved illustrations by Peter Barker-Mill, 1937. (Sotheby's)   £462

Geoffrey Chaucer, edited by Arundel del Re, Troilus and Criseyde, number 149 of 225 copies, wood-engraved pictoral title, 5 full-page illustrations and pictorial borders by Eric Gill, 1927. (Sotheby's)   £800

George Stubbs, The Anatomy of the Horse, 1st Edition, 24 engraved plates, J. Purser for author, 1766. (Christie's) £1,500

Elizabeth, Petra, Joanna and David Gill, and Stephen and Mark Pepler, A Christmas Book, 18 wood-engraved illustrations by the authors, 1919. (Sotheby's) £99

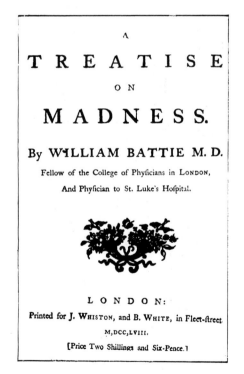

The English Midwife, containing directions to midwives, 7 folding plates, 23 wood-cuts in text, Rowland Reynolds, 1682. (Sotheby's) £650

William Battie, A Treatise on Madness, 1st Edition, wood-cut ornament at end of most sections, J. Whiston & B. White, 1758. (Sotheby's) £270

W. H. Scott, British Field Sports, 1818. (Sotheby's) £80

Edward Lear, A Book of Nonsense, 54 pen
and ink drawings for 53 limericks with
text written below on three lines.(Sotheby's)
£17,600

The Song of Songs, number 740 of 740 copies,
19 wood-engraved illustrations by Eric Gill,
one full page, Golden Cockerel Press, 1925.
(Sotheby's)   £286

Carlo Ruini, Anatomia del Cavallo, Ingermita,
et Suoi Rimedii, 3rd Edition, 2 volumes in
one, 64 full-page woodcut illustrations, Venice,
F. Prati, 1618. (Sotheby's)   £1,320

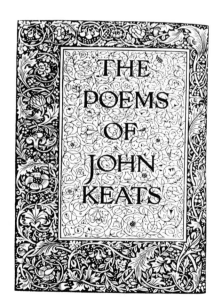

Hippopotami And Quack Medicine, charming
printed broadside illustrating 'Le Grande e
Maravigliose Virtu Del Dente Del Hippopotami
. . .', for Cesare Scaccioppa, Rome, 1625.
(Sotheby's)   £190

John Keats, 'Poems' edited by F. S. Ellis,
limited to 307 copies, this is no. 300, printed
in red and black, 1894. (Sotheby's)   £290

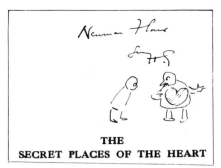

THE
SECRET PLACES OF THE HEART

H. G. Wells, The Secret Places of the Heart,
1st Edition, Presentation Copy, 1922.
(Sotheby's)   £65

Aristide Maillol, Virgil, The Eclogues, 43
woodcut illustrations, 3 initials, and press-
mark by Maillol, 1927. (Sotheby's) £605

Hugh Ronalds, A Concise Description of
Selected Applies, 1831. (Sotheby's) £500

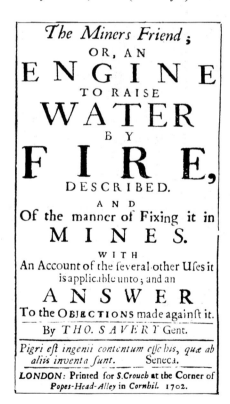

Thomas Savery, The Miner's Friend or An
Engine to Raise Water by Fire, 1st Edition,
S. Crouch 1702. (Sotheby's)   £1,200

N. Heideloff, Gallery of Fashion, volume V-
IX, 5 volumes in 2, April 1798-March 1803.
(Sotheby's)   £2,800

BOTTLES

A hobby far more profitable than the highly speculative art of panning for gold in British rivers has been growing steadily in the past few years — that of literally digging up the rubbish of yester-year.

I have heard figures quoted of over two million pounds' worth of relics being unearthed each year, mostly in the form of bottles which have a ready market in both this country and the U.S.A. No expensive metal detectors are needed to reap this harvest, just a pair of wellies, a fork and a little detective work in finding out where the old rubbish dumps are.

Collectors have found a most profitable site in the search for whisky, gin, wine and beer bottles to be under and around river bridges, for it was common practice for the homeward bound tippler to sling the empty over the parapet where it was likely to become lodged in the mud directly below or close to the banks. A study of the river current may help to pinpoint a likely spot for rubbish to have built up over the years.

Household rubbish dumps often yield an amazing assortment of bottles and containers. The bottles most often found are the stone ginger beers with transfer printing or the pale green glass Hiram Codd's lemonade bottles with marble stopper. (Many of these Codd's bottles are found with the neck broken off and the marble missing for, understandably, the children of the household would take the marble out before the bottle was disposed of). A complete Codd's bottle will always fetch a few pounds and a rare example like the cobalt blue illustrated, can be worth around £125. Patent medicine, ink and poison bottles also have their special examples which will fetch good prices.

Early light amber glass 'Bovril' jar.
£2

Green glass wine bottle, 1707.   £800

Cobalt blue bottle marked 'Poison'.
£15

Sheared top sauce bottle of green tinted glass.   £3

Codd's 'light bulb' bottle with black marble stopper.
£25

Dutch engraved bottle by Willem van Heemskerk with dark emerald green body, 1689, 33cm. high.
£6,380

BOTTLES

Dark green glass pickle jar, 1880.   £9

18th/19th century Indian blue glass hookah bottle with flaring ridged neck, 7½in. high.   £242

Sealed and dated wine bottle inscribed Saml. Whittuck, 1751, 9in. high.   £340

17th century Dutch sealed wine bottle shoulder applied with armorial seal, 9½in. high.   £1,320

Sealed wine bottle, 1741, 9¼in. high.   £225

Gigantic green glass bottle, mid 17th century, 15in. high.   £40

Etched and polished internally decorated bottle and stopper, incised Marinot, 13.2cm. high.   £3,200

Early sealed wine bottle, circa 1683, 6in. high. £820

H. Codd's cobalt blue marble stoppered bottle.   £125

BOTTLES

1st century A.D. small blue glass bottle with squat pear-shaped body, 3in. high. £700

Serving bottle, dark olive green with opaque white inclusions, Shropshire, circa 1800, 12.5cm. high. £190

Sealed onion form wine bottle, inscribed Ed. Jones/Burton, 1737, 19cm. high. £180

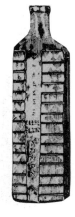

Clarke's clear fluid ammonia bottle. £12

Early sealed wine bottle, seal inscribed 'Robt. Tanner 1725', 8¾in. high. £275

Bung stopper mineral water bottle. £4

Blown-in mould bottle in green colour, New England, circa 1825, 6¼in. high. £375

One pint brown glass beer bottle. £5

Attractive Pekin glass bottle of transparent amber coloured metal, Qianlong period, 20.3cm. high. £300

American blown three-mould bottle in olive green glass, circa 1830, 17cm. high. £125

Rare early sealed and dated onion form wine bottle, dated 1699, 13cm. high. £1,000

Sealed wine bottle with short tapering cylindrical neck, 7in. high, circa 1725. £400

Codd's amber glass mineral bottle. £55

19th century Indian glass hookah bottle with bell-shaped sides, 7in. high. £99

Codd's glass mineral bottle with amber stopper. £20

Red glass Barrel Bitters bottle, American, circa 1860-80, 9¼in. high.£17

French blown-in mould Pocahontas bottle, circa 1830, 2 x 2¼in. £210

Cobalt blue bottle marked 'Not to be Taken'. £6

BRONZE ANIMALS

Bronze groups of animal sculpture became a popular art form in the 19th century. When Antoine-Louis Bayre exhibited his 'Tiger Devouring a Gavial' at the Salon of 1831 it caused a commotion in the French art world. The general enthusiasm led to other artists adopting animals as the subject of their work and so a group emerged to become known as — les animaliers.

For the first time, animals were depicted in art as they are in nature: docile, active, resting, feeding, dramatic in combat and always in realistic detail.

Notable artists from this period include P. J. Mene, Isadore Bonheur, Jules Moigniez and Christophe Fratin.

Bronze model of a running hare. (Sotheby, King & Chasemore)   £60

Bronze group of a standing coursing greyhound with a hare in its mouth, by P. J. Mene, 5in. high. (Sotheby, King & Chasemore)   £150

Oriental bronze group of an elephant being attacked by two tigers. (T. Bannister & Co.)   £200

Bronze figure of a stallion by P. J. Mene, signed, 8½in. long. (Sotheby, King & Chasemore)   £500

Large bronze figure of the Huntsman's Horse after J. Willis Good, 12½in. wide.(Boardman's)   £720

Bronze figure of a grazing goat by Antoine Louis Barye, 3¾in. long, signed. (Sotheby, King & Chasemore)   £280

16th century Paduan bronze model of The
Capitoline Wolf, by Severo da Ravenna,
14cm. wide. (Christie's)   £1,760

Japanese bronze model of a crawling monkey,
18in. long. (Hall Wateridge & Owen)   £240

Bronze model of a stretching dog, 7½in.
long. (Sotheby, King & Chasemore)   £260

Viennese cold-painted bronze model of a
cat, 6½in. long. (Sotheby, King & Chasemore)
                                        £25

French cast bronze rabbit on black marble
base, signed F. Pautrot, circa 1861, 5½in.
long. (Robert W. Skinner Inc.)   £335

Bronze model of the Lion and Serpent by A.
L. Barye, 6¼in. high. (Sotheby, King &
Chasemore)   £480

Bronze figure of a charging elephant by
Barye, 7½in. wide. (Sotheby, King & Chasemore)   £580

Bronze group of a bull and a recumbent
cow, 16in. long. (Sotheby, King & Chasemore)   £420

BUCKLES

Buckles have presented an interesting fashion feature throughout the centuries. Essentially a piece of jewellery, they have been styled for daywear and to sparkle in the evening. They were worn at the belt, on a garter at the knee and on shoes. It is reported that men wore buckles as an indication of their social status and some were so large, they almost covered the whole instep.

Buckles were often included in a parure — a set of matching jewellery — and reflect the changing styles. Examples include those made of precious metals and set with gem-stones and the rather ornate Victorian style of gilt, silver filigree, beads or jet.

Emphasis was placed on the use of metal during the Art Nouveau period and it is buckles from this period that have become most popular with collectors today.

Liberty & Co. 'Cymric' silver and enamel belt buckle of butterfly shape, Birmingham, 1902, 9.25cm. wide. (Sotheby's)   £170

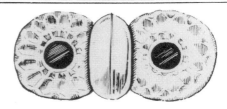

Liberty & Co. silver and enamel belt buckle in the form of two flowers, Birmingham, 1909, 8.25cm. wide. (Sotheby's)   £40

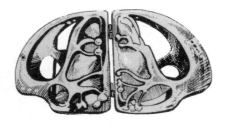

Theodor Fahrner silver and stone buckle, London, 1902, 6.75cm. wide. (Sotheby's)   £165

William Comyns silver belt buckle, London, 1901, 7.25cm. wide. (Sotheby's)   £60

Liberty & Co. silver belt buckle, 11cm. wide, Birmingham, 1902. (Sotheby's)   £200

French Art Nouveau belt buckle, 7.5cm. wide, circa 1900, gilt teeth. (Sotheby's)   £265

BUCKLES

Rare early 19th century Swiss buckle, enamelled with white and black flowers. (Taylor Lane & Creber) £160

Unusual belt buckle by H. Hobson & Sons, Birmingham, 1910, 7cm. wide. (Phillips)£70

Large Art Deco rose-diamond, enamel, gold and silver gilt buckle by Cartier. (Christie's) £750

Art Nouveau silver buckle by William Comyns, London, 1898, 13cm. wide. (Phillips)   £130

Art Nouveau belt buckle, 7.75cm. wide, probably American, circa 1900. (Sotheby's) £90

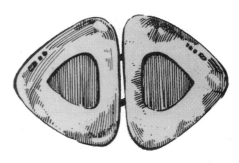

Silver and enamel buckle, 7.7cm. wide, circa 1903, London. (Sotheby's) £45

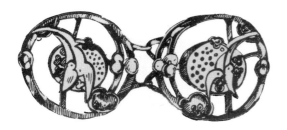

Liberty & Co. silver and enamel belt buckle, Birmingham, 1906, 8.75cm. wide. (Sotheby's) £525

Gold buckle by Myer Myers, New York, circa 1765. (Sotheby's) £5,375

The earliest tickets in use were punch types originated by Bell Punch Co. Ltd. of London. More recent issues are still reasonably common though will in time become more rare and thus appreciate in value. The current price is around 2 pence each but earlier issues which relate to tramway operators can fetch up to 50 pence each.

Edmondson printed tickets are on thick card and have been used by the railways since they were developed by a ticket office clerk on the Newcastle and Carlisle Railway. It was unusual for them to be used by bus or tram operators thus the illustrated example from Leicester is worth up to 30 pence.

The Gibson and T.I.M. types are from the earliest machine system for ticket issue developed in the 1920's. The tickets illustrated are much more recent and are worth only a penny or so each while the fragile nature of pre-war examples ensures a value upwards of 30 to 50 pence.

The Insert tickets of the Setright company have also been around from the 1920's and examples illustrated are recent issues currently worth typically no more than 5 pence each.

Following on from Inserts, Setright developed its Speed System, the 6 examples shown represent something of the development of this still very much alive system. Tickets are generally worth only 1 or 2 pence each.

The Ultimate system was introduced by Bell Punch company in the late 1940's. Fully preprinted tickets from rolls were issued from a machine. Most tickets are single issues, but double issues (i.e. 2 tickets joined together) are not uncommon; the latter are preferred by some collectors. Ultimates are now giving way to new electronics based machines. Typical prices are 1 to 2 pence each.

Willebrews, from Williamson the printer, have gone out of fashion now. A column of fares along one or both edges was cut by a machine so that the last fare showing represented the fare paid. Collectors' price about 2p.

The rarer and larger tickets are worth more than the usual 'everyday' issues and are many and varied; price typically 5 to 50 pence though some may be worth more.

Tickets issued for special occasions are becoming more numerous. They celebrate centenaries, last rear entrance bus in service and other such events. Prices currently range from 5 to 50 pence on the occasions that dealers have such tickets available but, with limited issue, they are bound to escalate in price within a few years of issue.

Setright Speed — West Midlands PTE.
Predecimal issue.   2p

Setright Speed — Nesbit Brothers.
Decimal issue.   2p

Special Issue — this one marked the last of Leicester's
rear entrance buses.   30p

Punch Type — early issue
for joint tram services of
Blackpool and Lytham St.
Annes.   50p

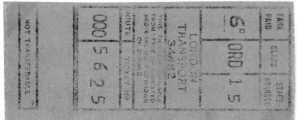

Gibson — these are widely used by London Transport.
                                           40p

Double Ultimate — Lancaster City.
Decimal issue.   2p

Prepaid — typical prepaid card ticket. This one
from Bournemouth.   2p

Punch Type — one of the few decimal
issues of this type. 'R' denotes Return. 2p

BUS TICKETS

Autofare — modern ticket for one-man operated buses. 2p

Punch Type — early issue showing principal stopping points tramway route. 50p

Punch Type — typical predecimal issue. 'S' denotes Single. 2p

Ultimate — typical later predecimal issue. 2p

Ultimate — more detailed issue. 2p

Edmonson — usually used by railway companies. This is from Leicester trams. 30p

Setright Insert — fare date printed by machine on hatched area. 5p

Setright Speed — recent decimal issue. 2p

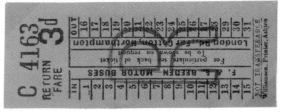

Setright Speed — predecimal issue. 2p

Punch Type — early issue. 2p

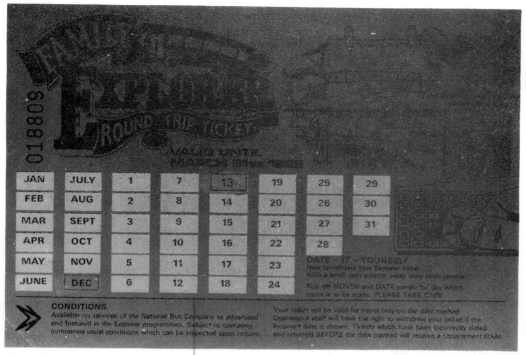

Large Card Type — National Bus Company explorer ticket. Passenger rubs off date with a coin. Valid for one day only.   35p

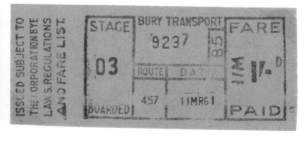

Multiple Journey Ticket — one from a vast variety available to all collectors. 35p

Setright Speed — recent decimal issue. 2p

T.I.M. — machine prints all the information.   40p

BUS TICKETS

Setright Insert — Isle of Man issue. 5p

Ultimate — double issue (worth 6d) from Blackburn. 2p

Ultimatic — issued from desk mounted machine at booking office. 2p

Setright Speed — Scottish decimal issue. 2p

Special Issue — issued in connection with an open day to mark the operator's centenary.
20p

Punch type — composite issue covers single or return journeys. 2p

Autofare 3 - issued by one of the new generation of electronic ticket machines. 2p

Ultimate — 'Stock' type which can be used by any operator. 2p

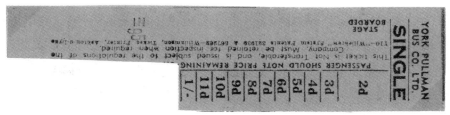

Willebrew — the machine cuts the table of fares below the value of actual fare paid. 2p

SP 09178

1D TYNESIDE P.T.E.
Issued subject to Bye-laws & Regulations

Single	EXch.	Return

Williamson   Ashton

Ultimate — single issue is most common version of this type.   2p

HYLTON & DAWSON

Nᵒ 13019

TEN TRIP TICKET

CONDUCTOR WILL PUNCH ONCE FOR EACH JOURNEY | PRICE ▶ |

| 10 | 9 | 8 | 7 | 6 | 5 | 4 | 3 | 2 |

Ten Trip Ticket — with cancellation spaces for journeys subsequent to the First.   30p

---

A

5439   Burwell & District Motor Service

SINGLE

58p		5p
56p		6p
54p		7p
52p		8p
50p		9p
48p		10p
46p		11p
44p		12p
42p		13p
40p		14p
38p		15p
36p		16p
34p		17p
32p		18p
30p		19p
28p		20p
26p		21p
25p		22p
24p		23p

Not transferable and must be retained for inspection. Issued subject to the regulations of the Company.
Williamson, Printer, Ashton

5439

A

Willebrew — decimal issue. 2p

Ij 7821   Ij 7821

EMERGENCY TICKET   **EMERGENCY TICKET**

1p		19p	19p		1p
2p		20p	20p		2p
3p		21p	21p		3p
4p		22p	22p		4p
5p		23p	23p		5p
6p		24p	24p		6p
7p		25p	25p		7p
8p		26p	26p		8p
9p		27p	27p		9p
10p		28p	28p		10p
11p		29p	29p		11p
12p		30p	30p		12p
13p		31p	31p		13p
14p		32p	32p		14p
15p		33p	33p		15p
16p		34p	34p		16p
17p		35p	35p		17p
18p		Return	Return		18p

VALUE OF TICKET SHOWN BY PUNCH HOLES. Not Transferable. Issued subject to regulations.

SELNEC P.T.E. CENTRAL DIVISION

PASSENGER   **CONDUCTOR**

Williamson, Printer, Ashton   Williamson, Printer, Ashton

Duplex — Emergency issue only used when usual machine fails.   30p

---

N 8211

CUMBERLAND
Motor Services Ltd.

TOUR

DATE

PICK-UP AT

TIME	**SEAT**

This ticket is issued subject to the conditions printed on back.
C & Williamson, Printer, Ashton

Setright Insert — special issue for pre-booked tours.   5p

BUTTER STAMPS

Butter stamps have a lot to commend them as suitable objects for collecting. They are small, quite readily available and offer an attractive range of interesting motifs.

Most commonly made of sycamore with a turned wood handle and a hand carved design on the base, the topic of the design will help to identify the source: a swan and bullrushes suggests a riverside farm, a sheep — a hill farm, and so on.

A popular American butter stamp bears a tulip motif and other themes include birds, dates, wheatsheaves, a heart and even a little motto entreating one to 'Eat Good Butter'.

Less common examples in boxwood and those designed to commemorate a special event are of particular interest to the collector.

19th century American butter stamp, carved with a lamb, 3in. diam. (Robert W. Skinner Inc.) £150

Sycamore wood butter marker, circa 1830, 5in. diam. (Christopher Sykes) £38

19th century American wooden handleless butter stamp with incised anchor, 3½in. diam. (Robert W. Skinner) £40

19th century American wooden butter stamp carved with a running fox, 2½in. diam. (Robert W. Skinner Inc.) £80

19th century American wooden butter stamp of shell design, 3½in. diam. (Robert W. Skinner Inc.) £55

19th century American wooden butter stamp with incised deer, 4in. diam. (Robert W. Skinner Inc.) £165

19th century American wooden butter stamp showing a bird on a branch, 3in. diam. (Robert W. Skinner Inc.) £120

19th century American wooden oval butter stamp with carved eagle standing on a globe, initials on either side, 5½in. long. (Robert W. Skinner Inc.) £190

19th century American wooden butter stamp carved with a cow, 3½in. diam. (Robert W. Skinner Inc.) £80

BUTTONS

Most highly prized are the 18th century sets of silver buttons and those beautiful silver and enamel buttons from the Art Nouveau period but, these are quite rare and a good representative collection might include buttons in pewter, copper, cloisonne, steel, ivory, bone, horn, glass, china, jet, amber, wood — and many more.

People very seldom throw buttons away and many a good collection has been started after the casual purchase of an old 'household' button tin or box at a jumble sale. Once buttons have been sorted for resale they, obviously, come a bit more expensive.

When you consider the immense number of buttons produced over hundreds of years, in an almost infinite range of shapes, sizes and materials, it follows that button collecting has become one of the most popular hobbies today.

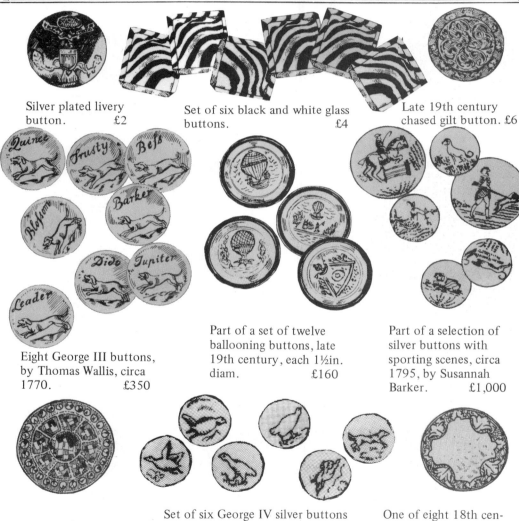

Silver plated livery button. £2

Set of six black and white glass buttons. £4

Late 19th century chased gilt button. £6

Eight George III buttons, by Thomas Wallis, circa 1770. £350

Part of a set of twelve ballooning buttons, late 19th century, each 1½in. diam. £160

Part of a selection of silver buttons with sporting scenes, circa 1795, by Susannah Barker. £1,000

One of a set of twelve Georgian cut steel buttons, about 1800. £60

Set of six George IV silver buttons embellished in relief with birds, a hare and hound, 1in. diam., by W. W., London, 1823. £150

One of eight 18th century buttons, by Saml. Wheat, circa 1755. £130

Cameras were first produced on a commercial scale at the end of the 19th century and the Victorians quickly developed a passion for the art of photography. Their veritable mania for documentation led them to record all manner of events from the Grand Tour to the day a young man paraded proudly in his first pair of long trousers.

Today, as the race goes on to develope smaller, lighter, slimmer, fully automatic cameras, the trade in old plate cameras and all the paraphernalia of the Victorian studio, is thriving. Made with the precision of scientific instruments most of these cameras are still in usable condition but they have taken on more than a utilitarian appeal and are now treasured for their intrinsic quality.

A few years ago a good Victorian brass and wood plate camera could be bought easily for as little as £10; after all, who wanted old cameras? Then a few enthusiasts began collecting in a serious way and, suddenly, plate cameras were changing hands at ten times as much.

Even some cameras made as recently as ten years ago have acquired a commercial value to collectors — often far in excess of the guide lines worked out by manufacturers for trade-in prices on new equipment.

One of the rarest examples to come on to the market was the Sutton Panoramic Wet Plate Camera which fetched £11,000 at auction, the resulting publicity bringing two more to light which also sold for about the same figure. Although these were exceptional prices, there are many cameras, like the Powell's stereoscopic camera or the Compur Leica, which sell for well over £1,000.

Most, however, change hands for a good deal less than this, but still at prices which would send anybody up into the loft for a search.

Rare Dallmeyer miniature wet-plate camera, circa 1862, 2 x 3¾in. (Sotheby's)   £1,100

Postcard size Tropical Soho stereoscopic reflex camera. (Christie's S. Kensington) £3,700

Wet-plate camera by W. W. Rouch, London, circa 1864, 5 x 5in. (Sotheby's)   £700

W. Watson & Sons stereo tailboard camera, 3¼ x 6¾in., circa 1900, in leather case. (Sotheby's) £240

A rare Richard's Homeos stereoscopic camera, 17 x 24mm., with twin Krauss-Zeiss Tessar 28mm. f 4.5 lenses, French, circa 1914. (Sotheby's) £770

A Watson & Sons hand and stand camera, 4½ x 6¼in., with lens in Bausch & Lomb shutter, English, circa 1920. (Sotheby's) £209

A W. Watson Alpha Hand and stand camera, 4¾ x 6½in., with 6½in. Watson Holdstigmat F6.5 lens, English, circa 1895. (Sotheby's) £220

Voigtlander prominent folding camera, 6 x 9cm., circa 1933, in original leather case. (Sotheby's) £220

A tailboard folding field camera, 4¾ x 6¼in., P.A.C.S.A. lens with Waterhouse stops, English, circa 1870.(Sotheby's) £121

A Belliene stereo camera, with twin Zeiss 110mm. f/1.8 lenses, in leather case, French, circa 1900. (Sotheby's) £250

VEF Minox sub-miniature camera, 8 x 11mm., Latvian, circa 1939. (Sotheby's) £200

A Bosco stereo camera, 3¾ x 6½in. on roll film, the two lenses with guillotine shutter, German, circa 1905. (Sotheby's) £121

CAMERAS

Newman & Guardia Nydia folding plate camera, 3¼ x 4¼in., in original leather case, circa 1905. (Sotheby's) £170

A. C. Lawrance 'Clifford' drop-plate camera, 4 x 5in., with Goerz Doppel-Anastigmat, 150mm. lens, English, circa 1890. (Sotheby's) £165

ICA Universal Juwel 440 folding plate camera, 13 x 18cm., Germany, circa 1925. (Sotheby's) £170

Ensign Tropical special reflex camera, 3¼ x 4¼in., in teak body, circa 1930. (Sotheby's) £150

Thornton Pickard amber folding field camera, circa 1895, 6½ x 4¾in. (Sotheby's) £60

Newman & Guardia New Ideal Sibyl folding camera, 3¼ x 4¼in., circa 1925. (Sotheby's) £80

A Kodak no. 1 camera, with 57mm. f 9 periscopic lens, guillotine sector shutter, 17cm., American, circa 1880. (Sotheby's) £800

Canon model 7 35mm. camera, 24 x 36mm., circa 1962, in leather case. (Sotheby's) £300

A Sinclair Tropical Una hand and stand camera, 3¼ x 5¼in., with Zeiss f/6.3, lens in Newman & Sinclair shutter, English, circa 1925.(Sotheby's) £715

Sanders & Crowhurst 'The Birdland' reflex camera, 4 x 5in., circa 1908. (Sotheby's) £160

A stereoscopic sliding box camera, with two simple lenses, in mahogany body on baseboard, 9in. long, English, circa 1860. (Sotheby's) £462

Marion's metal miniature camera, 1¼ x 1¼in., in mahogany case, circa 1884. (Sotheby's) £1,400

Prestwich Manufacturing Co. 35mm. hand-crank movie camera, circa 1915, 18 x 24mm. (Sotheby's) £240

Early Sinclair Una hand and stand camera, 3¼ x 4¼in., and six plate holders, circa 1905. (Sotheby's) £90

Zeiss Ikon contaflex twin lens reflex camera, 24 x 36mm., German, circa 1935. (Sotheby's) £450

Newman & Guardia folding reflex camera, 2½ x 3½in., circa 1925, in original leather case. (Sotheby's) £180

A J. H. Dallmeyer transitional wet/dry plate tailboard camera, 4¼ x 7in., with Ross 4in. lens, English, circa 1880.(Sotheby's) £264

A rare J. Frennet stereo reflex camera, 7 x 15cm., with twin Zeiss Protarlinse 244mm. lenses, Belgian, circa 1900. (Sotheby's) £220

CANE HANDLES

Walking sticks have been with us for thousands of years — arousing in man an acquisitive instinct for just about that long.

Sticks were made from cane or a variety of woods and decorated with many materials but, it was usually the cane handle which received most attention to detail and design. The most elegant sticks have tops mounted in gold, silver or porcelain and many more versatile sticks are designed to conceal gadgets such as a snuff box, a watch or even a hidden camera.

During the second half of the 19th century glass walking sticks were made at the Nailsea glass works near Bristol. These glass sticks were hung on the wall in the belief that they had the power to ward off disease from the household.

Walking stick with wood shaft and handle and horn ferrule, circa 1900, 88.4cm. long. (Sotheby's)   £143

Early 18th century German gilt metal finial from a jester's stick, 4¾in. high. (Sotheby's)   £1,210

Late 19th century malacca walking cane with scrimshaw ball-grip set with a compass, 81.5cm. long. (Sotheby's)   £132

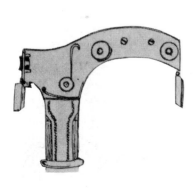

Ben Akiba miniature walking stick camera. (Christie's S. Kensington)   £3,400

Japanese carved ivory cane top, in the form of a lion's head. (Robert W. Skinner Inc.)   £40

Bent cane walking stick handle, 9in. long. (Christopher Sykes)   £11

CAR MASCOTS

These decorative symbols introduced around 1905, are usually made of cast metal though sometimes of wood or glass.

Of the wide range of designs, including those issued by car manufacturers, such as, the Rolls Royce Spirit of Ecstasy and the American company Lincoln's greyhound, the magnificent mascots designed by the French glass artists Sabino and Lalique are the most highly prized.

Many car owners had mascots made to their own designs and these offer a great variety of interesting subjects for the collector.

A nickel plated **'Minerva'** car mascot. (Sotheby's) £150

Lalique **'Cinq Chevaux'** glass car mascot, marked, 1920's, 16.5cm. wide. (Sotheby's) £638

'Mickey Mouse' glass car mascot, stamped Walt Disney Productions, circa 1940, 5¼in. high. (Sotheby's) £77

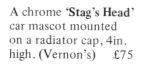

A chrome **'Stag's Head'** car mascot mounted on a radiator cap, 4in. high. (Vernon's) £75

Red Ashay glass car mascot in the form of a **'Woman's Head'**, 23cm. wide, 1930's.(Sotheby's) £330

A standing figure of the **'Esso Man'**, 5½in. high. (Vernons) £125

CARD CASES

In the days when polite society expected printed notice of an intended visit, the calling card played a vital role. It is said that the fasionable ladies of the 19th century, anxious to impress others with their status, would display cards presented to them by those of considerable social consequence, in a large open dish placed on the drawingroom table. The most important being well to the top.

Cards were often delivered by a footman but the common practice was to carry several personal cards in a case.

Card cases are almost always of slim and rectangular shape and made from a variety of materials such as gold, silver, ivory, tortoiseshell, Tunbridgeware, mother-of-pearl, papier mache and leather. They are often beautifully decorated and sometimes marked with the original owner's monogram or inscribed to commemorate an event.

Victorian Tunbridgeware card case with geometric patterns. £20

Austrian silver and enamel rectangular cigarette and card case, stamped. £150

Victorian diamond pattern mother-of-pearl card case, 4½in. tall. £25

Silver card case by Taylor & Perry, Birmingham, 1842, 9.2cm. high, stamped with views. £143

Fine Victorian card case embossed with a view of King's College Chapel, Cambridge. £240

Shaped rectangular card case by Hilliard & Thomason, Birmingham, 1885, 9.8cm. high. £70

The standard design of our modern playing cards originated in Rouen during the 15th century. Since then, we, like every other nation in the world, have used them for simple amusement and as a means of disposing of family fortunes.

Playing cards were produced in vast quantities from the beginning and as early as 1628 the volume of foreign imports was disturbing British producers to such an extent that they persuaded Charles I to grant them the protection of a Royal Charter. By the beginning of the 18th century card-playing had become a national mania — prompting Queen Anne to impose a tax of sixpence on each pack — enough, you might say, to make that particular Royal flush...

Not all cards are the same, however, for there are different systems in parts of France, Spain, Switzerland and Italy. Indian cards are often circular and have eight to 20 suits with 12 cards in each. Chinese cards are long and narrow like book marks, while the Japanese variety are small pieces of board known as Mekuri Fuda. As can be seen from the illustrated examples early educational cards are rare and valuable.

Perhaps surprisingly, age is not the greatest indication of value, many of the old packs selling for modest sums. It is often the most recent editions which have attracted the attention of collectors, like those produced for the Kennedy Presidential Campaign in 1963, or an advertising pack made in 1959 by an American firm specialising in cashmere sweaters.

Question and Answer Cards — 40 engraved cards of 50 each with a question or answer, 55 x 45mm., Germany, circa 1700. (Sotheby's) £110

Rebus Cards — 11 engraved cards, each describing a different vice or virtue, 115 x 75mm., J. Wallis, 1791. (Sotheby's) £93

Marlborough's Victories — 52 engraved cards each with scene relating to War of the Spanish Succession, captions below, 92 x 61mm., Christopher Blanchard, circa 1708.(Sotheby's) £2,600

Natural History Cards — 12 cards each with an engraved illustration of an animal, coloured by hand and a rhyme below, W. Tringham, circa 1780. (Sotheby's)   £95

Musical Pack — 32 lithographed cards, each with a section of a dance tune in the lower half and miniature card or court figure in the upper half, 93 x 61mm., Germany, circa 1860. (Sotheby's)   £187

Educational Cards — complete set of 52 woodcut cards, each with decorative border of flowers etc., with improving mottoes about learning and gaming, coloured through stencils, 86 x 57mm., circa 1680. (Sotheby's)   £1,200

Russian Alphabet Cards — complete set of 28 engraved cards, 27 with an illustration of a street seller, caption with initial letter and street cry, 186 x 118mm., Moscow, circa 1830. (Sotheby's)   £1,050

Court Game of Astrophilogeon — complete pack of 60 engraved cards, 30 with maps, 30 with pictorial representations of constellations, 95 x 63mm., Stopforth, circa 1830. (Sotheby's) £210

Jeu Des Drapeaux — complete set of 32 engraved cards, depicting French, Russian, German and English armies, 435 x 543mm., after 1814. (Sotheby's) £105

Magic Cards — 12 litho cards each with illustration coloured by hand with concealed image, 115 x 76mm., H. G. Clarke & Co., circa 1850. (Sotheby's) £80

Joan of Arc Transformation Pack — 52 lithographed cards, the court cards with full length coloured figures the remainder with humorous scenes incorporating the suit signs, 103 x 71mm., Paris, Grimaud, circa 1850. (Sotheby's) £77

CARNIVAL GLASS

Carnival glass was distributed in fairly substantial quantities throughout Europe and America. As the name suggests, it was designed to be given away as prizes at fairgrounds and is usually presented in the form of a bowl or flower vase.

The main characteristic of this inexpensively produced pressed glass is the colour. Mainly orangey/red, blue, gold or green with an iridescent hue. Most pieces show a great deal of moulded decoration.

Examples are still fairly plentiful and most are moderately priced. Although a bright orange carnival 'type' of glass is produced today in Czechoslovakia, it is of inferior quality and is easy to distinguish from the earlier pieces.

Victorian mauve carnival glass dish. £15

Orange carnival glass vase. £10

Victorian purple carnival glass bowl with a wavy edge. £18

Northwood purple carnival glass punchbowl and stand with cups, Ohio, circa 1910, 10in. high. £165

An attractive pair of iridescent carnival glass vases, circa 1890, 10½in. high. £25

Victorian mauve carnival glass bowl. £10

CHAMBER POTS

The chamber pot or 'po' — from the French pot de chambre — was usually supplied as part of a toilet set consisting of a jug, basin, soap dish and slop pail. The quality of material and design varies enormously and includes the simple transfer printed earthenware pot, the better quality and colourful Mason's ironstone pot and the elegant fine porcelain pot enamelled and gilded by a factory such as Limoges. Chamber pots were also made of silver and gold.

Most collectible pots, apart from the obvious, are those bearing some kind of novel decoration like the frog illustrated or those with a portrait of Napoleon or a watching eye painted on the inside on the bottom surface. Early 19th century potters produced many pots bearing an inscription — some amusing, some crude and these too are highly collectible.

Late Victorian chamber pot with floral decoration. £7

A superb George I silver chamber pot, 26oz., 1722.   £4,000

Mason's ironstone chamber pot of octagonal shape with serpent handles. £50

An early 19th century chamber pot made at the Bristol pottery.   £100

19th century Peruvian silver potty, 27½oz.   £360

Frog chamber pot bearing the transfer portraits of Napier and the King of Abyssinia.   £190

Nostalgia always plays a large part in the appeal of children's books and good period illustrations make them almost irresistible. A children's book in good condition, with its original dust cover and illustrations by one of the famous names is priced above pearls.

There are some artists whose work alone sells a book — Lear, Cruikshank, Tenniel, Ernest Shepherd who illustrated so many of A.A. Milne's books, Arthur Rackham, E.H. Detmold, Jessie M. King and Kay Neilsen (a man, by the way). Fairy story books by Andrew Lang were often illustrated by people like Austen Dobson, Kate Greenaway, T. Bowick, Linley Sanbourne and Randolph Caldecott.

Early children's books like Hornbooks and Chapbooks are of course immensely valuable but they do not turn up every day and when they do the prices they fetch ensure that they will be bought up by libraries or learned institutions.

Ordinary buyers come into their own however with Victorian children's books and with those written later. If you fancy Victorian books look for good, colourful bindings and follow one author if possible. Adventure stories like those by Henty have a strong following.

Condition here is again all important and because the books were often given rough handling by their original owners those in pristine condition are very rare — and consequently very highly priced when they come up for sale.

New Dialogues for the Amusement of Good Children by Dorothy Kilner, 1st Edition, seven wood-engraved illustrations, original printed wrappers, 12mo, Tabart and Co. 1805 (Sotheby's)   £187

Mother Goose Nursery Rhymes, file copy, illustrated by John Hassall, stained, 4to, 1918. (Sotheby's)   £33

Kate Greenaway and George Weatherly, 'Dame Wiggins of Lea and Her Seven Wonderful Cats', edited by John Ruskin, large paper copy, illustrations, original cloth, gilt, George Allen, 1885. (Sotheby's)   £50

Mrs E Lucas, Translator, 'Fairy Tales' by Hans Christian Andersen, coloured frontispiece, decorated title and 90 illustrations, slightly worn, t.e.g., Dent, 1899. (Sotheby's)　£55

Mother Goose's Rag Book, illustrated by Hilda Cowham, slightly soiled, 4to, 1917. (Sotheby's)　£49

W. Heath Robinson, Illustrator, 'Danish Fairy Tales and Legends', sixteen plates, original cloth gilt, slightly soiled, Bliss, Sands and Co., 1897. (Sotheby's)　£45

Andrew Lang, 'The Yellow Fairy Book', 1st Edition, no. 107 of 140, large paper copy, numerous illustrations by H. J. Ford, original boards, worn and soiled, 1894. (Sotheby's)　£55

James Greenwood, 'The London Vocabulary, English and Latin put into a New Method, proper to Acquaint the Learner with Things as well as Pure Latin Words', 11th Edition, 26 woodcut illustrations, decorations, half calf, C. Hitch, 1749. (Sotheby's) £80

H. G. C. Marsh, Baby's Diary, 1910; Toddles, 1911; Babies Both, 1916, another issue, circa 1920, Benny and Bunny, 1916; Baby's Diary, 1917, 6 volumes, illustrated by H. G. C. Marsh, 8vo and 4to, 1910-17. (Sotheby's) £20

Hans Christian Andersen, 'Out of the Heart, Spoken to the Little Ones', translated by H. W. Dulcken, 1st English Edition, wood-engraved frontispiece and fifteen plates printed in colour, original cloth, gilt, Routledge, 1867. (Sotheby's) £32

Chapbooks, 'The Banjo Songster'; 'Watty and Meg'; 'Peep at the Fair' and twelve others, fifteen works in one vol., contemporary half morocco, slightly rubbed. (Sotheby's) £85

Fairy Tales From Past Times — 'Mother Goose' 1814, 'King Pippen' 1814, 'Tommy Thumb's Song Book' 1814, 3 vols., wood engraved illustrations, original printed wrappers, 32 mo, Glasgow 1814. (Sotheby's) £55

The Universal Primer, or A New And Easy Guide to the Art of Spelling and Reading, woodcut picture alphabet of 24 letters, 24mo, John Marshall, c. 1785. (Sotheby's) £121

George MacDonald, 'Dealings with the Fairies', 1st Edition, engraved frontispiece and 11 plates after Arthur Hughes, slightly spotted, original cloth gilt, 1867. (Sotheby's) £170

H. W. Dulcken, Translator, 'What the Moon Saw' by Hans Christian Andersen, 1st English Edition, numerous wood engraved illustrations, Routledge, 1866. (Sotheby's) £32

Caroline Peachey, Translator, 'Later Tales of Hans Christian Andersen published between 1867 and 1868', 1st English Edition, 8 engraved plates, Herbert Bowes Lyon's copy with inscription, Bell and Duddy, 1869. (Sotheby's) £60

Norman and Lena Ault, series of 12 watercolour drawings to illustrate 'Sammy and the Snarleywink' three framed and glazed, three mounted and one soiled. Drawings probably by Lena Ault and text by her husband. (Sotheby's) £75

The Child's New Book of Pictures, 28 of Dean's picture sheets mounted on linen, coloured by hand, original cloth, worn, oblong 4to, Miller, Toy Warehouse, circa 1850. (Sotheby's) £132

Batman Annual, 1961-64, Batman with Robin, 36 issues, Silver Anniversary Issue 1964, World's Finest Comics, 31 issues, 1960-70. (Sotheby's) £20

Superman, 75 issues, numbers 161-270, 1963-73, Superman Annual No. 7, 1963. (Sotheby's) £28

The Playtime Book, illustrated by Herouard, 4to, 1927. (Sotheby's) £16

Robert Louis Stevenson, 'A Child's Garden of Verses', illustrated by George Robinson, one of 250 copies on vellum, cloth, New York, 1896. (Sotheby's) £115

Wonder Woman Annual. (Sotheby's) £12

Susan Robinson, a series of autograph manuscript Fairy Tales, each written in an 8vo notebook; a volume of manuscript verse, disbound; and further manuscripts and seven other tales, all on sheets extracted from 4to notebooks, prepared for publication, and typed copies of five of the tales, circa 1900. (Sotheby's) £88

The Fantastic Four, numbers 2-111, 1962-71, 75 issues only; Fantastic Four Annual, numbers 3-8, 1965-70, 5 issues only. (Sotheby's) £42

CIGAR BANDS

Bands, like cigars, come in all sizes and sets illustrate every subject under the sun. Flags, flowers, butterflies, Roman Army Standards, scenic views, cavalry, vintage cars, pipes, famous painters, the Dutch cycling team, old theatre posters to name but a few from an infinite range.

A set can comprise of anything from six to 1,000 bands but 80 per cent of sets were issued in 24's, 36's and 48's.

It is impossible to put a price on these collector's items as they are rarely sold; exchange being the preferred method of acquiring a coveted band.

For collectors from Iceland, Malta, France, East & West Germany and America the British stamp is considered a number one trading item, stamps for bands, but usually it is bands for bands.

Rulers of the Netherlands by Hoogeboom, 24 in set.

Life of Thailand by Alto, 24 in set.

Horse Breeds by Lugano, 24 in set.

Old Watches by Alto, 24 in set.

Old Posters by Balite, 24 in set.

Vintage Cars by J. Kramer, 36 in set.

Views of Amsterdam by Nederlandsche Munt, 24 in set.

History of Mode by Senator, 24 in set.

Breeds of Cats by Spanera, 24 in set.

Roman Army Standards by Henri Winterman, 12 in set.

Personalities by Capote, 24 in set.

World Leaders by Saelens, 24 in set.

Views of Israel by Lugano, 24 in set.

German Cavalry by Ritmeester, 24 in set.

Capitals of Europe by Jubile, 24 in set.

Pipes by Nicoletto, 24 in set.

Abbeys of Belgium by Mercator, 24 in set.

Composers by Hoogeboom, 24 in set.

CIGARETTE CARDS

Cigarette cards were the 'commercial breaks' of the 1870's until the end of the Second World War. During that time more than 5,000 sets of cards were produced ranging in subject over every possible aspect of life and interests from royalty to railway trains.

Before the arrival of the cardboard slide-action packet, cigarettes were presented in a thin paper packet with a piece of card inserted to protect the cigarettes from damage.

American manufacturers with a keen eye for the promotional main chance were the first to put a picture on the cards and around 1885 W.D. & H.O. Wills of Bristol became the first firm to issue these cigarette cards in Britain. They were an immediate success and soon eagerly collected by youngsters throughout the land.

Many of the cards were of high artistic merit and since most offer some information on the subject illustrated on the other side, a collection soon became an important source of general knowledge on an abundant range of subjects and made up a richly illustrated history of the times. Early cards show a preference for Kings and Queens and famous statesmen but later issues encompass an endless variety of topics — Sports Personalities, Air Raid Precautions, Stars of Screen and Stage, How to Swim, Do You Know and so on.

Nowadays collectors tend to be of more mature years and collections very valuable assets indeed. A complete set of Taddy's Clowns issued early this century in a series of twenty sold recently for the amazing sum of £2,000. It is important always to bear in mind that the condition of cigarette cards has a direct bearing on their value and dog eared, creased or marked sets are worth considerably less than those in pristine condition.

Champions of 1936 — Series of 50. 1936. £12

Air-Raid Precautions — Series of 50. 1939. £6

Footballers in Action — Bolton v. Notts Forest — Series of 50. 1928. £18

Robinson Crusoe — Series of 100. 1928. £40

CIGARETTE CARDS

Wonderful Century — Series of 50. 1937.
£3

Birds & Eggs — Series of 50. 1906.   £35

Empire Exhibition Scotland 1938 — Series of 25. 1938.   £3

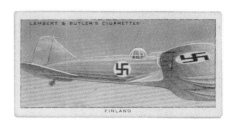

Aeroplane Markings — Series of 50. 1937.
£6

Fables and their Morals — Set of 100. 1922.
£18

Speed — Series of 50. 1930.   £15

The Reason Why — Series of 100. 1924. £12

Fish & Bait — Series of 50. 1910.   £8

Strange Craft — Series of 50. 1931.   £5

Film, Stage & Radio Stars — Series of 50. 1935.   £5

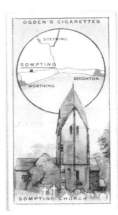

By The Roadside — Series of 50. 1932.   £10

Clowns & Circus Artistes — Series of 20.   £2,000

Famous Jockeys — Series of 25. 1910.   £100

Time & Money — Series of 50. 1908.   £25

Boy Scouts — Series of 50. 1911.   £40

Photocards — Rosella Towne — Continuous Series. 1939.£8

Army, Corps & Divisional Signs 1914-18 — 2nd Series 51 to 150. 1925.   £8

CIGARETTE CARDS

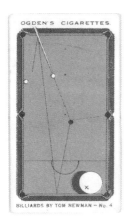

Billiards — Series of 50. 1928. £18

Actors Natural & Character Studies — Series of 50. 1938. £4

Association Cup Winners — Series of 50. 1930. £6

British Birds — Series of 50. Cut-outs. 1923. £5

Air-Raid Precautions — Series of 50. 1938. £5

Army, Corps & Divisional Signs 1914-18 — Series of 50. 1924. £5

Pin-Up Girls — Series of 12. 1953. £2

Cathedrals & Abbeys — Series of 50. 1936. £9

Arms and Armour — Series of 50. 1909. £75

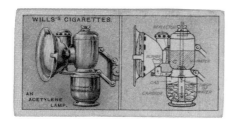

Do You Know? — 4 Series of 50. 1922-33.
£5—£8 Set

The 'Queen Mary' — Series of 50. 1936. £6

Flags & Funnels of Leading Steamship Lines
— Series of 50. 1906.   £50

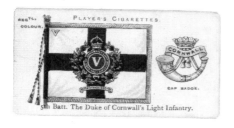

Hidden Beauties — Series of 25. 1929. £3

Regimental Standards & Cap Badges — Series
of 50. 1930.   £6

Poultry — Series of 50. 1931.   £6

Ocean Greyhounds — Series of 50. 1938. £6

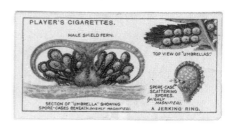

Dogs — Series of 50. 1936.   £5

CIGARETTE CARDS

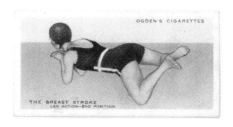

How to Swim – Series of 50. 1935. £3

Boy Scouts – Series of 50. 1912.   £40

Birds' Eggs – Series of 50. 1904.   £25

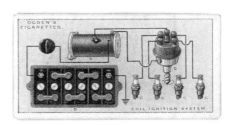

Applied Electricity – Series of 50. 1928.
£12

A Road Map of Scotland – Section 16 of
50. 1933.   £25

Famous Scots – Series of 50. 1933.   £4

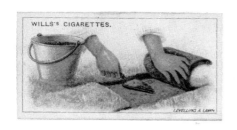

Gardening Hints – Series of 50. 1923. £5

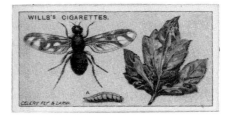

Garden Life – Series of 50. 1914. £5

Broadcasting — Series of 50. 1935. £5

Stars of Screen & Stage — Series of 48. 1935. £5

Wild Flowers — Series of 48. 1939. £2

Tricks & Puzzles Series — Set of 100. 1933. £4

British Born Film Stars — Series of 50. 1934. £9

Types of the British Army — Series of 50. 1898. £350

With Captain Scott at the South Pole — Series of 25. 1908. £35

Sporting Personalities — Series of 48. 1936. £2

Women on War Work — Series of 50. 1916. £80

CIGARETTE CARDS

Lawn Tennis Strokes —
Series of 30. 1924/25. £14

Music Hall Artistes — Series
of 50. 1913. £75

Kings of Speed — Series
of 50. 1939. £3

Cope's Golfers — Series of
50. 1904. £275

Household Hints — Series
of 50. 1925. £14

Heroes — Series, unnumbered
50 — 2nd 51-75. 1916-17.
£80 and £65

Cathedrals — Series of 25.
1939. £5

British Warriors — Series of
50. 1912. £75

Boxer's — Series of 125.
1915. £250

CIGARETTE CASES

Many people are collecting cigarette cases. They have the advantage of being small, reasonably easy to find and, in use, re-create the sophistication of the time of their origin.

Early examples tend to be in traditional style and demonstrate the delicate craftsmanship of the silversmith and engraver. It was not until after it became fashionable for women to smoke that we see the bold and colourful cases of the modernist era.

Enamel cases of the '20's were most popularly decorated with a thin lacquer and patterns of shiny metal or contrasting enamels. Plain enamel cases were often highlighted with a rhinestone or turquoise.

Cigarette cases were considered an essential piece of equipment and one interesting example was produced in the form of an evening bag incorporating a compartment for powder and lipstick.

Silver Art Nouveau cigarette case, Birmingham, 1905, 9cm. high.   £110

Engine-turned oblong cigarette case, with secret compartment, London, 1922, 3¾in. wide.£495

Oblong silver cigarette case engraved on both sides, London, 1883, 2oz., 8.6cm. high. £20

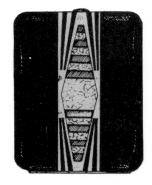

Silver and enamel cigarette case, 8cm. wide, Glasgow, 1926.   £100

Austrian rounded rectangular silver cigarette case designed by Georg Anton Scheidt, 8.8cm. wide.   £129

Eggshell lacquer modernist cigarette case, late 1920's, 11.6cm. wide.   £200

CIGARETTE CASES

Enamel cigarette case with risque scene, Birmingham, 1905, 9.1cm. high. £605

Shaped rectangular cigarette case by George Unite, Birmingham, 1882, 10cm. high. £42

French Art Deco lacquered cigarette case in sunburst design, 1920's, 8.2cm. long. £180

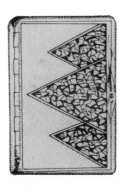

Eggshell lacquer modernist cigarette case, 11.6cm. wide, late 1920's. £550

German enamelled cigarette case on silver coloured metal, circa 1910, 9.4cm. high. £770

Silver and eggshell lacquer cigarette case, 8.2cm. wide, 1926. £220

Early 20th century German enamel and silvered metal cigarette case, 9cm. high. £360

A Faberge cigarette case enamelled in white and green with gold mounts. £1,600

German cigarette case, circa 1910, 10.5cm. long. £60

CIGARETTE PACKETS

Sixty or seventy years ago small boys used to stand outside tobacconists asking 'Got any fag cards, mister?'. In the late forties youngsters went around picking up empty packets and tearing off the fronts. Cards had been discontinued during the war and the packet front was a sort of substitute.

Things are on a firmer footing now with over 100 serious collectors in this country. There is also a keen following abroad, especially in Brazil, Czechoslovakia, Hungary and the U.S.A.

The formation of the British Cigarette Packet Collectors' Club in 1980 coincided with the publication of the one and only book on the subject of cigarette packet design, Cigarette Pack Art by Chris Mullen, published by Hamlyn. The club was the brainchild of Mr Nat Chait, a retail tobacconist from Richmond in Surrey whose knowledge of the trade over many years is unsurpassed, while his collection of items of pre-1914 vintage is probably the finest in the country.

Collectors ages range between 9 and 69. Collections range in size from a few hundred to tens of thousands. The current world record holder, Mr Vernon Young, has in excess of 60,000. Compared with cigarette cards prices are low for the hobby is relatively new, and as a consequence the field for research is large. Cigarettes have sold in Britain since 1851. General awareness regarding their packaging did not come about for almost 100 years.

Further information regarding the collectors' club can be had from Mr Hilary Humphries, 15 Dullingham Road, Newmarket, Cambs. CB8 9JT.

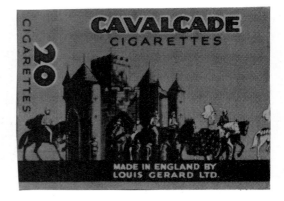

'Cavalcade', packet of twenty cigarettes by Louis Gerard Ltd., circa 1950.   70p

'Nutcracker', packet of five cigarettes at 1d. by Gallaher, circa 1900.   £5

'White Horse', by Rothmans, packet of twenty cigarettes, 1950.   70p

'**Apple Blossom**', packet of ten cigarettes at 3d., by Kriegsfeld & Co., circa 1910. £5

'**The Middies**', packet of twenty cigarettes by the Lauralf Cigarette Co., Charing Cross, circa 1930. £3

'**Roberts Navy Cut**', packet of five cigarettes at 1d., by Roberts & Sons, circa 1900. £5

'**New Alliance**', packet of five cigarettes at 1d., by David Corre & Co., circa 1902. £5

Bacon's '**Gold Flake**', packet of twenty cigarettes by Bacon Brothers, Cambridge, 1950. £2.50

'**Turkish Blend**', packet of twenty cigarettes by B. Morris & Sons Ltd., 1970. £1

'All Gay', packet of five cigarettes at 1d., by W. J. Harris, circa 1900. £5

'King Midas', packet of five cigarettes at 1d., by S. Mitchell & Son, circa 1900. £5

'The Don', packet of five cigarettes at 1d., by J. J. Holland, circa 1900. £5

'Rich Uncle', packet of five cigarettes at 1d., by S. J. Gore & Co., circa 1900. £5

'Navy Cut', packet of twenty cigarettes, by the Army & Navy Stores Ltd., circa 1935. £3

'At Ease', packet of ten cigarettes, Cope Bros., circa 1905. £5

CIGARETTE PACKETS

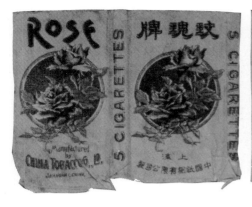

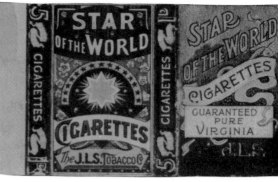

'Rose', paper packet of five cigarettes at 1d., by China Tobacco Co., circa 1900.   £5

'Star of the World', packet of five cigarettes at 1d., by J. L. S. Tobacco Co., circa 1900.   £5

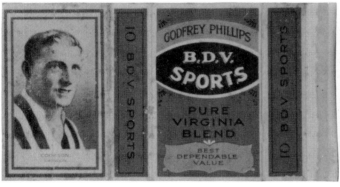

'B.D.V. Sports', packet of ten cigarettes by Godfrey Phillips, 1933.   £1

'Ark Royal', packet of twenty cigarettes, by the Premier Tobacco Co., 1953.   70p

'Robin', packet of twenty cigarettes, by Ogden, 1950.   30p

'Gainsborough', packet of ten cigarettes by Cohen, Weenen & Co., 1902.   £5

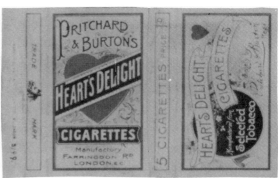

'**Bird in Hand**', packet of five cigarettes at 1d., probably by Lambert & Butler, circa 1900. £5

'**Heart's Delight**', packet of five cigarettes at 1d., by Pritchard & Burton, circa 1900. £5

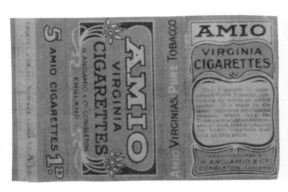

'**Amio**', packet of five cigarettes at 1d., by H. Andiamo & Co., 1906. £5

'**The Greys**', packet of twenty cigarettes by Godfrey Phillips, 1953. 30p

'**Bandmaster**', packet of five cigarettes at 1d., by Cohen, Weenen & Co., 1897. £5

'**Ironsides**', packet of seven cigarettes at 1d., by A. Baker & Co. Ltd., circa 1900. £5

CIGARETTE PACKETS

'**Jolly Sailor**', packet of five cigarettes at 1d., by Churchmans, 1897. £5

'**Player's Medium Navy Cut**', packet of twenty cigarettes by John Player, 1955. 20p

'**Dandy Dan**', packet of five cigarettes at 1d., 1899, by A. H. Franks. £5

'**Bobs**', packet of five cigarettes at 1d., by Symonds & Co., Kings Cross, circa 1900. £5

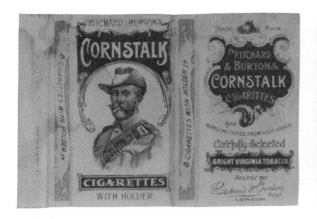

'**Cornstalk**', packet of five cigarettes at 1d., by Pritchard & Burton, circa 1900. £5

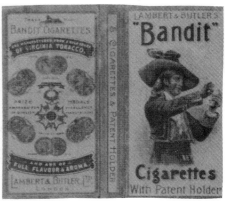

'**Bandit**', packet of five cigarettes at 1d., by Lambert & Butler, circa 1900. £5

'Clipper', packet of twenty cigarettes by John Player, 1939. £1

'Lucky Dream', packet of twenty cigarettes by Lucky Dream Cigarette Co., 1950. £1.50p

'Island Queen', packet of twenty cigarettes by P. J. Carroll & Co. Ltd., circa 1935. £2

'Turf', cigarette packet slide, Film Favourites, 1947. 30p

'Kyprinos Cyprus', packet of twenty cigarettes, by the Cyprus Cigarette Co., 1960. £1

'Grand Parade', packet of twenty cigarettes, by P. J. Carroll & Co., 1953. 50p

CIGARETTE PACKETS

'Kensitas K4's', packet of twenty cigarettes by J. Wix & Sons Ltd., circa 1940.   £1

'Tenner' Green Label, packet of fifteen cigarettes, by Churchman, 1940.   50p

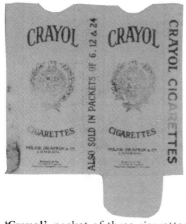

'Crayol', packet of three cigarettes by Major Drapkin & Co., circa 1900.   £5

'Diamond Navy Cut', packet of five cigarettes at 1d., by S. Cavander & Co., circa 1900.   £5

'Turf', packet of twenty cigarettes by Carreras Ltd., 1947.   30p

'Pall Mall De Luxe', packet of twenty cigarettes, by Rothmans, 1950.   £1

CLARICE CLIFF

Clarice Cliff, who was apprenticed to A.J. Wilkinson Ltd., and later became art director at both the Royal Staffordshire Pottery and a subsidiary company Newport Pottery, produced vases, jars and tableware in a glazed pottery painted in combinations of vibrant yellow, orange and red, or purple, green, blue and orange. These works are distinctive not only in colour content but often in shape. One of the better known examples is a tea set moulded in the shape of corn on the cob and painted yellow.

Patterns to look for include Bizarre, Inspiration Bizarre, Biarritz, Crocus and Fantasque. Although most pieces are easy to identify and there are still many good examples on the market, trade tends to be between collectors and the prices high.

Newport pottery 'bizarre' coffee pot, designed by Clarice Cliff, 1930's, 19cm. high.   £110

Clarice Cliff 'bizarre' vase, 21cm. high, 1930's.   £45

Wilkinson Ltd. 'bizarre' lemonade set of seven pieces, 1930's, designed by Clarice Cliff.   £396

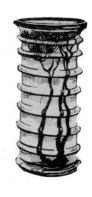

Large Clarice Cliff vase with baluster body, 1930's, 41cm. high.   £140

Newport pottery 'bizarre' two person breakfast set, designed by Clarice Cliff, 1930's.   £300

Newport pottery vase designed by Clarice Cliff, 1930's, 29cm. high.   £143

CLOISONNE

Cloisonne is a technique of enamelling developed in the 10th century. It consists of soldering fine wires on to a solid base to form a pattern of small cells which are then filled with coloured enamel: the wire acting as a wall to prevent adjacent colours from running together. When fired, the wires remain visible and become an integral part of the design.

This method differs from Champleve enamel where actual depressions are cut into the metal base and then filled with enamel paste and fired as before.

Although a few older pieces are to be found, most of the examples seen today date from the 19th century when enamel was returned to popularity by Alexis Falize. He was a French silversmith who began importing and selling Chinese cloisonne articles while also adapting the technique for his own products.

16th century cloisonne enamel censer and cover of squat bombe shape, 15.3cm.   £396

Late 19th century Chinese cloisonne opaque enamel on copper vase of baluster form, 6in. high.   £45

Late 19th century Japanese cloisonne opaque and transparent enamel on copper jar, 3½in. high.   £80

One of a pair of late 19th century turquoise ground cloisonne wall plates, 30.5cm. diam.   £230

Slightly cracked cloisonne vase with full body enamelled with cranes, circa 1900, 13cm. high.   £165

One of a pair of 19th century Chinese cloisonne camels, 41cm. high.£1,440

COMICS

The authors and artists who worked for the comic strip paper publishers are now being recognised as masters of their craft and their works are eagerly sought after. One of the most popular artists is Dudley Watkins who drew Desperate Dan for the 'Dandy', Lord Snooty for the 'Beano' and many other comic strips and story illustrations for D. C. Thomson.

Roland Turner who drew several issues of the 'Super Detective Library' and 'Thriller Picture Library' is another artist whose work is in great demand and any comic containing examples of his art commands a premium price.

The most widely collected comics are the 'Beano', 'Dandy', 'Film Fun', 'Eagle', 'Radio Fun' and 'Knockout' (along with their annuals, produced in the autumn of each year.)

Whilst story papers are best represented by 'Magnet', 'Gem' and D. C. Thomson's Big Five — 'Adventure', 'Hotspur', 'Rover', 'Skipper' and 'Wizard', a study of the catalogues will show that most of these comics and story papers had vanished by the end of the early 1960's (only the 'Beano' and 'Dandy' are still going strong) and it is largely true that collecting interest fades somewhat after this time. However, the 1960's are not without their notable examples of comic art. The ill-fated boy's magazine the 'Ranger' which only lasted for forty weeks in 1965-66 contained the now legendary Trigan Empire, magnificently drawn by Don Lawrence printed in full colour. The comic 'TV21' (1965-69) specialises in comic strips, best of Jerry Anderson's TV series 'Thunderbird', 'Fireball XL5', 'Sting Ray' and 'Super Car' and copies of this comic changes hands at up to £3 each.

To bring us up-to-date '2000 A.D.', with its science fiction comic strip, has become something of a cult and early issues, only five or six years old, may bring up to £2 each.

The Dandy, Dec. 21st 1957. £1.50

The Beano Comic, July 30th 1938. £300

Film Fun.   80p

Lucky Lester's Lone Hand.   £2

The Nelson Lee, Dec. 15th 1928.   £1.50

The Wizard, April 26th 1952.   65p

Knockout, Feb. 7th 1959.   80p

The Union Jack.   £2

Radio Fun, Oct. 15th 1938.   £30–£50

The Magnet, Jan. 15th 1921.   £2

The Champion, Dec. 21st 1946.   80p

The Victor, June 25th 1966.   40p

The Pilot, Oct. 5th 1935.   £5–£15

Lion, Jan. 17th 1953.   80p

The Kinema Comic, Jan. 30th 1932. £2–£4

The Surprise. £2

The Greyfriars Herald, July 17th 1920. £1.50

Pluck. £2

The Pioneer, Feb. 10th 1934. £5–£15

Adventure, June 26th 1948. 90p

The Boys Realm, Dec. 22nd 1928. £1.50

COMMEMORATIVE CHINA

Although there were fairly limited productions of mugs and similar objects to commemorate the Coronations of George III, George IV and William IV, it wasn't until Victoria came to the throne that manufacturers realised that the population at large was willing to spend vast amounts on souvenirs of the occasion. Having established the market, the flood gates opened for vases, pipes, tobacco jars, teapots, plates, doorstops, biscuit tins and the like to commemorate anything from a national occasion to the opening of a local park. Politicians, military events and even notorious crimes and criminals were not immune from commemoration in one form or another, which leaves a vast array of articles to be collected today. Most will cost only a few pounds, but some, like Victorian Coronation mugs in particular (but not those made for the Jubilee), are quite rare and have fetched well over £500.

'**Caroline**' mug, body printed in black, circa 1820, 2¾in. high. (Sotheby's) £240

Rare and very large commemorative punchbowl, 1743, 15½in. diam. (Sotheby's) £374

Very rare '**Queen Victoria**' child's mug, circa 1837-38, 3in. high. (Sotheby's) £170

'**Queen Caroline**' plaque of rectangular shape, circa 1820, 11.2cm. wide. (Sotheby's) £165

Rare late 18th century American commemorative earthenware dish, 14¾in. diam. (Sotheby's) £132

Rare '**Victoria R.**' jug, possibly Scottish, with faceted body, circa 1838, 17.5cm. high. (Sotheby's) £143

Rare Staffordshire pearlware commemorative bowl, circa 1793, 8¾in. diam. (Sotheby's) £231

A rare **Coronation Day** teapot and cover, transfer-printed in black with two portraits of Queen Victoria and Windsor Castle, 1838, 24.8cm. (cracked). (Sotheby's) £200

'Victoria Regina' commemorative mug, 1837, 3in. high. (Sotheby's) £420

Good and rare Sunderland **'Coal Trade'** jug, circa 1820, 17.2cm. high. (Sotheby's) £100

Copeland commemorative tyg painted with panels of **Queen Victoria, Britannia, etc.**, 1900, 14cm. high. (Sotheby's) £154

Unusual commemorative mug showing **'Queen Victoria and Prince Albert'**, 1840, 12.5cm. wide. (Sotheby's) £165

One of a rare pair of commemorative children's plates, circa 1840, 13.2cm. diam. (Sotheby's) £231

Coalport jug, commemorating the **'Shropshire Election of 1841**, 29cm. high. (Phillips) £320

Very rare commemorative bowl made for **'Seven Incorporations of Dumfries'**, circa 1820-25, 18.3cm. diam. (Sotheby's) £77

'Queen Caroline' jug, bat-printed in black with two portraits, circa 1820, 8.8cm. high. (Sotheby's) £143

Commemorative creamware mug with portrait of 'George IV', circa 1800, 14.5cm. high. (Christie's) £440

Pearlware teapot and cover depicting the 'Battle of Trafalgar', circa 1806-10, 4¾in. high. (Sotheby's) £165

Rare Dutch commemorative plate with portraits of 'William IV, Princess Anne and Princess Caroline', 1747, 22.5cm. diam. (Phillips) £850

Very rare commemorative shaving bowl and stand, 1840 for the marriage of 'Victoria and Albert'. (Sotheby's) £286

Unusual 'Albert' plate moulded in light relief, circa 1840, 18.1cm. diam. (Sotheby's) £121

Mug made to commemorate the Coronation of 'Queen Victoria'. (Sotheby's) £600

Rare commemorative jug, 5½in. high, probably 1832. £310

Commemorative mug made for the Coronation of 'Queen Victoria', 1838, restored, 8.8cm. high.(Sotheby's) £495

COPPER & BRASS

Copper and brass have been used for making an enormous range of generally functional household articles on a commercial scale for over 300 years. Originally there were many flaws on the surface but this was alleviated with improved production methods in the 18th century.

Be it candlesticks or kettles, trivets or jelly moulds, a choice often has to be made as to what to collect but all will enhance the home if you don't mind the cleaning.

With early pieces it is often the patina built up over centuries which accounts for most of the value so care in cleaning is recommended.

There are many reproductions on the market, some very difficult to identify so don't hesitate to ask in antiques shops. Most dealers are willing to pass on the benefit of their experience and knowledge and all are obliged to give an accurate description.

Late 19th century brass coal scuttle.   £30

A set of brass fire implements.   £45

A large solid copper 19th century wash boiler, 20in. diam.   £55

Antique brass door knocker, 8in. high, with circular brass plate.   £48

Set of three graduated antique copper jugs, 8in. to 11in. high.   £130

19th century globe-shaped copper tea urn.   £125

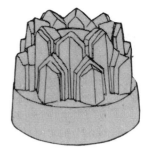

Stylish brass jardiniere, about 1900, with three supports and pierced workband round the body. £30

Late 18th century pierced brass footman with shaped front legs. £120

19th century copper jelly mould. £34

Copper and brass jardiniere on stand, Austrian, circa 1910, 53in. high. £465

Art Deco brass sparkguard carved with a peacock. £50

20th century copper washing dolly. £16

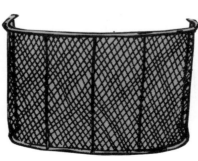

Four gallon copper measure. £100

19th century brass fireguard. £40

19th century copper preserve pan with two handles, circa 1840, 13¾in. diam. £85

COPPER & BRASS

Victorian brass trivet with screw on legs. £20

Victorian brass inkstand, circa 1850. £12

Pair of Victorian iron and brass fire dogs. £16

Late 19th century metal milk container. £50

20th century pressed brass magazine stand. £15

Brass electric kettle designed by Peter Behrens, circa 1920, 22.75cm. high. £132

W. Benson copper and brass kettle and burner, 11½in. high, 1890's. £115

Brass chamberstick with a drip pan. £16

Victorian brass watering can. £30

CORKSCREWS

Although corkscrews were first introduced around the middle of the 17th century, the most common examples date from the 1850's.

At first they were a simple steel spiral fixed to a wooden handle, later more intricate designs emerged incorporating handles made of inlaid or engraved silver, brass, ivory and horn, often in the shape of animals and birds. Many handles were fitted with a brush at one end for dusting the neck of the bottles.

Any corkscrew combined with a gadget is of interest to collectors and these generally date from the Victorian period when the craze for new inventions was at its height.

Pocket boxwood cork-screw and holder. £5

Lignum vitae corkscrew with brush handle.   £15

Large pocket folding steel corkscrew.   £10

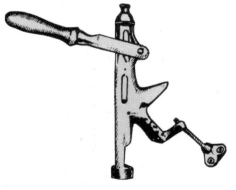

Johnnie Walker Scotch advertising corkscrew with brush handle.   £20

Impressive Victorian brass and cast iron corkscrew with beech-wood handle, 12in. high.   £85

Wine taster's tap screw with brush handle. £45

CORKSCREWS

Excelsior Lever simple
corkscrew.   £160

Unusual brass Victorian corkscrew.
                    £160

Unusual twist spring steel
corkscrew.   £10

19th century iron cork-
screw with wooden
handle.   £10

19th century cast iron bar corkscrew with round knob wooden
handle, 6in. high.   £95

Dutch silver corkscrew by
Hendrik Smook, Amster-
dam, 1753.   £650

Fine 19th century iron
corkscrew with brush
handle.   £25

Steel rack and pinion hand corking
device, 6¼in. high.   £275

Mid 19th century rare
bronze corkscrew,
possibly French.£1;050

CORKSCREWS

Early steel corkscrew.
£180

Georgian pocket steel corkscrew and holder.
£25

Rare corkscrew marked Bonsa.
£310

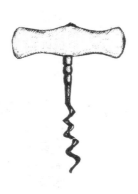

19th century iron corkscrew with ivory handle.
£30

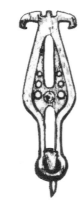

Crown cork remover. £10

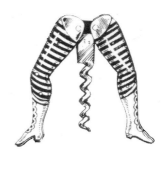

German pocket corkscrew in the form of a can-can dancer's legs.
£55

J. H. Perille's patent single side lever corkscrew. £125

Wier's patent corkscrew of 1884, single form.
£50

Late 18th century example of the first patented cork-screw in this country. £180

COSTUME

Period costume has always held a fascination for collectors so it comes as no surprise when a garment one or two hundred years old fetches a high price.

The current trend, however, shows some astonishing prices paid for clothes from as recent a period as the 1950's.

Elegant dresses of the 20's, 30's and 40's are eagerly sought after by the fashion conscious to be worn today and, all but the rare and flimsy, are likely to be in wearable condition. From the 1900's onward fashionable women were known to change their clothes up to four times a day leaving us the legacy of a multitude of garments showing scant signs of real wear. The named labels to look for are Dior, Cheruit, Chanel, Nini Ricci and Fortuny 'Delphos'.

Clothes that once belonged to well known personalities fall into a category of their own and fetch the high prices of a specialised market.

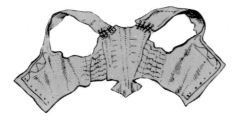

Pair of late 18th century stays of white linen with silk binding, circa 1790. (Phillips) £580

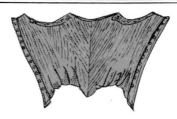

Natural linen corset, boned, lined with linen, circa 1780. (Bonham's) £90

Pair of Queen Victoria's bloomers. (Bonham's) £210

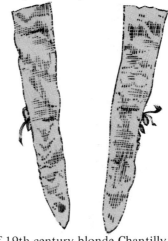

A pair of 19th century blonde Chantilly stockings with side lacings, 78cm. long. (Phillips) £105

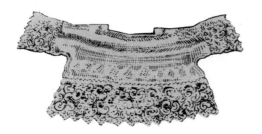

Rare late 17th century alb of crimped linen and lace, circa 1690. (Phillips) £1,900

Marilyn Monroe's pink-mesh bra. (Sotheby's) £520

A red beaded georgette dress, the bodice with white bands in a vermiculated pattern, 1920's. (Sotheby's) £198

A Cheruit evening coat of bright yellow silk, circa 1920. (Sotheby's) £55

A gold, white and black beaded dress and jacket, the dress with simulated V-neck, 1920's. (Sotheby's) £308

A gold sequinned and beaded black satin evening dress probably by Christian Dior. (Sotheby's) £60

A maroon and black shot silk dress, the bodice with front buttoning, 1865. (Sotheby's) £55

A black, white and eau-de-nil beaded dress, the shoulders with an overlapping leaf design, 1920's. (Sotheby's)£308

A silver and white beaded dress, the bodice and panelled skirt with a zig-zag design. (Sotheby's) £99

A black taffeta short evening dress probably by Christian Dior, 1950's. (Sotheby's) £38

A black georgette dress with vertical lines of black beads, 1920's. (Sotheby's) £110

A Christian Dior pink net and sequinned evening dress with V-neck. (Sotheby's) £100

A Nini Ricci full length black velvet evening dress with heart-shaped bodice, 1940's. (Sotheby's) £110

A Chanel opalescent sequinned long dress and jacket, 1920's. (Sotheby's) £700

A Chanel sequinned long evening dress with narrow straps, circa 1930. (Sotheby's) £330

A French beaded dress, the slate blue muslin ground covered with a vermiculated pattern, 1920's. (Sotheby's) £330

A gold lace long evening dress and jacket, the dress with short sleeves and an asymmetrical top tier. (Sotheby's)£187

An unusual polychrome and gold thread long satin evening dress, 1920's.(Sotheby's) £242

A Christian Dior two-piece evening dress with black printed clouds and spots on a white ground.(Sotheby's) £66

A gold, black, silver and white beaded dress, the V-neck flanked by gold flashes, 1920's.(Sotheby's) £308

A Coco Chanel black satin and tulle evening dress, 1930's. (Sotheby's) £385

A painted and printed brown chiffon dress and cape, painted by Elaine Bodley, 1920's. (Sotheby's)   £93

Printed silk two-piece bodice and skirt, with purple violet sprigs, circa 1895. (Sotheby's)   £110

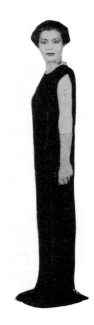

A shaded blue and silver beaded dress reputed to be by Chanel, 1923. (Sotheby's)   £55

Lady's quilted dressing gown with frilled collar and cuffs, 1870's. (Sotheby's)   £150

A Fortuny 'Delphos' dress of black satin, circa 1920, unlabelled. (Sotheby's)   £660

COSTUME DESIGNS

Artists have been illustrating their designs for stage sets and costumes since formal dramatic ballet was introduced at the French court in the 16th century. In those days the drama was performed by sovereign and courtiers dressed in incredibly sumptuous and exotic costumes. These early designs are extremely rare and most are in private collections or museums.

Most works available today date from the late 19th or 20th century and price will depend largely on the merit of the artist and the production. It is particularly interesting to find a design complete with instructions for material and colours to be used for best effect.

Alexandre Benois costume design for Parpagnol, 1946, 12½ x 9½in. (Sotheby's) £242

Costume design for a Grenadier from Le Regiment qui Passe, 15¼ x 7in. (Sotheby's)   £176

Leon Bakst costume design for Andre from La Boutique Fantasque, 1918, 17¼ x 11in. (Sotheby's)   £3,080

Costume design for Martha from 'Khovanshchina', by Matislav Doboujinsky, pencil, coloured crayons, signed and dated 1948, 13½ x 10½in. (Sotheby's)   £396

Costume design for the Mad Hatter from Alice in Wonderland by G. Sheringham, pencil and watercolour, 7¾x x 4½in. (Sotheby's)   £120

Costume design for a female dancer in blue from Ghost Ballet by Doris Zinkeisen, pencil, watercolour, gouache and silver paint, signed and titled, 15 x 10½in., 1933. (Sotheby's)   £140

150

COSTUME DESIGNS

Costume design for the Hollyhock Fairy by Cecil Beaton, watercolour and gouache, signed, 10¼ x 8in. (Sotheby's) £180

One of six costume designs for girls in evening dress and Spanish style costume, 13 x 10in. (Sotheby's) £220

Costume design for Diana from Le Reveil de Flore by Albert Rutherston, pen and ink, watercolour and silver paint, signed — 14½ x 9¾in. (Sotheby's) £550

A. Benois costume design for a young girl, dated '52, 9 x 6¼in. (Sotheby's) £209

Fashion design by Erte, brush and indian ink, watercolour and gold paint, signed, 13½ x 10¼in. (Sotheby's) £550

Alexandre Benois costume design for Von Rothbart as an owl, dated 1946, signed, 9½ x 6½in. (Sotheby's) £396

Leon Bakst costume design for one of the Boy Brigands, signed, 10½ x 7¼in. (Sotheby's) £572

Costume design by F. Leger, for Goliath, dated Dec. '36, 12 x 10in. (Sotheby's) £2,200

Costume design by B. Bilinsky for the prison watchman in La Princesse Cygne, 19¼ x 12¼in. (Sotheby's) £242

Costume design for 'La Fauve', by Freddy Wittop, pencil and watercolour, signed, titled and inscribed in French, 32.5 x 25cm. (Sotheby's)   £242

Costume design by Cecil Beaton for My Fair Lady, signed, 13½ x 5¾in. (Sotheby's)   £385

Costume design for a gypsy from The Infant's Birthday, by Rex Whistler, pencil, watercolour and gouache, 43.3 x 21.5cm. (Sotheby's)   £360

One of three costume designs for La Baronne Sandore from L'Argent, 14 x 10¾in. (Sotheby's)   £143

Design for a pioneer's outfit, 1926, 13½ x 8¾in. (Sotheby's)   £880

A. Benois costume design for a court lady from Le Bourgeois Gentilhomme, 1932, 11¾ x 9in. (Sotheby's)   £220

Costume design for a young peasant from 'Petrouchka', by A. Benois, pencil, indian ink, watercolour, signed, 12¼ x 9in. (Sotheby's)   £700

Three new ideas for designs, 1. Girl with Plumes, 2. 'Rose de France', 3. The Serpent Dress, watercolour and gold paint, each inscribed, 12¾ x 9¾in. (Sotheby's)   £297

Costume design for an Old Woman by Jose-Maria Sert, oil on paper, 26¾ x 20in. (Sotheby's)   £99

COSTUME DESIGNS

Costume design for a female guest in 'The Cakewalk' by Leon Bakst, signed and dated 1913, 11¼ x 9½in. (Sotheby's) £3,000

Alexandra Exter design for two Duelling Figures, signed, circa 1926, 21½ x 18½in. (Sotheby's) £3,740

Costume design for the Coster Girls from My Fair Lady, by C. Beaton, 19 x 17in. (Sotheby's) £297

Costume designs for the Queen of Printing and her Attendant by Dolly Tree, 14¼ x 10¼in. (Sotheby's) £132

Leon Bakst costume design for the Negro Dancer from Le Dieu Bleu, 1922, 25½ x 18½in. (Sotheby's) £19,250

Costume design for the Persian Fan by Hugh Willoughby, 27.5 x 18.5cm. (Sotheby's) £242

Costume design for Margot Fonteyn as the 'Image of Beauty' in the White Scene by Sophie Fedorovitch, 12½ x 9½in. (Sotheby's)£140

Alexandre Benois costume design for a jester from Sadko, signed, dated 1930, 12½ x 9in. (Sotheby's) £462

One of six costume designs by I. Segalle for Dick Whittington, 1935, 15 x 10½in. (Sotheby's) £16

CRESTED CHINA

The value of crested china may be determined by three factors: theme, rarity and condition in that order. The most popular themes are: The Great War, Buildings; Animals (including birds); Transport; Memorials; Statues, Cartoon/Comedy Characters; Comic/Novelty; Sport; Alcohol and Musical Instruments. This list is by no means exhaustive but it does cover the main spheres of interest among collectors. Rarity is self-explanatory; a 'Bomb Thrower' is rarer than a 'Cenotaph' and therefore is worth more. These two factors may be summed up as 'Collectibility', for example a scarce animal would be worth far more than, say, a unique billiken because there is far more demand for the animal from theme collectors. Thus supply and demand play an important part. It should always be borne in mind that even the most attractive and rare crested cup and saucer will never be worth more than a few pounds whereas a rare military piece could command as much as £100.

Condition is the third factor which affects price. Crested china produced by other manufacturers was never as fine as that of the Goss factory. The other producers were not interested in the high standard that Goss set himself, they were only concerned with jumping on the crested china bandwagon and producing wares as quickly and as cheaply as possible for the profitable souvenir trade which was rapidly developing.

Having made the point that crested china factories were not that particular about the quality of their products it follows that many pieces were substandard even before leaving the factory. Such manufacturers' imperfections do not affect value, however, damage occurring in the period subsequent to manufacture such as cracks or chips affect value considerably.

Model of the 'Forth Bridge' by Carlton China, 166mm. long.   £25

Children Playing in the Sand, by Grafton China.   £30 each

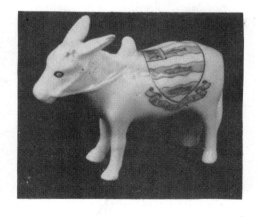

Donkey, by Arcadian China.   £15

Figure of **Lady Godiva** by Arcadian China, 75mm. high.   £20

Model of a goose by Balmoral China, 155mm. high.   £12

Cream jug, transfer printed with two hens, by Arcadian China. £2

Grenade with flames at top by Aynsley China, 88mm. high.
£15

Seaside souvenir of a **Bathing Machine**, 65mm. 65mm. high, by Arcadian China.   £3

Tent with open flaps, by Aynsley China, 75mm. high.   £6

Arcadian, **St. Paul's Cathedral**.
£15

Children on a ski-ing slope.
£10

Willow Art, **Solomon's Temple**.   £30

CRESTED CHINA

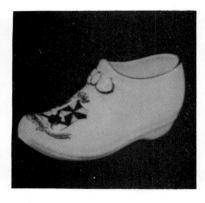

Snooker Table by Botolph China, 100mm. long. £35

Model of a sitting bear, 80mm. high. £5.50

Lancashire Clog by Albion China, 80mm. long, £3.50

Model of a fierce **English Bulldog**, by Anglo Heraldic Co., 112mm. long. £10

Mary Queen of Scots Chair, by Willow Art. £4

Model of a **Lifeboatman** by Arcadian China, 85mm. high. £4.50

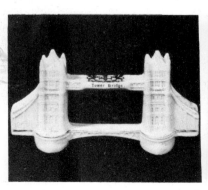

Model of **Tower Bridge** by Alexandra China, 140mm. long. £15

Billikin by Grafton China. £5

Model of a **Tank** by Arcadian China. £10

156

CUPS & SAUCERS

A major advantage of collecting cups and saucers is the certainty that, wherever you shop, you will be offered at least one example to look at and talk about. The variety is infinite with pieces in every price range from a few pounds to thousands.

This would be an excellent field for a beginner who can start by buying inexpensive items, then, as knowledge is gained from experience, can move on and up a league. At the top of the league, there are rare and exquisite pieces to tempt even the most discerning of established collectors.

One can soon become a specialist by buying to a theme. Perhaps you will buy only blue and white or the work of a particular factory; it may be the decorative style, colour tones, or, you may choose to build a collection around something as unusual as moustache cups. These were introduced around 1855 and produced by many of the well known porcelain factories in Britain. The design incorporates a ledge to support the moustache and keep it dry.

Be on the lookout for early saucers which don't have a well in which to rest the cup, or even earlier cups which don't have handles and rest in saucers which resemble small bowls.

Cups and saucers from the 1930's have become highly collectible and those by the notable potter Clarice Cliff whose work continued into the 1950's are very desirable collectors' items indeed. The style is very distinctive with bold design in bright colours.

Incidentally, in the days before cups had handles, it was considered the height of elegance to drink from the saucer!

Royal Worcester teacup and saucer. (R. H. Ellis & Sons) £21

Longton Hall teabowl and saucer painted with flowers and branch, circa 1755. (Christie's) £220

Swansea tea cup and saucer. (Russell, Baldwin & Bright) £420

Mid 19th century Dresden topographical cup and saucer with gilt borders. (Sotheby's) £180

Swansea cabinet cup and saucer painted by Wm. Pollard, circa 1820. (Sotheby, King & Chasemore) £650

Vienna Du Paquier beaker and saucer with silvered rims, circa 1730-35. (Christie's) £2,000

Minton reticulated teacup and saucer, impressed marks. (Christie's)   £110

A Derby teabowl and saucer of octagonal shape, 1750-55. (Sotheby's)   £210

Worcester teacup and saucer decorated in floral festoons, circa 1775. (Phillips)   £150

Early Ginori armorial beaker and saucer, circa 1745. (Christie's)   £1,200

Sevres coffee cup and saucer with paintings of landscapes and birds, circa 1760. (Christie's)   £95

Paris Napoleon portrait coffee can and saucer, circa 1805, saucer repaired. (Sotheby's) £440

Longton Hall blue and white teabowl and saucer, circa 1755. (Christie's)   £462

Berlin cabinet cup and saucer, dated 1829, cup with portrait of young man. (Sotheby's) £180

Meissen teabowl and saucer gilt with chinoiserie figure, birds and plants, circa 1730. (Christie's)   £500

DECANTERS

Over the years decanters have changed shape in accordance with styles and a good representative collection will include as many different shapes as possible. The best known are ships' decanters — or Rodneys, mallet shaped decanters, taper decanters perhaps in blue or green, and square decanters — shaped to fit into decanter boxes for fortification during the days of coach travel.

These boxes became less popular when the tantalus with its locking frame system was introduced in the mid 19th century. The tantalus, a case in which decanters are visible but locked up, takes its name from Tantalus, the son of Zeus who, as a punishment, was made to stand in water that ebbed when he would drink, overhung by grapes that drew back when he reached for them!

Art Deco mallet-shaped decanter. £25

Lalique glass decanter, bulbous body with tapering neck, 32cm. high, 1920's. (Sotheby's) £165

Victorian pear-shaped decanter, 22.5cm. high. £20

Large cut glass decanter and stopper, circa 1820, 11¾in. high, chipped. (Sotheby's) £209

Enamelled decanter and stopper for 'Port', by Wm. and Mary Beilby, circa 1765. (Christie's) £2,400

Lalique glass decanter, signed, 1920's, 25.5cm. high, sides moulded with masks. (Sotheby's) £190

DECANTER LABELS

Decanter labels have always struck me as very worthwhile articles to collect, for not only are they small and reasonably plentiful, but there are also rare examples worth hundreds which add spice to the search. They are made in a variety of materials, including silver, enamel, porcelain and Sheffield plate and come in a variety of shapes including oval, shield and rectangular.

Dating from about 1730, they were used in wealthier homes to identify the contents of the opaque bottles of the period, while lesser mortals made do with stuck-on handwritten parchment labels.

Most were individually made until the Victorian period, when mass production took over, but their real demise followed the Grocers' Licences Act of 1860, which allowed wine to be sold in single bottles, provided a paper label indicated their contents.

There are, of course, numerous modern die-stamped reproduction labels to be found, but these are fairly easily distinguishable from the heavier original examples.

A more watchful eye is necessary, however, to spot old labels (usually Madeira) renamed with more saleable titles like brandy or whisky. This practice is indicated by very thin metal on the face, and sometimes old lettering may even be revealed by huffing on the surface.

The rarest labels are those made of Battersea enamel (and I mean Battersea enamel made from 1753 to 1756, not the many other forms of enamel which have attracted the name). The originals are usually quite large, about 7.5cm. across, with a wavy outline, and could be worth hundreds of pounds.

George III wine label for Port, by John Whittingham, London, 1792. (Lawrence Fine Art) £35

One of a pair of William IV labels in vine leaf form by G. White, Birmingham, 1838. (Parsons, Welch & Cowell)£80

Pair of George III plain crescent shape wine labels, circa 1790. (Lawrence Fine Art)£100

George III wine label for Brandy, by Wm. Snooke Hall, 1817. (Lawrence Fine Art) £55

Rare Battersea bottle ticket of vine leaf form, by James Gwin and Simon-Francois, Ravenet, circa 1755, 7cm. wide.(Sotheby's) £1,250

DECOYS

The ancient hunter in search of food, practised decoying by imitating the sounds that animals make. Then, observing that a bird feeding or swimming on a pond represented safety to other birds, he fashioned the decoy.

The first decoys were of primitive style, fashioned from mud and reeds but now decoy making has become the art of professionals.

Decoys are mainly used on estuaries and ponds. They are made of wood and painted in traditional colours with flat paint. They are generally larger than life size; sometimes by half the natural size, sometimes twice as large, for out on the rough water, the larger decoys are spotted sooner.

Decoys of many species may be found. The gulls and crows were often placed on the banks near to where the duck decoy was tethered in order to improve the setting.

Pied-Billed Grebe — in summer plumage, by Harold Haertel, Dundee, Illinois, signed and dated 1975. (Wm. Doyle Galleries Inc.) £235

Goldeneye Drake — by O. S. Bibber, Maine, head turned to right, original paint with some working repaint on body. (Wm. Doyle Galleries Inc.) £175

Goldeneye Drake — miniature, maker unknown, mounted on wood base, paint excellent, bill tip chipped. (Wm. Doyle Galleries Inc.) £150

Coot — by Madison Mitchell, Havre de Gras, Maryland, crack in neck. (Wm. Doyle Galleries Inc.) £50

Pintail Drake — with turned head, miniature by Ward Bros., Chrisfield, Maryland, excellent condition. (Wm. Doyle Galleries Inc.) £450

Old Squaw Drake — possibly by Ben Holmes, Stanford, Connecticut, hollow with mostly working repaint. (Wm. Doyle Galleries Inc.) £400

Pintail Hen — with turned head, miniature by Ward Bros., Chrisfield, Maryland, excellent condition. (Wm. Doyle Galleries Inc.) £350

Blue Wing Teal Hen — by Mason Decoy Co., Detroit, Michigan, standard grade, glass eye, worn and /or chipped in numerous places. (Wm. Doyle Galleries Inc.) £185

Eared Grebe — in summer plumage, by Harold Haertel, Dundee, Illinois, signed and dated 1975. (Wm. Doyle Galleries Inc.) £300

161

Black Duck — in preening position, possibly by Bob White, Tullytown, Pennsylvania, excellent original condition. (Wm. Doyle Galleries Inc.) £115

Lesser Yellowlegs — from Knotts Island, North Carolina, original, worn condition, iron bill. (Wm. Doyle Galleries Inc.)£500

Black Duck — probably by Hays Decoy Co., Missouri, right glass eye missing, some wear to paint on body. (Wm. Doyle Galleries Inc.) £75

Black-Bellied Plover — with applied wings from South Jersey, bill replaced. (Wm. Doyle Galleries Inc.) £250

Canada Goose — by A. Elmer Crowell, East Harwich, Mass., original paint on back of body and on head, oval stamp on bottom. (Wm. Doyle Galleries Inc.) £2,750

Dowitcher — by David Ward, fine decorative maker. (Wm. Doyle Galleries Inc.) £80

Broadbill Drake — by Ward Bros., Maryland, signed on bottom and dated 1937, completely repainted. (Wm. Doyle Galleries Inc.) £285

Black Duck — by A. Elmer Crowell, East Marwich, Mass., oversized body, oval stamp on bottom. (Wm. Doyle Galleries Inc.)£1,700

Black Duck — by Joe Lincoln, Accord, Maine, original paint, worn and chipped in spots on body, large check running full length of base. (Wm. Doyle Galleries Inc.) £1,200

Merganser Drake — by Harry Shourds, Tuckerton, New Jersey, completely repainted. (Wm. Doyle Galleries Inc.) £150

Merganser Drake — by Hurley Conklin, Manahawkin, New Jersey. (Wm. Doyle Galleries Inc.) £135

Merganser Hen — in preening position, probably from Nova Scotia, original paint with working repaint to white. (Wm. Doyle Galleries Inc.) £225

Black-Bellied Plover — in feeding position. (Wm. Doyle Galleries Inc.) £100

Canada Goose — by Oliver Lawson, Chrisfield, Maryland, signed on bottom and dated 1965, unusual preening position with intricate carving of wings and primaries. (Wm. Doyle Galleries Inc.)£1,250

Sandpiper — tinny, factory made, in excllent original paint and original stick. (Wm. Doyle Galleries Inc.) £135

Merganser Drake — possibly by Lloyd Parker, Parkertown, New Jersey, completely repainted. (Wm. Doyle Galleries Inc.)£115

Black Duck — in preening position, by A. Elmer Crowell, East Harwich, Mass., this decoy has never been rigged. (Wm. Doyle Galleries Inc.) £10,000

Brant — by Dave Cochran, Blue Point, Long Island, circa 1860-80, root-head from the collection of Malcolm Fleming, Bellport, New York. (Wm. Doyle Galleries Inc.) £200

Mallard Duck — from Illinois River area, maker unknown, original paint with repaint to breast. (Wm. Doyle Galleries Inc.) £125

Broadbill Drake — by A. Elmer Crowell, East Harwich, Mass., excellent original paint, head turned slightly to right, large oval stamp on bottom. This decoy has never been rigged. (Wm. Doyle Galleries Inc.) £4,500

Mallard Drake — in sleeping position, by Robert Elliston, Bureau, Illinois, old working repaint. (Wm. Doyle Galleries Inc.) £525

Hudsonian Curlew — in running position from eastern shore of Virginia. (Wm. Doyle Galleries Inc.) £325

Herring Gull — very rare, in juvenile plumage, made and used by G. E. Wallace, game warden from Barnegat, New Jersey, circa 1900. (Wm. Doyle Galleries Inc.) £1,700

Hudsonian Curlew — in running position from eastern shore of Virginia. (Wm. Doyle Galleries Inc.) £50

Broadbill Hen — maker and region unknown, probably working repaint. (Wm. Doyle Galleries Inc.) £85

Canvasback Hen — probably by the Ward Bros., Chrisfield, Maryland, in excellent condition. (Wm. Doyle Galleries Inc.) £225

Goldeneye Drake — possibly from Massachusetts, old working repaint. (Wm. Doyle Galleries Inc.) £70

DECOYS

Green Wing Teal Drake — excellent paint. (Wm. Doyle Galleries Inc.) £100

Goldeneye Hen — from Maine, with working repaint to body and head. (Wm. Doyle Galleries Inc.) £80

Broadbill Hen — by Mason Decoy Co., Detroit, Michigan, standard grade glass eye, right eye cracked, original paint on body with much flaking. (Wm. Doyle Galleries Inc.) £85

Black-Bellied Plover — from New Jersey, mostly worn original paint. (Wm. Doyle Galleries Inc.) £200

Great Blue Heron — by Hurley Conklin, Manahawkin, New Jersey, checks in body and weathered original paint. (Wm. Doyle Galleries Inc.) £600

Greater Yellowlegs — in sleeping position, decorative, from New England. (Wm. Doyle Galleries Inc.) £135

Canvasback Drake — from Maryland, paint in good condition and may be original. (Wm. Doyle Galleries Inc.) £80

Goldeneye Drake — by Ken Gleason, Connecticut, 1975. (Wm. Doyle Galleries Inc.) £175

Herring Gull — from Sag Harbour, Long Island, circa 1890. (Wm. Doyle Galleries Inc.) £185

Lesser Yellowlegs – possibly by Joe King, Manahawkin, New Jersey, bill tip missing, shot scars, large check on body, old coat of shellac. (Wm. Doyle Galleries Inc.) £135

Black-Bellied Plover – by A. Elmer Crowell, East Harwich, Mass., full sized, original paint, filler chipped from part of each leg, oval stamp on carved clam shell base. (Wm. Doyle Galleries Inc.) £6,000

Quail – male, by Lloyd J Johnson, Bay Head, New Jersey, signed on bottom 1960, original condition. (Wm. Doyle Galleries Inc.) £250

American Bittern – from New England, decorative. (Wm. Doyle Galleries Inc.) £120

Sanderling – in feeding position, Quogue, Long Island, circa 1900, of cork, extremely old and worn. (Wm. Doyle Galleries Inc.) £250

Black-Bellied Plover – from Virginia, original paint. (Wm. Doyle Galleries Inc.) £100

Black-Bellied Plover – from New Jersey, entirely repainted, with check along left side of body, much flaking. (Wm. Doyle Galleries Inc.) £70

Hudsonian Curlew – in running position, body made in two parts. (Wm. Doyle Galleries Inc.) £115

Lesser Yellowlegs – decorative copy of the style of William Bowman, Lawrence, Long Island. (Wm. Doyle Galleries Inc.) £135

DE MORGAN

Towards the end of the 19th century many European potters were experimenting with the old Italian and Islamic methods of painting pottery with metallic lustre.

William De Morgan the English ceramic designer, was one of the first to achieve success in this field and his work has a distinctive and rare quality.

Throughout his working life he teamed up with other well known artists such as William Morris, Joe Juster, Halsey Ricardo and Frederick and Charles Passenger to produce vases, tiles and dishes.

His first pottery workshop was at Chelsea, his second at Merton Abbey near London and the third, which closed down in 1907, was at Fulham. His early tiles are unmarked but subsequent marks from Merton Abbey 1882-1888, show W. De Merton Abbey, with a sketched abbey within a rectangle. Marks from the Fulham factory include, DM over a tulip and William De Morgan & Co., Sands End Pottery, Fulham.

De Morgan lustre deep charger decoration by Charles Passenger, 46.5cm. diam. (Christie's) £3,000

William De Morgan lustre plate decorated by Charles Passenger, circa 1898-1907. (Sotheby's) £650

De Morgan lustre charger painted in pink and copper lustre, 36cm. diam., slightly cracked. (Christie's) £130

De Morgan two-handled oviform vase with garlic neck, 44cm. high. (Christie's)£33

De Morgan jardiniere, bell body with twin lug handles, 21.5cm. high. (Sotheby's) £286

William De Morgan oviform vase painted by Joe Juster, 15cm. high. (Phillips) £360

DINKY TOYS

Few toys on the market have such appeal for the male of the species as the ubiquitous Dinky toy cars with their instant ability to evoke the memories of aching knees and multiple pile-ups created at the back of the throat.

Marklin and Bing and Georges Carette were among the first to produce tin plate model cars but it was the American firm of Tootsie Toys who produced the first die cast models just prior to the first World War.

For some unknown reason they didn't catch the public interest at the time but when Hornby, the model train people, started to produce the famous Dinky Toys in the mid 30's they really caught the imagination and started the boom in collecting.

One of six Dinky army vehicles and artillery. £60

One of five Dinky lorries and vans, 1937-60. £60

Part of a lot of thirteen sports and racing cars by Dinky, circa 1937-60.   £60

Meccano Dinky toy with metal wheels, circa 1935, rear doors repaired.   £165

Red Cross vehicle by Dinky.   £3

Post war Dinky van with 'Shell' insignia. £3

Toy Bentalls removal van. £55

Dinky model of a Holland Coachcraft van No. 31. £100

Meccano two-seater non-constructional sports car in original cardboard box, circa 1934, 8¾in. long. £280

A collection of six Dinky London taxis. £110

Pre-war model of a Dinky sports coupe, 1933. £200

Dinky toy, A.E.C. double-decker bus with Dunlop Tyres slogan, circa 1938. £48

Royal Air Mail Service car by Dinky, slightly worn. £60

Dinky super toy Weetabix Guy van, No. 514, in cardboard box, 5¾in. long. £135

Post war Dinky racing car. £7

Pre-war Dinky model of an open two-seater car, 1933-35. £240

Part of a lot of eight commerical vans and lorries by Dinky. £100

Part of a lot of six Dinky buses, circa 1937-60. £40

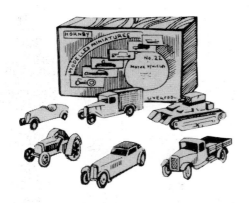

Set of Hornby vehicles in original box. £1,460

Dinky 28a Type 1 square yellow van. £240

Post war Dinky transporter. £3

One of a collection of five commercial vehicles by Dinky. £800

Few people would argue the point that the fourth son of Elias and Flora Disney, born on Sunday, December 5th 1901, at 1249 Tripp Avenue, Chicago, has made the greatest contribution to the world of fun and laughter.

His formative years were spent on the family farm at Marceline in Missouri, a small town beside the Atchison Topeka and Sante Fe railway, where on hot summer days he would walk for miles through the woods, watching the animals, on his way to cool off in the languid waters of Yellow Creek.

Success on a small scale came when he was just nineteen when a number of his cartoons were published in his school magazine at the McKinley High.

From newspaper delivery boy to handyman at a jelly factory he eventually became a cartoonist on the Kansas City Star when he was just nineteen.

After one or two setbacks Mickey Mouse evolved in 1928 and the rest is history.

The full commerical qualities of the character were seen from the beginning and toys from this era can now be worth amazing money. Only recently a Mickey Mouse organ grinder, just 6in. long, made by Distler in 1930, sold for over £2,000.

The market for Disney products has always been universal and enthusiastic and eager collectors of Disneyana can be confident of a wise investment set for a rosy future.

Unusual tinplate and composition Minnie Mouse and pram, probably by Wells, 7½in. long, circa 1933. (Sotheby's)   £900

'King John' original Walt Disney celluloid from 'Robin Hood', framed and glazed, 13¼ x 16½in. (Sotheby's)   £80

Seven Walt Disney opaque glass ornaments, circa 1935, 4½in. to 7in. (Sotheby's) £300

'The Three Caballeros', an original Walt Disney celluloid, signed, 18 x 16in., framed and glazed. (Sotheby's)   £1,210

'Jiminy Cricket', original Walt Disney celluloid, framed and glazed, 16¼ x 17½in. (Sotheby's) £264

Back and front of German tinplate Mickey Mouse mechanical bank, circa 1930, 6¾in. high. (Sotheby's) £187

Pinocchio doll, with clock-work movement within the articulated legs, circa 1942., 7½in. high. (Sotheby's)£150

Original Walt Disney celluloid showing five characters from 'Ferdinand The Bull', framed and glazed, 18 x 16½in. (Sotheby's) £242

Pinnochio doll by Ideal Novelty & Toy Co., 7¼in., circa 1945. (Sotheby's) £120

American Mickey & Minnie Mouse, plaster painted models, 9in. high, circa 1945. (Sotheby's) £66

'The Moles', a celluloid taken from 'Song of the South', framed and glazed, 12¼ x 10½in. (Sotheby's) £38

American Mickey and Minnie Mouse, two Fun-e-Flex painted wooden toys, circa 1931, 6¾in. high. (Sotheby's) £110

Walt Disney rug in tufted cotton, showing characters from his films, 1950's, 104 x 70in. (Sotheby's) £200

'Felix the Cat', large plush-covered toy with cloth bow tie, 28½in. high, circa 1930.(Sotheby's)£550

'Donald Duck', original Walt Disney celluloid, framed and glazed, 16½ x 17¾in. (Sotheby's) £187

Glazed earthenware musical jug depicting the 'Three Little Pigs', circa 1935, 10in. high. (Sotheby's) £110

'Brer Bear', a celluloid taken from 'Song of the South', framed and glazed, 12¼ x 10½in. (Sotheby's) £99

'The Three Caballeros', three plaster figures of Disney characters, circa 1950. (Sotheby's) £66

Original Walt Disney celluloid 'Bambie', framed, 18¼ x 20¼in. (Sotheby's) £264

'Happy', original celluloid from 'Snow White and the Seven Dwarfs', framed and glazed, 15 x 13in.(Sotheby's) £385

Original Walt Disney celluloid of 'Grumpy', framed and glazed, 15 x 13½in. (Sotheby's) £242

Mickey Mouse, stuffed toy by Dean's Rag Book Ltd., circa 1930, 6¼in. high. (Sotheby's) £120

Alarm clock, clockface depicting the Three Little Pigs, circa 1935, 6in. high. (Sotheby's) £120

'Minnie Mouse', stuffed toy by Dean's Rag Book Ltd., circa 1930, 7in. high. (Sotheby's) £71

'Faline', original Walt Disney celluloid, framed and glazed, 12¼ x 10½in. (Sotheby's) £110

Mickey Mouse glass car mascot, base stamped 'Walt Disney Productions, 6¼in. high, circa 1940. (Sotheby's) £77

One of two original Walt Disney celluloids of 'Thumper's Girl Friend', framed and glazed, 12¼ x 10½in. (Sotheby's) £242

DOLLS

From the 17th to the early 19th century, ownership of fine looking dolls expensively dressed in silks was generally the prerogative of fashionable society ladies. Some even had two, one clad in the latest haute couture while the other sported a risque negligee. Most children, on the other hand, had to be content to play with dolls made of simply painted wood or rags, very few of which have managed to survive all the loving care lavished upon them.

It wasn't until the mass production methods of the Victorian age that young girls were provided with something a little more lifelike, with bisque china head and limbs and hair that you really could comb. No doubt their popularity was partly brought about by Queen Victoria, who was an avid collector of dolls, dressing many of them herself.

American composition character doll 'Bobbie-Mae', circa 1940, 12in. high, in original box. (Theriault's)   £95

Very rare late 19th century black bisque doll, impressed 7 1302 Dep S & H, 19½in. high. (Sotheby's)   £4,180

19th century miniature papier-mache doll with kid body, circa 1850, 7½in. high. (Theriault's)   £220

American composition character doll by Effanbee, circa 1940, 17in. high, dressed in formal wear. (Theriault's)
                              £235

French bisque automaton fashion doll, probably Vicky, circa 1875, 15in. high. (Theriault's)   £1,010

Italian all cloth doll with felt face, by Lenci, circa 1925, 17in. high. (Theriault's)   £445

Rare French shoulder bisque Oriental doll in original clothes, circa 1860, 13in. high. (Sotheby's) £3,850

Bisque headed character doll by Armand Marseille, circa 1920, 12in. high, in excellent condition. (Theriault's) £445

American wooden character doll by Albert Schoenhut, circa 1915, 18in. high. (Theriault's) £235

German bisque child doll with wooden body, circa 1915. 18in. high. (Theriault's) £600

Bisque character doll by J. D. Kestner, Germany, circa 1915, 15in. high. (Theriault's) £285

American plastic character doll, with soft head, circa 1962, 12in. high. (Theriault's) £160

American artist all bisque doll in one piece by Jeanne Orsini, New York, 1920, 7in. high. (Theriault's)£350

Large French bisque bride doll with kid body, 26½in. high, circa 1875. (Sotheby's) £1,870

Rare Jumeau 19th century Bruno Schmidt bisque Oriental doll, Germany, 16in. high, in original dress. (Sotheby's) £1,100

American artist all bisque doll 'Little Bo Peep', 1981, 10in. high. (Theriault's) £205

All bisque character doll by J. D. Kestner, circa 1915, 'Our Baby', 10in. high. (Theriault's) £270

French bisque child doll, beautifully dressed, by Jules Steiner, circa 1890, 19½in. high. (Theriault's) £1,645

19th century miniature papier-mache doll with kid body, circa 1850, 7½in. high. (Theriault's) £220

German bisque character doll with papier-mache body, 8in. high, by Heubach, circa 1915. (Theriault's) £110

19th century all china doll in one piece, circa 1885, 12in. high. (Theriault's) £190

German all bisque miniature doll, 7in. high, by Kestner, circa 1910. (Theriault's) £175

French bisque character doll with mohair wig, by A. Marque, early 20th century, 22in. high. (Theriault's) £24,050

French bisque child doll by Emile Jumeau, France, circa 1880, 15in. high. (Theriault's) £1,455

Rabery and Delphieu bisque doll with jointed body, in ivory satin dress, 28in. high. (Sotheby's) £286

German bisque character doll by Heubach, circa 1915, 9in. high, with 'googly eyes'. (Theriault's) £380

American artist all bisque doll 'Miss Muffet' 1981, on purple tuffet, 7in. high. (Theriault's) £125

French all bisque miniature doll, circa 1880, in 'Jester' costume, 6in. high. (Theriault's) £300

American composition personality doll by the Reliable Toy Co., circa 1935, 17in. high. (Theriault's) £125

German all bisque miniature doll, probably by Kestner, 8in. high. (Theriault's) £205

Rare late 19th century Bruno Schmidt bisque Oriental doll, Germany, 16in. high, in original dress. (Sotheby's)£1,100

Rohmer china head doll with wooden joints, circa 1866, 14in. high. (Sotheby's) £1,540

Amerian plastic character doll with bendable knees, circa 1965, 7½in. high. (Theriault's) £315

German bisque miniature doll, circa 1920, with papier-mache body, 6½in. high. (Theriault's) £125

German bisque miniature doll by J. D. Kestner, circa 1900, in crocheted dress, 8in. high. (Theriault's) £330

French Bru Jeune bisque doll in original silk dress and bonnet, 16½in. high, circa 1875. (Sotheby's) £3,080

Jumeau phonograph bisque doll in original dress and straw bonnet, circa 1895, 24in. high. (Sotheby's) £1,650

Late 19th century American cloth Folk Art doll, 23in. high, in original plaid dress. (Theriault's) £175

German bisque child doll with brown head and body, by Kammer & Reinhardt, circa 1915, 22in. high. (Theriault's) £725

Late 19th century Simon & Halbig bisque Oriental doll, 12in. high. (Sotheby's) £880

Steiner Patent walking bisque doll in blue dress with lace overdress, 15in. high, circa 1880. (Sotheby's) £528

English cloth character doll by Chad Valley, 18in. high, with mohair plaited wig. (Theriault's) £425

French FG bisque fashion doll in original blue dress, 16in. high, circa 1875. (Sotheby's) £880

American plastic character doll, by Madame Alexander, New York, circa 1966-68, 8in. high. (Theriault's) £350

German all bisque figure, circa 1915, 18½in. high. (Theriault's) £475

French bisque lady doll, circa 1870, 19in. high, with kid and wooden body. (Theriault's) £1,455

Two German all bisque miniature dolls, 5in. high, circa 1900, with mohair wigs. (Theriault's) £205

Unusual French bisque doll, circa 1870, 17in. high, in original shot-silk dress. (Sotheby's) £286

Rare Jules Steiner Bourgoin bisque portrait doll in original suit, circa 1880, 29in. high. (Sotheby's) £3,850

German bisque character doll by Heubach, circa 1915, 10in. high. (Theriault's) £315

French bisque lady doll, circa 1875, 18in. high, with wooden body. (Theriault's) £1,770

Huret bisque doll with sock-
eted head and jointed body,
circa 1860, 17½in. high.
(Sotheby's)　　£6,820

Rare negro bisque doll, probably
French, circa 1870-85, 16in.
high. (Sotheby's)　　£1,760

Bisque child doll by Emile
Jumeau, France, circa
1880, 17½in. high.
(Theriault's)　　£1,770

American composition child
doll, with mohair wig, circa
1940, 21in. high.(Theriault's)
　　£95

American composition character
doll, 14in. high, circa 1940, in
original clothes. (Theriault's)
　　£190

American plastic character
doll, 'Prince Charming', by
Madame Alexander, circa
1950, 18in. high.
(Theriault's)　　£315

French bisque novelty doll,
torso forming sweet con-
tainer, 18in. high, circa
1890. (Theriault's)　£665

Steiner Patent walking bisque doll
in original dress and jacket, circa
1860, 15¼in. high. (Sotheby's)
　　£1,045

Steiner talking bisque doll
in original lace dress, circa
1880, 17½in. high.
(Sotheby's)　　£572

DOLLS' HOUSES

Early 'baby houses' were designed to be a plaything for adults. They were furnished with precious miniature pieces made of silver and other fine materials. Many contain examples of early hand blocked wallpaper and fabrics.

They were thought to have originated from Germany and kitchens complete with all the utensils were being exported from there as early as 1660. The dolls' house, as a toy for children, was kept in the nursery and furnished for play.

A catalogue of the Dolls' Houses at Bethnal Green Museum in London, illustrates houses from 1673 to 1921 and offers an invaluable insight into contemporary life of the times.

The outside of some houses also give a good idea of the lifestyle with carriages, carts and trains set in the landscape.

19th century wooden Mansard roof doll's house with painted brick front, 23¾in. high. (Robert W. Skinner Inc.)   £115

American diorama of an early 19th century hallway, circa 1950, fitted with dolls and furniture, 19½in. wide. (Robert W. Skinner Inc.)   £70

Early 20th century American wooden gabled roof doll's house with glass windows, 24¾in. high. (Robert W. Skinner Inc.)   £115

A late Victorian wooden doll's house in the shape of a two-storey villa, with pitched slate roof, front divided and hinged, 71 x 33cm. (Sotheby's)   £440

Large doll's house in the form of a two-storey suburban house with arched roof, English, circa 1930, 45in. high by 73in. long. (Sotheby's) £500

A model doll's house of Harethorpe Hall, a two-storey mansion, with painted brick front, 23 x 47 x 13in. deep.(Sotheby's) £396

A lithographic paper on wood doll's house, with steps leading to front door, 13in. high, American, circa 1910. (Sotheby's) £150

Victorian painted doll's house with porticoed doorway flanked by columns, English, circa 1890, 32½in. high by 37½in. wide.(Sotheby's) £800

Doll's house copied from original family house, with Gothic shaped door, gabled roof and two chimneys, English, circa 1910, 33in. high by 39½in. wide. (Sotheby's) £800

A lithographic paper on wood doll's house with decorative front porch and balcony, 12½in., German, circa 1915. (Sotheby's) £150

DOOR STOPS

Such is the multitude in variety and composition of door stops, particularly from the 19th century, that one is left to wonder why the Victorians were so keen to keep all their doors ajar.

Due to their function, they are usually heavy and made of cast iron, lead or brass in many forms such as animals, fruit, flowers, fish or in representations of famous people of the day; Wellington, Albert or Victoria. Even Jumbo the notable elephant from London Zoo was immortalised after he was exported to Barnum & Bailey's Circus in America, where he met his untimely death trying to charge a steam train.

Doorstops are also found made of green glass in the shape of a beehive or of Nailsea glass from Bristol with air bubble decoration.

A solid cast brass standing plaque, stamped on back 'Crowley & Co., Manchester', circa 1860, 9in. long, 7in. high. £20

Victorian brass dog door stopper. £24

Heavy cast iron door stop of a zebra, circa 1820, 10½in. long, 8in. high. £40

Victorian cast iron door stop, 9in. high. £24

A 19th century brass dolphin door stopper. £48

A historical cast brass door stop of King George IV leaning on a pillar, 7½in. long, 8in. high. £50

DOULTON

If you have a compelling urge to collect Doulton pottery, it is more than likely that you will run out of money before you run out of Doulton products.

Established in 1826, the firm at first specialised in commercial stoneware but went on to produce a multitude of household articles and ornaments at their factory in Lambeth High Street, London.

In fact, so prolific and varied was the output that Doulton pottery has become synonymous with the all embracing phrase 'Victoriana'.

When young Henry Doulton took over from his father, John, he was quick to recognise the talent available on his doorstep at the Lambeth School of Art, and employed the skills of many students in decorating his wares; notably the Barlow sisters Hannah and Florence.

Their forte was drawing animals and country scenes, freehand, onto the stoneware while it was still soft, then rubbing pigment into the lines. Hannah's work can be identified by the monogram B.H.B. with the first initial reversed, and Florence by her initials F.B. and F.E.B. Examples of their work will fetch many times the price of ordinary Doulton ware.

Another talent was one, George Tinworth, employed from 1866 to 1913. He specialised in modelling small figures of mice and frogs in the guise of cricketers or musicians.

In 1901, Edward VII granted the firm a Royal Warrant, therefore, pieces bearing the title Royal Doulton are of 20th century origin.

A Doulton moon flask decorated by Frank A. Butler, 33cm. high. (Christie's)　£220

Unusual Doulton stoneware jug, circa 1895, 9in. high, decorated by F. Barlow. (Sotheby's)　£170

Unusual Doulton 'Dickens' jug, after a design by Noke, 10½in. high, circa 1936. (Sotheby's)　£180

Royal Doulton figure of Lady A. Nevill, designed by M. Davies, 1948, 25cm. high.(Phillips)　£280

A Doulton oviform vase decorated by H. Barlow and E. E. Stormer, 25.5cm. high. (Christie's)£130

Early Doulton stoneware candlestick group, 1879, 16cm. high. (Sotheby, King & Chasemore)£260

Unusual Royal Doulton 'Sung' vase, painted by Arthur Charles Eaton, 25cm. high, impressed 6-25. (Phillips) £750

Royal Doulton figure of Annabella designed by L. Harradine, dated for 1939, 13.5cm. high. (Phillips) £160

Royal Doulton twin-handled loving cup 'The Three Musketeers', 25cm. high. (Phillips) £220

Doulton Lambeth vase by Mary Mitchell, 1881, unsigned, 27cm. high. (Phillips) £150

Doulton group of 'Music & Literature Albert Embankment', circa 1880, 17.8cm. long. (Sotheby's) £720

Doulton stoneware biscuit barrel, 6¾in. high, dated 1880. (Sotheby's) £115

Royal Doulton jug of a Regency beau. (McCartney, Morris & Barker) £120

Royal Doulton figure of a Churchillian bulldog, circa 1940, 6in. high. (Sotheby's) £60

Rare Royal Doulton character jug of Field-Marshal Smuts, 1946, 17cm. high. (Phillips) £620

EGG CUPS

Egg stands were originally crude wooden stands designed to be kept in the kitchen. As they developed, simple egg cups were often created to sit in the holes and these became more decorative when egg stands found their way into the breakfast rooms of the nation.

Silver examples usually date from the last quarter of the 18th century but it wasn't until the 19th century, when members of the household could boil their own eggs on a little spirit stove set on the sideboard, that egg cups came into their own.

The variety is endless as is the price range, yet it is interesting to note that the boiled egg and its accompanying container has yet to find widespread popularity in America.

19th century Staffordshire blue and white egg cup. £3

Rockingham porcelain egg cup, circa 1835, 11cm. high. £125

One of a set of six silver egg cups by John Tapley, 1843, 15oz. £150

19th century Satsuma egg cup with floral decoration on a cream ground. £5

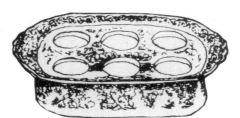

19th century Spode blue and white egg stand. £20

One of a pair of Victorian pewter egg cups, circa 1884. £25

One of a set of six mid 19th century silver egg cups. £160

One of a pair of 19th century silver gilt egg cups on bases. £175

One of four egg cups by Rebecca Emes and Edward Barnard, London 1814. £95

ELECTRIC LIGHT BULBS

One Otto Von Guericke, a contemporary of Robert Boyle, is generally regarded as producing the first light from electricity back in the 17th century when he discovered that by holding the hands firmly against a revolving ball of sulphur, the friction produced a dull glow.

It wasn't, however, until the electric arc was discovered early in the 19th century by Sir Humphrey Davy, that a practicle source of artificial light was established.

Light bulbs themselves date from about 1841 when an American inventor named Starr found that a bright light could be produced by sending an electric current through a piece of carbon.

This idea was further developed independantly by both Edison and Swan who made filaments from such diverse materials as carbonised bamboo and treated cotton thread. Such light was regarded with fascination and carbon filament lamps were tremendously popular from 1880 until the turn of the century.

The big breakthrough came in 1906 when the General Electric Company found that by using a tungsten filament sealed in a glass bulb, it not only produced a clear white light but used very little electricity as well.

This revolutionised the whole industry and created a massive demand, though doubts were expressed at the time as to the adverse effect all this powerful light would have on the eyesight of future generations.

Swans Electric Lighting Company light bulb, circa 1882, 3½in. high. (Sotheby's)   £170

Early electric light bulb, probably by Lane Fox, with plugged base and looped element, 5½in. high. (Sotheby's)   £170

Late 19th century 'Sunbeam Lamp' electric light bulb, with lobed element, 11in. high. (Sotheby's)   £210

ENAMEL

Real Battersea enamel was made in Battersea, at York House for only three years from 1753 to 1756, and it would be an understatement to say that pieces produced there at that time are extremely scarce. The term Battersea has come into popular use by the trade to describe most enamel boxes and trinkets, despite the fact that they are more likely to have been made at Wednesbury, South Staffordshire, Bilston or even last week in Czechoslovakia. Old examples should be surfaced with a substance similar to opaque glass applied over a copper base.

Pieces with any age are expensive trinkets but extremely pleasing. Decorated with a wide variety of subjects encompassing landscapes and seascapes, the most tender-hearted of these are love tokens and souvenirs from popular resorts.

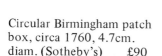

Circular Birmingham patch box, circa 1760, 4.7cm. diam. (Sotheby's) £90

German enamel snuff box, after Boucher, circa 1760, 8.2cm. wide. (Sotheby's) £1,300

Bilston oval enamel bonbonniere formed as a resting bull, circa 1800, 3.8cm. long. (Christie's) £480

Unusual circular German enamel snuff box with lobed bombe-shaped sides, circa 1750, 7.5cm. diam. (Sotheby's) £1,870

Staffordshire enamel sander, 18th century, with gilt metal mounts, 4.5cm. high. (Christie's) £170

Large pair of French or Swiss enamelled opera glasses, 11.5cm. high, circa 1875. (Sotheby's) £352

ETUIS

Etuis were often referred to as the Lady's Companion. They take the form of a small ornamental case designed to hang from a chatelaine worn at the waist, or simply to be carried in a pocket or purse.

They may be found in a variety of materials including, gold and hardstone, but are generally made in porcelain, ivory, painted enamel or silver.

They usually contain a multitude of manicure or sewing implements, together with a small snuff spoon, pencil, button hook or even a small fruit knife.

They saw their demise at the end of the 19th century, having been a symbol of feminine capability for over two hundred years.

Bilston enamel rainbow etui case, 4½in. high, circa 1765-70.(Sotheby's) £275

Mid 18th century etui, oval tapered body, fully fitted. (Sotheby's) £286

Furstenberg shaped oblong gold mounted etui, circa 1760, 11cm. long.(Christie's) £100

French lacquered etui of tapering form, circa 1760, 9.6cm. high. (Sotheby's) £143

George II etui, circa 1745, in green shagreen case.(Phillips) £300

Gold mounted shagreen and enamel etui, late 18th century, Swiss, 4in. high. (Sotheby's) £350

FAIRGROUND GALLOPERS

One of the more recent areas for specialised collection is the fairground, offering a plethora of fine artwork, albeit primitive and brash. Of particular interest are the carved and painted animals and birds of the merry-go-round their glazed eyes and dazed expression no doubt reflecting something of the generations spent whirling around at high speed, while being simultaneously bombarded with the blast of a slightly off-key steam organ.

Prices vary depending very much on the condition and quality of the carving and polychroming. It is pleasing to know that the art in their creation still survives having been handed down from generation to generation.

Early 20th century English polychromed carved wood fairground galloper, 2ft. 10in. wide. £165

Small wooden carousel galloper, 41in. long, circa 1930. £190

Early 20th century English fairground galloper with flowing mane and glass eyes, 64in. long. £418

One of a pair of 19th century carved carousel horses with brass harnesses and saddles, 46in. long. £465

Superb Victorian merry-go-round peacock of carved wood, 82in. high overall, with original brass pole, circa 1850. £650

English carved wood carousel galloper with leather saddle and bridle, 66in. long, circa 1920. £200

FAIRINGS

If you had gone to a travelling fair in the 1860s and had proved your prowess on the hoopla stall, chances are that you would have returned home the proud owner of a small china figure bearing a humorous and probably slightly risque legend on the base. These are referred to nowadays as "fairings".

Most are about 4in. high and stand on rectangular bases measuring 2in. by 3in. Subjects include themes like courtship, marriage, politics, war, childhood and animals behaving as people. In all, there are over 400 different types.

With something so typically English as fairings, it comes as a surprise to learn that most were made in Germany, and the two main manufacturers were Springer and Oppenheimer of Elbogen, and Conte and Boehme of Possneck. Of course, it was all a matter of getting down to a price, for the same objects could be bought in the shops for a copper or two, and the German manufacturers had perfected cheap mass production methods without losing on quality.

The manufacturers have obviously borrowed many of their ideas for fairings from such printed materials as sheet music covers. Two, entitled 'Pluck' and 'The Decided Smash' are copies from the cover of a popular song sheet of the time called 'Full Cry Gallop'. In the case of 'Slack' and 'How's Business', these are very good copies of each side of a Staffordshire mug. 'Champagne Charlie is my name' represents George Leybourne making popular the song 'Champagne Charlie' in the 1860s. There are also a few scenes of the Franco-Prussian War which include 'English Neutrality attending the Wounded'.

'I'm First Sir'.   £25—£45

'Robbing The (Male) Mail'. £45—£75

'After Marriage'.   £25—£45

'A Cat, A Cat'.   £25–£45

'Now They'll Blame Me For This'.   £75–£100

'A Spicey Bit'.   £25–£45

'That's Funny, Very Funny! Very, Very Funny!'   £45–£75

'Modesty'.   £75–£100

'Adolphus Won't Tell Papa'.   £250–£750

'Our Best Wishes'.   £150–£250

'The Organ Boy'.   £150–£250

'Oysters, Sir?' (Also captioned 'Oesters, Mynheer?')   £25–£45

'When A Man's Married His Troubles Begin'. £25—£45

'Much Ado About Nothing'. £45—£75

'A Nip On The Sly'. £45—£75

'Beware Of A Collision'. £150—£250

'You Dirty Boy'. £25—£45

'The Surprise' (Also captioned 'Wet Reception'). £150—£250

'Morning Prayer'. £25—£45

'Returning At One O'Clock In The Morning'. £25—£45

'A Pastoral Visit By Rev. John Jones'. £15—£20

'English Neutrality 1870/71 Attending The Sick And Wounded'. £150–£250

'Happy Father. What Two? Yes Sir. Two Little Beauties'. £45–£75

'God Save The Queen'. £75–£100

'What Peace When The Old Girl Sleeps'. £25–£45

'Twelve Months After Marriage'. £15–£25

'His First Pair'. £45–£75

'Vy Sarah You're Drunk'. £45–£75

'The Orphans'. £45–£75

'Shamming Sick'. £75–£100

'After You My Dear Alphonso'.
£100–£150

'Dick Whittington And His Cat'. £15–£25

'Children's Meeting'. £25–£45

'The Last In Bed To Put Out The Light'. £15–£25

'All Over'. £250–£750

'Am I Right, Or Any Other Man'. £150–£250

'O', Do Leave Me A Drop'.
£75–£100

'Baby's First Step'.£25–£45

'The Shoemaker In Love'.
£250–£750

'Hit Him Hard'.   £150–£250

'Stop Your Tickling Jock'.
£45–£75

'A Swell'.   £25–£45

'Please Sir, What Would You
Charge To Christen My Doll?'
£100–£150

'Truly Any Form Is Not
Evil'.   £75–£100

'Attack'.   £45–£75

'What Is Home Without A
Mother-in-Law?' £25–£45

'Who Is Coming?' £45–£75

'Three O'Clock In The Morning'.
£25–£45

FANS

Most eighteenth century fans are either delicately hand painted or those referred to as brise fans, which are composed of overlapping sticks radiating from a pivot and joined with ribbon threaded through slots at the top.

Many of the fans seen today date from the 19th century and, as a rule, do not fetch the very highest prices unless they are made from the finest of materials, incorporate precious metal and stones or are connected with the Empress Eugenie, who was partly responsible for their return to fashion in the Victorian era. Fans became such an important fashion feature that no expense was spared in their design and decoration.

Lace fans with mother-of-pearl mounts were popular from about 1860, until the vogue for all things Oriental popularised large silk fans decorated with birds and flowers in the Japanese style. These were followed by sequinned fans of black and white lace, and large Spanish types with ebony sticks.

The fan, originally a simple and effective gadget, was often modified to incorporate functions other than its original cooling system, e.g. a concealed mirror, peep holes, eyeglasses and even a weapon for self defence — a stiletto!

Particularly popular now are those rich plume fans of Art Deco design made during the brief fan revival of 1925-30.

Of the numberless fans on the market many are of very poor quality indeed and do not merit a place in a collection. However, with so many to choose from, it should not be difficult to find good examples of most periods at a reasonable price.

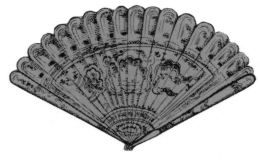

Mid 19th century lacquered Chinese brise fan, 23.5cm. long. (Sotheby's)   £143

Leaf painted fan, circa 1760, with carved mother-of-pearl sticks, 10¾in. wide. (Christie's S. Kensington)   £750

Framed Chinese ivory brise fan with finely pierced and draped central shield, circa 1795, 19in. wide. (Robert W. Skinner Inc.)   £85

Lace fan with mother-of-pearl sticks, circa 1890, 27cm. long. (Sotheby's)   £66

FANS

Rich black ostrich feather fan, tortoiseshell sticks. (Alfie's Antique Market)   £40

Historical fan painted with the coronation of Charles of Austria as King of Spain, circa 1703, damaged. (Sotheby's)   £210

Early 19th century Chinese lacquer brise fan, black sticks painted in shades of blue, red and green, 20cm. long. (Sotheby's) £605

Late 19th century Japanese ivory fan decorated in Shibayama style, 38cm. long. (Sotheby's)   £88

18th century chinoiserie 'peep-hole' fan decorated with mother-of-pearl, 29cm. long. (Sotheby's)   £198

Early 20th century yellow feather fan with floral decoration. (Phillips)   £30

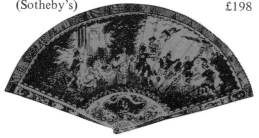

Early 18th century Vernis Martin brise fan, 21cm. long. (Sotheby's)   £605

Late 19th century Chinese ivory brise fan with carved bead, 28cm. long. (Sotheby's)   £220

Mid 19th century Chinese silver filigree and enamel fan, slightly damaged, 28.5cm. long. (Sotheby's)   £242

Tiffany & Co. fan with lace wing, veins of incised mother-of-pearl. (Phillips)   £60

Chinese ivory and feather fan with pierced and carved sticks and guards, 23cm. long, circa 1830. (Sotheby's)   £99

French mother-of-pearl fan with pierced sticks, circa 1860, signed Mabel, 26.8cm. long. (Sotheby's)   £265

Fan painted with watercolour and with gilt and mother-of-pearl sticks, 1895, 34cm. long. (Sotheby's)   £198

Mid 19th century Chinese parcel gilt filigree brise fan, 19.5cm. long. (Sotheby's)   £352

Late 19th century French mother-of-pearl fan, leaf painted with a watercolour, 25.2cm. long. (Sotheby's)   £88

Pierced ivory fan with chinoiserie vignettes on blue-ground paper mount, circa 1760, 29.5cm. long. (Sotheby's)   £1,110

If you had been in the unfortunate position of having your "one up and down with outside loo" burst into flames prior to about 1830 you would have been at the mercy of the private fire brigades employed by insurance companies.

If the outside of your house did not display the firemark of the first brigade to arrive, legend has it that their first priority was to sell policies to the neighbours and to blazes with you! It is also rumoured that particularly unscrupulous companies sent runners to impede the progress of rival brigades.

The earliest firemarks were of lead, often bearing the policy number, and these are naturally rare, for I assume they melted if a fire occurred. Later firemarks were of copper, tin or zinc and occasionally of terracotta or porcelain.

National Insurance Company of Ireland.   £50

Large engraved brass **London & Lancashire Fire Insurance Company** wall plaque, 16in. wide.   £125

Hants, Sussex and Dorset Security mark.   £600

Royal Exchange mark.   £100

Porcelain firemark of the **Athenaeum Fire Office.**   £900

Farmers Insurance Company copper plate.   £60

Firemark of the **London Assurance Fire Office**, in lead, circa 1720, 7in. wide. £600

Central Insurance Company plate. £70

Salamander Fire Office Society firemark, circa 1822, lead, 6¾in. wide. £300

Lead example of the firemark of the **Worcester Fire Office, 1790**. £1,000

Bristol Crown Fire Office mark, circa 1718, lead on wooden mount, 6½in. wide. £225

Convexed oval firemark of the **Phoenix Fire Office, 1782**. £750

London & Lancashire copper plate. £75

Sun Fire Office firemark, in lead, circa 1710, 5¾in. wide. £75

Rare Insurance firemark **Bath Sun Fire**. £125

Australian copper insurance firemark, **'Victoria'**. £48

London Assurance mark, 11in. diam. £60

Sun Fire Office, 1710. £50

Lead firemark of the **West of Scotland Insurance Company**. £850

Royal Exchange Assurance plate. £160

Early 19th century seven point star firemark of the **Suffolk and General County Amicable Insurance Office (1799-1848)**. £800

Hand-in-hand **Fire and Life Insurance Society** mark, in lead, 8in. wide. £250

Manchester **Fire and Life Assurance Company** plate. £75

Bath Fire Office mark in painted lead, 6½in. wide. £325

FISHING REELS

The sport of angling has been a rich source for the collector ever since the days of dear old Isaac Walton. Be it salmon flies, plugs, spoons, spinners, floats, gaffs or even weights there are specialist collectors for all.

Specimen fish have always been popular set amidst realistic fauna, particularly those mounted in bow fronted glass cases. Rods, too, have a serious following some collecting only roach poles while others seek nothing but greenheart rods with fine silver ferrules.

Fishing reels, however, seem to have a wider appeal perhaps because they can easily be displayed or simply admired for the ingenuity of their design, each for a specific job.

Brass and wooden reel by Wilkes Sprey Brand, 3in. diam.   £25

Fine 19th century solid brass trout reel, 2½in. diam.   £40

Fine cow horn and brass fishing reel, circa 1830, 4½in. diam.   £45

Rare 2¾in. 'Silex Multiplier' spinning reel, stamped D. W., with ebonite handle.   £242

19th century all brass trout reel, circa 1810, 2¼in. diam.   £40

Unusual narrow-drum 'perfect' trout reel of aluminium and brass, marked Hardy Bros., Alnwick.   £219

FLAGS

The attraction of collecting flags is that you can start with those little paper efforts which are bought on flag days to make you immune for the rest of the day, through all those souvenir pennants from far flung places and progress to those massive trade union banners as high as a house; though the real collectors seek military or national flags.

Be they in the form of silk cigarette cards, post cards or the real full size thing it is immediately noticeable how many countries have apparently disappeared completely, particularly in relation to those dating prior to the first World War.

Early American flags, count the stars, will always have a ready market as will Regimental flags especially if they have seen action.

Confederate Battle Flag, red field with a diagonal cross of blue on white. (Robert W. Skinner Inc.) £1,500

An early Nazi Police car flag, being the old Prussian Police Eagle with motto 'Gott Mit Uns'. (Wallis & Wallis) £155

A Nazi D.A.F. district banner, red ground, the top left hand corner with brown panel stitched with district 'Munster 7'. (Wallis & Wallis) £155

An early American flag, circa 1800, with a blue field containing fifteen white stars. (Robert W. Skinner Inc.) £250

GAMES

Before television and radio brought entertainment into the home, board and table games had an important role to play in family life. Many games survive, some in remarkable condition, and most have the potential to entertain if not to challenge the intellect.

Emphasis was placed on education as well as entertainment and many Victorian children's games were devised to combine a degree of random luck with the development of a good basic general knowledge of historical events, countries of the world, national costume etc. Children were not encouraged to play games on a Sunday unless, of course, they were on a religious theme like Noah's Ark.

A high price is more likely to be paid for a game when it is in the original box, complete with original components.

French 'Jeu de Course' game, circa 1900, 10½ x 10½in.   £45

W. Gamage set of conjuring tricks, circa 1915, 17¼in. wide.   £120

French tinplate 'Jeu de Course', circa 1900, 18in. diam.   £100

A fine English ivory chess set, the Kings surmounted by Maltese crosses, circa 1840. £275

Victorian coromandel wood games compendium in box, 13½in. wide.   £500

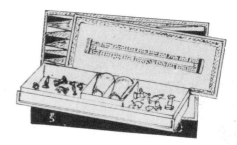

20th century sandalwood and ivory Indian games box, 18in. wide.   £250

GAMES

French faience chess set, made in Gien in the 19th century. £2,500·

Two from a set of twelve late 19th century carpet bowls, 8.2cm. diam. £80

Fine boxed set of graduated pyramid and ABC picture blocks. £50

19th century papier mache games box by Jennens & Bettridge's, 11¼in. wide. £250

Victorian child's snakes and ladders game, 16¾in. square. £18

American set of 'Snow White' picture bricks, circa 1946. £40

English ivory chess set by Fisher, circa 1890. £200

Complete set of wooden skittles, circa 1875. £20

GAMES

Unusual mid 19th century roulette game in painted wooden box, 18½in. wide.   £70

Set of eleven coloured carpet bowls.   £80

Mid 19th century artist's paintbox, 1ft. 10in. wide, English.   £260

Antique decorated wood 'Pope Joan' game, 10in. diam., circa 1870.   £38

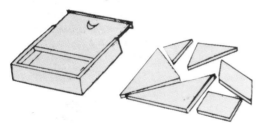

Victorian child's wooden puzzle in box.   £5

Child's game 'Lamplough's Model Cricket'.   £90

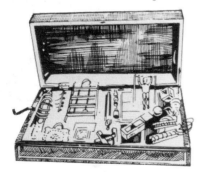

19th century compendium of Chinese ivory puzzles and games, in black lacquered box.   £180

1940's Mahjong set in carved wooden cabinet.   £65

GLOVES

An example of how the wearing of gloves has been influenced by the changing dictates of fashion may be seen in some early 17th century examples. They were often slit to show a ring, elaborately decorated, fringed and scented, going up to the elbows — and worn by men! Throughout the 17th and 18th centuries long gloves were held secure at the elbows with a glove band or string made of ribbon or plaited horsehair.

The range of materials include, a great variety of animal skins, embroidered satins, velvet, knitted silks, worsted cloth and strong washable cotton. There was also a colour code of sorts. According to the fashion of the day — colours were for daywear, white for the evening and lavender for weddings.

There are any number of good examples on the market and the knitted or crocheted gloves of the late Victorian early Edwardian period are still very moderately priced.

Lady's embroidered white kid hawking glove, mid 18th century, German or Austrian. £360

Pair of men's kid gloves said to have belonged to Edward VII. £40

One of a pair of 19th century Indo-Persian chain-mail gauntlets, made from butted rings of steel and brass formed to create a python-skin pattern of diamonds with dotted centres. £120

A pair of 17th century Dutch lady's kid gloves, circa 1635. £1,050

Early 17th century kid glove. £180

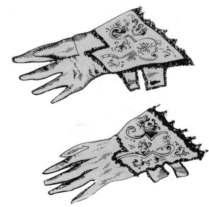

Pair of early 17th century gauntlets of white kid, cuff applied with ivory silk and sequins. £180

GOLDSCHEIDER

The Goldscheider factory of Vienna was founded in 1886 by Friedrich Goldscheider.

Production continued after his death in 1897, under the supervision of his widow and his brother Alois until 1920, when his two sons Marcel and Walter took the business over. Marcel left in 1927 to start the Vereinigte Ateliers fur Kunst and Keramic.

The art nouveau and art deco figures produced from the turn of the century, always incorporate the human form and are the pieces most desirable to collectors.

There are several marks for Goldscheider most including the name and another shows the Imperial Eagle along with the initials F.G.

Goldscheider earthenware mask, modelled as a woman, 1920's, 30.5cm. high. (Sotheby's) £110

Goldscheider 'bat girl' with winged cape, 1930's, 46.25cm. high. (Sotheby's) £572

Large porcelain figure by Friedrich Goldscheider of a young man seated on a chair, 21in. high. (Phillips & Jolly) £960

Goldscheider pottery figure of a young girl with flowers, 39.8cm. high. (Christie's) £432

Goldscheider earthenware nude figure holding a blue cloak, 1930's, 41.75cm. high. (Sotheby's) £341

Goldscheider cold-painted low-fired figure of a fairy, modelled by E. Tell, circa 1900, 76.25cm. high. (Sotheby's) £360

Had you been a turn of the century holidaymaker, the chances are that, in addition to sticks of rock, you would have carried home an example of the work of William Henry Goss.

A Londoner, born in 1833, he started business in 1858 producing fine china in the Copeland style. He might have gone on forever as just another china man had he not been interested in heraldry, and had his eldest son, Adolphus, not had a passion for archaeology. By combining his manufacturing talent and those two great interests, Goss hit upon a unique and highly successful formula for the holiday trade.

The best china shops of the time had shelves crammed with his miniature models of Roman vases, tombs and lighthouses, together with detailed replicas of famous buildings, which are amongst the most sought after pieces of Goss available today.

He made models of 51 cottages between 1893 and 1929, all of which (bar the Massachusetts Hall and Holden Chapel) were British. The two exceptions, having been made specifically at the request of his Boston (U.S.) agent, are rarely found in this country.

The firm traded under the name of W.H. Goss & Sons and later W.H. Goss Ltd. Printed marks include W.H. Goss, with goshawk, wings outstretched.

A number of factories, well aware of the success of Goss china, went into production with similar models but these are generally of inferior quality but do change hands for the same high price as Goss. Other manufacturers' pieces are quite clearly marked so there need be no confusion between the two.

Charles Dickens' house, Gads Hill. £100

Ellen Terry's farm Tenterden, Kent. £275

Wordsworth's home, Dove Cottage. £375

Shakespeare's Home.   £50

GOSS

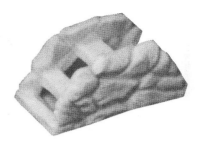

Queen Elizabeth Riding Shoe, 105mm. long. £85

Exeter Goblet, 130mm. high. £12.50

Cornish Stile, 72mm. long. £45

Newcastle Castle, 88mm. high. £150

Cat & Fiddle Inn, Buxton, 65mm. long. £185

The Old Horseshoe, 115mm. high. £7.50

Grinlow Tower, 95mm. high. £200

Eton Vase, 86mm. high. £4

Devon Cider Barrel, 60mm. high. £13.50

GOSS

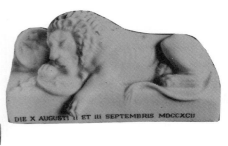

Thomas Hardy's birthplace Dorchester. £275

'Devil Looking Over Lincoln'. £60

Lucerne Lion. £80

Churchill Toby Jug. £100

Shakespeare's Home. (Late version). £35

Beccles Ringers Jug. £200

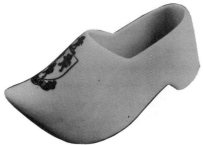

Hexham Abbey Frid Stool. £30

Dutch Sabot. £10

Nautilus Shell. £70

Kirk Braddan Cross. £60

Stornaway Highland Milk Crogan. £5

Bird's egg. £40

Ballafletcher cup. £20

Rye cannon ball on plinth. £85

Bournemouth pilgrim bottle. £10

Salisbury kettle. £5

Bust of Sir Walter Scott. £25

Stratford on Avon Toby jug. £40

Manx spirit measure. £5

Angel's head wall vase. £150

Windleshaw Chantry. £65

Abergavenny Ancient Jar.
£5

Melrose Cup. £30

Chicken Rock Lighthouse.
£20

W. H. Goss doll. £200

Cheshire Roman urn. £300

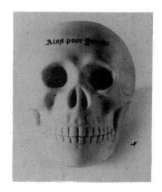

Yorick's Skull. £25

GRAMOPHONE NEEDLE TINS

There are many collectors of needle tins throughout the world as the collecting of gramophones and phonographs is a well established international hobby and the collecting of tins developed from this.

The City of London Phonograph and Gramophone Society caters for all these collectors from Australia, America, Holland, Germany and the United Kingdom. Auction houses in London regularly hold sales of all relevant items including tins.

It is only in the last few years that collecting gramophone needle tins, as a distinctly separate hobby from collecting gramophones and phonographs, has developed. The tins used to be found inside the machine or in the lid, so that many machine collectors already had some tins, and these made an ideal side collection as did the cutters, sharpeners and the record cleaning pads.

In their heyday, there were many hundreds of different brands produced and, because initially, each needle was only used once and then thrown away, the need arose to keep buying tins of 100 or 200 needles. The machines had no volume control, the tone being set by the needle, and most popular tones were medium, loud and extra loud.

The common brands were HMV, Songster, Columbia, Decca, Embassy and Edison Bell.

It is possible to build up a collection of 200 tins easily just by collecting variations of these six, and its an ideal start for novice collectors.

Collecting these tins has many advantages: their small size, ease of storage, relative cheapness, so the hobby is growing in popularity all the time.

Aeolian Vocalion — blue, pale blue and gold tin, large as it held 1000 needles, possibly German, 8cm./5cm./1.5cm. Very rare and attractive tin. £7—£10

Embassy 'Gramotube' — green and white tube 9cm. long with nozzle at end to dispense needles one at a time. Full instructions on the side of tin. Comes in different colours and tones, 200 or 150 needles, 200 extra loud needles from Redditch. £12—£17

Columbia Triple Tin — orange and gold tin, a round tin of 8cm. diam. and 1.5cm. deep. 3 compartments each of 200 needles of soft, medium and loud tones. A sliding top reveals the 3 sections. £5—£9

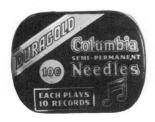

Columbia Duragold — green and gold tin, with Columbia trade mark, 'magic notes'. 100 semi-permanent golden needles. Very common.   50p–£1

Columbia Superbe — dark and light blue tin with magic notes. 200 loud needles.   50p–£1.50

Songster Bronze Pick-Up — blue and orange tin with Songster bird on branch. 100 pick-up needles for cinema use, made by J. Stead of Sheffield. £1–£2.50

Dog And Two Dogs — Natural Voice, red and white South African tin, found in many versions, usually with dog.   £1–£2

Edison Bell — brown and gold tin with bell in centre. 100 semi-permanent chromic needles.   £1–£2.50

Columbia De Luxe — orange and black tin with magic notes in orange circle. 200 de luxe needles. Attractive common tin.
                £1.50–£2.50

The Companion — green and dark green tin with space for local dealer's name and address. 200 pure tone needles.
                £1.50–£2.50

His Master's Voice — dark blue with world famous trade mark. Many variations and many copies, mainly German and S. African, 200 extra loud needles. £1–£3.50

Britannia (Minerva) — green, gold and yellow tin, a very attractive British picture tin. Produced in 1911 from The Minerva factory in Redditch, Worcs. 200 disc needles.
                £2–£4

Decca — purple and white tin with 1 large needle through name. Space for dealer's name and address or words 'She shall have music wherever she goes'. 200 needles. £2—£4

The Tungstyle — blue and white tin with HMV trade mark. Very thin tin, holding only 8 needles but each needle playing 150 times. Introduced in 1930's at 1 shilling and designed to fit in special clip in HMV gramophone. £2—£3.50

Embassy — bright yellow tin, red writing with Embassy 'eye' in centre of lid. Also found with ship in centre. Embassy being the cheap record label of Woolworths. Produced by The British Needle Co. of Redditch.£2—£4

Decca — green tin with white writing and black. 200 needles (soft). £2—£4

Solo — white or cream tin with record and sound box. 200 extra loud needles. £2—£3.50

Embassy — red tin with cabinet gramophone. Embassy eye on back of tin, 150 needles (loud tone). £2—£3.50

Beltona — blue tin and gold writing with face 'trade mark' — Euphonic brand name of tins. £2—£4

The 'Melba' Needle — blue tin with HMV trade mark. Rare early (about 1910) tin with the Melba needle written under the gramophone. 200 needles. £3—£5

Perophone — green, white and black tin with greyhound and record. Many variations, both in tin size and design. £2.50—£4.50

Arthurs Silver Steel — cream and red tin with name in red oval. Local brand, 200 needles, extra loud tone. £3—£5

Trutone Diamond Points — cream tin with highly decorated lid, often found with price 7½d. Many variations. £3—£5.50

Decca — orange and blue tin, very attractive with Decca 'lady' on lid. Dealer's name and address. 200 needles. £3—£5.50

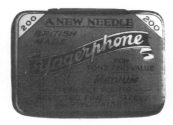

Needles for Disc Talking Machines — green and red tin with bird in red cross in centre. 200 sweet and clear full tone needles. £3—£6

Yagerphone — purple tin with gold and black writing. 200 medium tone needles. £4—£6

Chappell Golden Arrow — white tin with gold writing and golden arrow. 100 spear point needles. Rare make. £4—£6.50

'Red Ditch' — cream tin showing scene of Red Ditch (from which the town got it's name). 'SNEW' regd. trade mark. Rare picture tin, 200 needles. £4—£7.50

Lyric — red tin with white writing. Attractive picture of golden harp. 200 needles. £4—£7

Finest Steel Talking Machine Needles — red and green tin with Union Jack. Redditch made. Very rare. £4—£8

Sovereign Trutone — red and and gold tin with picture o of King George V. Only known Royalty needle tin. Pre-1936. 100 collar needles. £5—£8

Edison Bell 'Bell' — bell-shaped gold and green tin, 6cm. high, used to have stopper in top, again to dispense one needle at a time. Oval base has instructions on, 100 standard chromic needles, first introduced in 1933 at 1 shilling per 'Bell'. £10—£15

Golden Pyramid — golden tin with coloured section telling the tone. 200, 100 or 50 needles. Produced by The British Needle Co. Redditch. Designed to prevent spilling by delivering one needle at a time. £4—£8

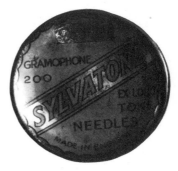

Sylvatone — blue round tin of 5cm. diam. Designed to prevent spilling. Many different brand names use this identical design eg.:- Fullotone, Nita, Wallis, Chorister etc. Sliding top to prevent spilling and dispense the needles. 200 extra loud tone. £5—£8

Marathon — grey German triangular tin, found in different tones, 2in. sides with white face. Most triangular tins are German. Rare 200 loud needles. £5—£9

5 Compartment HMV (Multi Compartment HMV) — there are 3, 4 and 5 compartment HMV's. All are very rare, the 5 is probably the rarest of the 3 tins. 15.5cm./4cm. The 5 contains 200 each of melba (blue), loud (red), piano (yellow), pianissimo (green) and the fifth compartment was used for used needles. The HMV dog and gramophone are shown on the 4 sections, the fifth says for used needles. Extremely rare. £12—£17

GRAMOPHONES & PHONOGRAPHS

The earliest record player, a phonograph, was invented by Thomas Alva Edison around 1877. This consists of a box structure housing the works, surmounted by a spindle, a needle lever and a horn. The record in the form of a cylinder is fitted to the spindle and when the works are cranked up, upon release of a catch the cylinder begins to turn, the needle moves onto the cylinder and the sound issues from the horn. It must have seemed like magic

The gramophone operating a sound system with flat discs followed in 1887, developed by Emil Berliner in America.

From the simple Pixie Grippa to the rare examples of early phonographs, this field of collection offers a vast range with something to suit whatever your budget.

Academy 78rpm gramophone with bell-shaped horn, circa 1930, 13in. square.(Sotheby's) £242

Edison diamond disc phonograph, model C19, American, circa 1915, in mahogany cabinet. (Sotheby's) £220

Gramophone Co. Ltd. Junior Monarch horn gramophone with Exhibition soundbox, circa 1910. (Sotheby's) £374

Edison Amberola 1A phonograph in mahogany cabinet, circa 1909, 49½in. high. (Sotheby's) £1,045

Edison opera phonograph with self-supporting Music Master laminated horn, circa 1912. (Sotheby's) £2,090

Edison Amberola Bi phonograph, Serial No. 4384, circa 1911, 50½ x 21½in. (Sotheby's) £1,210

221

Gramophone Company Style No 6 gramophone, circa 1900, in ornate oak cabinet. (Sotheby's) £748

Modern reproduction of a Berliner gramophone, Type B, in oak cabinet. (Sotheby's) £220

Edison Business phonograph, Model C, Serial No. 6421, in oak case, circa 1908. (Sotheby's) £264

Junior Monarch tin or brass horn, oak case, by Gramophone & Typewriter Co., 1904. (Capricorn Curios) £300

Aeolian-Vocalion gramophone in D-shaped sideboard, circa 1930, 47in. wide. (Sotheby's) £400

Zonophone gramophone in oak cabinet, 1912. (Capricorn Curios) £45

Gramophone & Typewriter Ltd. double-spacing Monarch gramophone in oak case, circa 1906. (Sotheby's)   £500

Gramophone & Typewriter Ltd. Junior Monarch horn gramophone, circa 1904, in carved oak case. (Sotheby's)   £300

HMV table grand, 109 Model, 1925. (Capricorn Curios)   £60

Edison Home phonograph, Model A, Serial No. 6221, circa 1898. (Sotheby's)   £352

Gramophone Company Style No. 5, trade-mark gramophone with Clark Johnson soundbox. (Sotheby's)   £715

Edison Amberola 30 phonograph, Serial No. 12866, circa 1915, 15½ x 15in. (Sotheby's)   £242

HAIR COMBS

Stage shows in the 19th century had, in much the same way as films and television do today, an incredible influence on fads and fashions of the period.

A prime example in Victorian times was Bizet's opera Carmen which opened in 1875 and prompted the popularity of large tortoiseshell combs worn in the Spanish style. They continued in fashion, although often of much smaller design, until the end of the century when the hair comb again received a boost in popularity as a result of the new designs created by the Art Nouveau movement.

Although most of those found today are plain tortoiseshell examples, costing a few pounds at the most, occasionally they can be seen decorated with gold and silver, or even semi-precious stones. These will obviously cost a lot more, depending on the design, with exceptional examples fetching a few hundred as opposed to a few pounds.

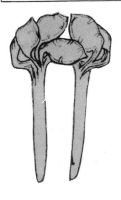

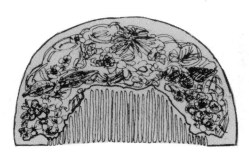

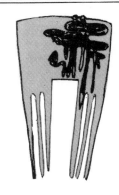

Art Nouveau comb of pale coloured horn. £45

Japanese blonde tortoiseshell hair ornament and pin, inlaid with gold, silver and mother-of-pearl. £200

One of a pair of French hair combs of horn adorned with silver lilies. £300

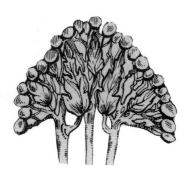

Carved horn, gold, enamel and mother-of-pearl hair ornament by Lalique, circa 1900, 17.5cm. wide. £1,600

Engraved tortoiseshell hair comb. £15

Good carved horn, enamel and moonstone hair comb, circa 1900, 13.1cm. wide. £575

HAT PINS

Hatpins have been in use to some degree since the 1880's. Originally sold in pairs, or in sets of three or four, they are usually about five to seven inches long with tops of silver, enamel, glass or semi-precious stones. Designs include butterflies, teddy bears, thistles, flowers, sporting themes, birds, shells and clusters of jewels. Some tops are hinged to give a snug fit close to the hat.

The original function of the hatpin was to anchor hat to hair and as hats got bigger, so did the hatpin. They began to look suspiciously like a dangerous weapon — resulting in a bill being read in America, proposing that, anyone wearing a hatpin more than 9in. in length would be required to carry a licence.

When very short hairstyles became fashionable in the 1920's the hatpin suffered something of a decline in popularity and those made after that date are generally of poorer quality.

Early 20th century yellow quartz hat pin. £4

Victorian green and white enamel hat pin. £5

Victorian carved jade hat pin in the form of a pig. £12

Art Nouveau style silver hat pin, circa 1905. £7

Edwardian glass flower cluster hat pin. £2

Early 20th century silver pique hat pin. £5

Edwardian painted glass hat pin. £3

Late 19th century cloisonne enamel hat pin. £10

HATS

Anyone who has become interested in hats can look forward to forming a thoroughly fascinating collection.

Most hats on the market today date from no earlier than the middle of the 19th century, however, this offers a range including, beautiful Victorian silk bonnets and little richly trimmed hats which were worn perched on top of the head, monumental Edwardian straw extravaganzas, and all of the attractive hats of the 20's, 30's and 40's.

Men's hats also make a marvellous collection and offer examples of the 18th century tricorne which was followed by the top hat made of beaver or felt, then the bowler, checked woollen caps, the summer straw boater and the trilby.

An enthusiastic collector may even attempt to determine the name of the original owner in the knowledge that the hats of the famous can be real collector's items.

Wedding bonnet of ivory georgette, about 1835-40. £45

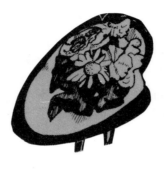

Edwardian straw hat trimmed with roses and daisies, circa 1910. £40

North American Athapaskan Indian beaded velvet cap. £150

Gentleman's finely quilted linen cap, mid 18th century. £341

Stovepipe bearskin hat belonging to Abraham Lincoln. £4,590

Carolean linen cap. £300

HORN

Horn is one of those materials which people seem either to dislike intensely or to collect avidly.

The range of objects of horn is almost limitless from spoons to mirror frames, from snuff boxes to chairs, from drinking vessels to chandeliers, and it is in this tremendous versatility that the chief attraction of the material lies.

Dividing horn into three categories we have articles made from treated horn (spoons, combs, shoehorns, snuff boxes, carved drinking vessels), those made of untreated — usually stags' — horn (chairs, tables, chandeliers, cutlery handles) and the grotesquely decorative (heads and skulls with antlers attached which adorn the walls of a few hunters' homes and those of many more would-be hunters).

Combs, spoons, fans, boxes, shoehorns and buttons are fairly widely available at reasonable prices, though spoons dating from the 16th and 17th centuries are rather more desirable and will fetch considerably more. Those having whistles incorporated in their handles are the best.

Powder horns make interesting collections, since many are finely carved and engraved with everything from flowers to coats of arms and hunting scenes.

It is not only the small objects to look for, however, for tables, chairs and chandeliers can also be found, their curiosity value ensuring a ready market.

19th century Japanese rhinoceros horn cup with flared rim, 4in. high. (Robert W. Skinner Inc.) £865

Silver mounted tapering cylindrical horn jug and two beakers by Chawner & Co., London, 1875. (Sotheby's) £320

Tiny Ozaki Kokusai study of an owl in staghorn. (Sotheby's) £10,500

One of a fine pair of buffalo horn armchairs.(Christie's) £1,900

Victorian brass and horn gong complete with hammer. (British Antique Exporters) £40

Bohemian carved staghorn powder flask. (Wallis & Wallis)£620

HORSE BRASSES

Horse brasses were thought to have originated over **4000** years ago in the near east and their symbolic designs to have evolved from the heraldic emblems on early horse armour. These decorative amulets were thought to have the power to deflect the gaze of the 'evil eye' from the wearer.

Handmade by gypsies and tinkers from sheet brass and sold at fairs up and down the country in the early 19th century they soon became very popular and were often awarded as prizes at agricultural shows and fairs. Demand eventually became so great that a more commercial method of production was sought resulting in the cast brass version making its first appearance around 1830 followed by a mass produced stamped brass as demand reached a peak at the end of Victoria's reign.

Early designs show acorns, flowers, wheatsheaves, trees, stags and fox masks with the later versions of 1840-1860 depicting portraits, county symbols, events and a variety of geometric designs. Of particular interest to collectors are those issued to celebrate Queen Victoria's Jubilee. A most attractive display can be made with Martingales, horse lames and even straps and buckles from Victorian harness.

It is something of a bonus if the brasses are still mounted on their original leather straps.

There is now almost a glut of modern horse brasses on the market but once you have handled and studied early brasses it will become easier to distinguish between the old and the new. As a broad rule, the modern version is mugh lighter in weight and shows no signs of rubbing on the reverse side.

Edward VII commemorative horse brass.£32

Horse brass depicting the Prince of Wales feathers.   £20

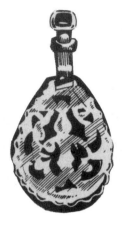

Large pierced horse brass in leather, circa 1870.   £30

Pierced brass on leather with brass buckle.   £30

Large horse brass mounted on leather.   £35

Pierced star horse brass, circa 1870.   £20

ICONS

Russian icons dating from the 10th to the 17th century are extremely rare and precious works of art. However, examples from a later period are more common and the high standard of their workmanship has guaranteed their continuing popularity with collectors.

Usually worked in tempera on wood, the subject is always of a religious or mystical nature showing representations of Christ, The Virgin, The Saints or scenes from a religious life. The majority of icon painters were monks and this work was often produced as part of the discipline of a life of contemplation.

Icons were sometimes set in a folding frame so that they could be carried from place to place. These frames are often of exquisite design and craftsmanship. A three-fold panel is called a triptych.

18th century Palekh School icon 'The Old Testament Trinity', 31.3cm. high. (Christie's) £1,026

Russian icon 'Christ Pantocrator', dated 1870, 21.2cm. high. (Christie's) £594

Icon of the Palekh School 'The Resurrection and Descent into Hell', circa 1800, 35.5cm. high. (Christie's) £702

The Kursk Mother of God, naturalistically painted, 1899-1907. (Sotheby's) £418

The Mother of God of the Sign, undated Moscow, early 19th century. (Sotheby's) £352

Christ Pantocrater, naturalistically painted, 1899-1907. (Sotheby's) £440

18th century Central Russian icon 'The Virgin of Smolensk', 31.2cm. high. (Christie's)£756

19th century Russian menological icon for the month of July, 41.5cm. high. (Christie's) £702

Moscow School icon 'The Metropolitan Philip' holding the Gospels, circa 1700, 32cm. high. (Christie's) £702

John the Baptist shown full length, 19th century. (Sotheby's) £440

17th century North Russian iconostasis panel 'The Apostle Peter', 94cm. high. (Christie's) £864

The Umilenye Mother of God, 17th century. (Sotheby's) £1,045

Late 17th century Russian icon 'The Apostles Peter and Paul', 31.2cm. high. (Christie's) £820

17th century Russian icon 'St. Nicholas' shown shoulder-high, 31cm. high. (Christie's) £410

17th century Russian icon 'Birth of the Virgin', 28.1cm. high. (Christie's) £756

19th century Palekh School icon 'The Resurrection and Descent into Hell', 34.1cm. high. (Christie's) £756

19th century icon 'The Virgin of Kazan' on ivory ground, 33cm. high. (Christie's)£1,836

19th century Russian icon of St. Nicholas, 101cm. high. (Christie's) £1,404

The appearance of the Mother of God, 18th century. (Sotheby's) £550

18th century Russian icon-ostasis panel 'The Evange-list St. Matthew', 53.5cm. high.(Christie's) £918

The Anastasis, the upper half centred by The Saviour, 18th century. (Sotheby's) £550

19th century Russian icon 'The Virgin of Kazan', circa 1900, 31.5cm. high. (Christie's)£1,458

Russian icon 'The Saviour', by Vladimirov, 1908-17, 32.1cm. high. (Christie's) £1,080

17th century Central Russian icon of Saints Samon, Gury, Aviv and Simeon the Stylite, 31.3cm. high. (Christie's) £518

Christ Pantocrator painted in traditional manner, Moscow, 1819. (Sotheby's)   £880

St. Nicholas, naturalistically painted and encased in a parcel gilt Oklad, Moscow, 1899-1908. (Sotheby's)   £1,012

The Kazan Mother of God painted on a gold ground, Kostroma, 1857. (Sotheby's)   £572

Saints Zosima and Savatti founders of the Solovki Monastery, 17th century. (Sotheby's) £880

11th/13th Byzantine steatite showing a representation of Hodegitria Virgin, 9cm. high. (Christie's)   £864

The Doctor Saints Cosmas and Damian, late 17th century. (Sotheby's)   £1,045

Christ Pantocrator, encased in a silver Oklad, Moscow, 1880. (Sotheby's)   £825

The Saviour, shown head and shoulders, 18th century. (Sotheby's)   £1,375

The Mother of God of the Sign, St. Petersburg, 1826. (Sotheby's)   £638

INROS

Most Japanese inros take the form of a decorative slim rectangular lacquered box. They will usually divide up into three to five sections slotting neatly together and strung on a cord threaded through slots in the sides.

They were used, by men, from the 16th to the 19th century for carrying the family seal, medicine or tobacco and were worn hanging from the belt alongside the sword.

The cords of the inro are secured by a bead (ojime) and attached to the girdle by a netsuke carved in wood or ivory.

A four-case gold Fundame inro decorated in gold and red hiramakie, signed Jokasai. (Christie's) £550

A Tamenuri four-case inro decorated in gold and silver hiramakie, signed Jokasai. (Christie's) £950

A four-case inro decorated in gold, silver, red, brown and black, signed Koryusai. (Christie's) £270

A four-case inro decorated in gold and silver togidashi, unsigned. (Christie's) £486

An unusual five-case inro signed Koma Koryu. (Christie's) £1,000

A three-cased Paulownia wood inro decorated in gold, silver and red. (Christie's) £216

A four-case circular Roiro-Nuri inro decorated with Kosekiko astride a horse. (Christie's) £1,100

An unusual cherry bark two-case inro signed Shigetsune, 19th century. (Christie's) £850

A two-case inro carved in high relief with a recumbent ox beneath a pine tree. (Christie's) £280

A rare five case inro decorated in iroe togidashi and kirigane, signed Shiomi Masanari. (Christie's)£4,200

An unusual shakudo and gilt nanako oval snuff box, 19th century. (Christie's) £320

A four-case inro signed Koma Koryu, saku with attached bead ojime. (Christie's) £756

A fine four-case inro decorated with three crows perched on a flowering plum branch. (Christie's) £2,600

A three-case wood inro carved in relief with a seated cat against a basket weave ground. (Christie's) £600

A four-case inro decorated in gold and silver hiramakie, 17th century. (Christie's) £220

A circular porcelain single-case inro, signed Tatsuke Tagamasu. (Christie's) £380

A four-case inro signed Koma Kyu-haku saku, late 19th century. (Christie's) £475

A well detailed three-case wood inro carved as a turtle, 19th century. (Christie's) £580

A fine Tsuishu single-case inro carved with a figure of Chokaro Sennin. (Christie's) £4,000

A rare four-case inro decorated with a kite modelled as a dancing man, signed Kajikawa saku. (Christie's) £7,200

A superb Roiro-Nuri sleeve inro inlaid in Somada style, 19th century. (Christie's) £3,200

A two-case Tsuikoku inro with attached hardstone bead ojime. (Christie's) £380

A fine four-case sleeve inro decorated with Daruma wearing a koromo. (Christie's) £3,200

A three case gold lacquer Fundame inro, inscribed Kenzan, probably 18th century. (Christie's)£300

IRONS

A wise buy for those with the collecting urge, would be old irons. They are comparatively cheap, fairly plentiful, and will form an interesting collection which is sure to increase in value. The variety of different types is staggering; from tiny curved 4in. lace irons to the enormous, professional Tailors Goose which can weigh anything up to 30lb.

It would appear that the practice of ironing clothes was known to the Chinese in the eighth century and introduced to Britain by the Viking invaders, who used a massive smooth stone resembling an inverted mushroom known as a 'sleek'.

Early flat irons were sold in pairs so that one could be reheating either on the stove or placed directly against the fire while the other was in use. They were heavy and the handles hot and awkward to manage. A set of irons with exchangeable handles was patented in America by a Mrs Potts in 1871.

In the 18th century, it was not uncommon for a household wash to be tackled only once every two or three months — an event presenting many challenges with fabrics requiring pleating, crimping, ruffling, goffering and finishing so that by the Victorian period every housekeeper worth her salt was armed with a battery of irons designed to cope with every conceivable task, even one with a tiny base and long handle for ironing hats.

If you keep your eyes open you can find old irons just about anywhere and, a few pounds will buy a simple cast flat (or sad) iron. Raise your sights and you can become the proud possessor of an interesting gas or methylated spirit model — or even a hollow iron complete with heating stone.

  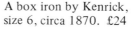

A box iron by Kenrick, size 6, circa 1870. £24

Victorian flat iron. £5

Petrol heated iron, by Coleman, model 8 'Instant Lite'. £25

Georgian brass goffering iron, circa 1830. £32

William Cross & Sons 'Hot Cross' gas iron. £10

An unusual brass iron of about 1720 with original stone. £75

IVORY

Ivory has been recognised as a perfect material for carving since ancient times and the art of the skilled carver has always been well appreciated.

Craftsmen used several kinds of ivory including, elephant tusks (the hard white ivory comes from the African elephant and the yellower from the Indian), and hippopotamus or walrus tusks to produce boxes, jewellery, knife handles, combs, buttons and statuettes and ornamental groups of particular beauty.

Ivory inlaid with designs in fine materials is known as Shibayama, named after the Japanese family Shibayama who excelled in this style of decoration.

There are many well produced fakes made of plastic on the market, but close examination of the surface may show a lack of the characteristic streaking or flecking of ivory. A test, which should be undertaken entirely at your own risk, is to place a hot needle pressed flat against the base of a suspect piece. Plastic will melt!

Early 19th century French prisoner-of-war Spinning Jenny, 5¾in. high. £375

Late 19th century French carved ivory figure of Cupid, 16cm. high. £418

Japanese ivory figurine, 6¾in. high. £100

Early 18th century Northern France ivory snuff rasp carved in relief, 7½in. high. £242

Late 19th/early 20th century Belgian five-man wood and ivory beggar band, 15.5.-17.5cm. £360

English Regency ivory bust of a lady, signed F. M. Jacobs Sc., 13cm. £95

IVORY

Hound-shaped carved ivory needlecase. £220

Carved ivory covered container of basket weave design, 4½in. high. £145

Ivory and gold pique patch box, mid 18th century. £70

Carved ivory female head by Julien Dillens, 55cm. high, circa 1900. £1,600

Japanese carved ivory sectional takarabune, 52cm. long. £1,200

Unusual Guangxu ivory acrobatic group of four articulated figures, 12.5cm. high. £165

Ivory figure of a young child by F. Preiss, inscribed, 9cm. high. £330

Ivory model 'Thoughts', carved from a model by F. Preiss, on green and black onyx base, 15.8cm. high. £1,430

Small ivory group of Kanzan and Jittoku with good detail, signed Yoshitomo. £187

Mid 19th cenurty French ivory group of two children, on gilt metal base, 9.5cm. high. £242

Attractive ivory group of four boys, signed, circa 1880-90, 3in. high. £310

Early 18th century ivory head of one of the Three Fates, inspired by Michelangelo, mounted as a seal. £308

JEWELLERY

Throughout the ages jewellery has been prized for both its decorative quality and the value of the materials used in its production.

Most of the collector's jewellery on the market today comes from the 19th and 20th century, mainly from the latter, and provides a rich variety of ingenious designs and fine craftsmanship.

A new collector would be well advised to study the subject well, learn to identify materials, styles and periods, and note important names such as Rene Lalique, Georges & Jean Fouquet, C.R. Ashbee, and Georg Jensen.

One of the greatest pleasures of collecting is to be able to use the pieces and this applies to jewellery more than most collectibles.

Lalique deep amber glass pendant, 5cm. high, 1920's. (Sotheby's) £180

French gold mounted diamond brooch in the shape of a bee with ruby eyes and double baroque pearl body. (W. H. Lane & Son) £370

Berlin iron brooch with ivory cameo, circa 1820. (Alfie's Antique Market) £95

Mid 19th century gold brooch designed as a kestrel with platinum leaves and stem. (Sotheby's) £200

Diamond brooch designed as a working model of a bicycle, circa 1900. (Sotheby's) £1,500

Silver brooch, circa 1885, of two crossed rackets and tennis shoe, English, 43mm. wide. (Phillips) £28

Silver gilt and plique-a-jour enamel brooch, circa 1905, 4cm. wide. (Sotheby's) £150

Arts & Crafts pendant possibly by Professor Joseph A. Hodel, 1.5cm. across. (Phillips) £80

Fahrner silver and opal pendant, circa 1900, 4.5cm. high. (Sotheby's) £340

Brooch in frog form, set with diamonds and with ruby eyes. (Sotheby, King & Chasemore)   £880

Russian niello bracelet, set with turquoise, St. Petersburg, 1884. (Vost's)   £130

Victorian pearl pendant brooch. (Lawrence Fine Art)   £150

Gold Art Nouveau brooch with rose-diamonds, in the style of Boucheron, circa 1900. (Locke & England)   £800

Diamond brooch in the form of an inverted crescent, in gold and silver setting. (Sotheby's)   £572

Georg Jensen brooch in silver coloured metal, 6cm. wide, 1920's. (Sotheby's)   £80

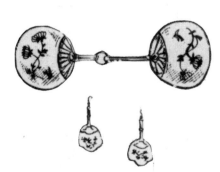

Art Nouveau pearl and enamel pendant, circa 1900. (Robert W. Skinner Inc.)£50

Enamel Chinese buckle and earrings. (Alfie's Antique Market)   £30

Diamond, dementoid garnet and gem set bird brooch. (Christie's S. Kensington)   £2,000

KEYS

These fine old keys come from lock sets which were designed to be both functional and attractive.

The old locks come on the market less frequently than the keys, most remaining united with their original door or chest, but keys are more plentiful and offer an interesting variety of designs.

They are most commonly made of steel, iron and brass though some unusual examples are in gilded wrought iron or pinchbeck. Great attention was given to the design of the 'bow', many are intricately designed and decorated with figures, birds, cherubs and heraldic motifs.

It will add interest to the collection if you know a little about the history of a key and obligingly, they occasionally have faded, written labels attached.

An 18th century cut steel key with a comb end, 5½in. long. £125

An 18th century cut steel key, 5¼in. long. £105

Early 17th century French steel key, 5½in. long. £660

17th century key, the head with geometric motif, 4½in. long. £45

Early 19th century iron key, 5in. long. £7

A small 18th century cut steel key, 4in. long. £6-

An extremely well made flintlock key pistol in the French style of circa 1640, 11in. long. £435

17th century steel key with geometric motif, 5½in. long. £65

LACE

There is Needlepoint and Pillow lace; and a lace that is a combination of both. There is rose point, point de neige, point d'Angleterre, point d'Alencon and point d'Argentan, and so on ad infinitum.

Most people start buying lace because they like it and want to wear it or use it in furnishings. This is as good a reason as any and as you handle lace and gain knowledge about it, you will become able to identify the country of origin, method of production and different designs. It is a good idea to read all you can about the subject, study patterns and even buy a magnifying glass so that you can closely examine the stitches used in a particular piece. Apart from the satisfaction of knowing your subject thoroughly you are less likely to overlook the early examples of Italian lace now fetching a small fortune.

Large chain point collar with scallop edge, circa 1840. £30

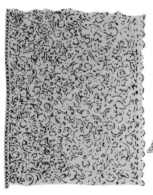

Italian 17th century flounce of point de neige. £3,400

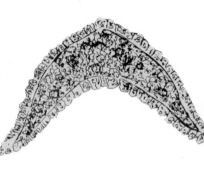

A collar of Punto in Aria edged with Genoese bobbin lace, circa 1650. £250

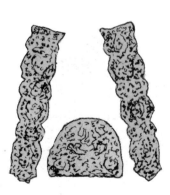

Pair of 17th century point d'Angleterre lappets and bonnet back. £200

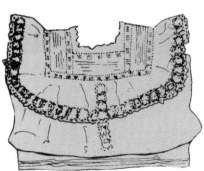

Late 19th century lace trimmed embroidered nightdress. £25

A Hollie Point baby's shirt and bonnet edged with Buckingham lace, 17th century. £175

LEACH

The English potter Bernard Leach was born in 1887. He spent his early years both in Japan and England, returning to Japan to teach engraving and design. His work was influential in the development of the Japanese folk art movement which gained recognition in 1929. In 1920 he started work at St. Ives in Cornwall, producing stoneware from local materials and re-introducing the art of marbled slip decoration.

The work of Bernard Leach and his pupils is noted for the vast range of decorative techniques. Marks include initials BL impressed within rectangle or painted and the work of the Leach pottery at St. Ives is marked with S and I crossed, with two dots, enclosed in circle or square, impressed.

While this is undoubtedly an expensive field of collecting it is one in which knowledge will be rewarded, for the reason that, the work of Leach is not immediately recognisable to the general public as a piece of such potential value.

Bernard Leach stoneware slab bottle with narrow neck, 19.4cm. high. (Christie's) £500

Important Bernard Leach cut-sided stoneware bowl, covered in olive celadon glaze, circa 1960, 31.5cm. diam. (Sotheby's) £2,400

St. Ives stoneware deep bowl decorated by Bernard Leach, 31.5cm. diam., centre showing an owl. (Christie's) £800

Bernard Leach stoneware vase of bulbous form, circa 1935, 18.5cm. high. (Christie's) £194

Bernard Leach stoneware vase of oviform, with everted rim, 34cm. high. (Christie's) £1,000

St. Ives preserve pot and cover decorated by Bernard Leach, 11.5cm. high. (Christie's) £150

LEAD SOLDIERS

In 1893, with the British Empire at its height, the firm of William Britain introduced a series of toy soldiers representing the regiments of the British army.

These were an immediate success and Britain's went on to increase their range, producing an abundance of military models including armies of other nations, tanks, gun units and army bands. Britain's continued to produce new models up until the time of the Coronation in 1953.

Early models fixed to a round base are more valuable than those on a rectangular base, and the stamp on the bottom will help to date the pieces. 'Copyright Wm. Britain' was used before 1912, and 'Britains Ltd.' before 1937. After this 'Made in England' was added. Although most sets change hands at less than £100, a set of Salvation Army Bandsmen recently made nearer £1,000.

A Britain's R.A.M.C. 4-horse covered ambulance waggon, original linen cover, with 2 A.S.C. drivers and 2 seated R.A.M.C. orderlies, all full dress, and R.A.M.C. officer, nurse and stretcher. (Wallis & Wallis) £80

Britain's Mounted Band of The Scots Greys, 6 instrumentalists on white horses, and one black drum-horse. (Wallis & Wallis) £65

A Britain's State Coach Set, George VI, comprising coach with 8 horses and 4 riders, 8 footmen, 5 footmen with swords, 4 'beefeaters', Household Cavalry escort of 1 officer and 4 troopers, in original box, no. 1476. (Wallis & Wallis) £80

Britain's Mountain Artillery battery, 4 mules with cannon parts, mounted officer and 6 other ranks. (Wallis & Wallis) £41

A Britain's armoured machine-gun carrier with driver and gunner and a vehicle only, a Tank Corps officer and 6 other ranks, rifles at the trail. (Wallis & Wallis) £26

Britain's Band of The 1st Life Guards, 11 mounted bandsmen, including drummer, in their box, no. 101; a Life Guards trooper in cloak. (Wallis & Wallis) £65

Ten mounted troopers of The 12th Lancers, movable arms, steel lances, and one mounted officer with sword at the ready, by 'Johilco', in their original painted colours. (Wallis & Wallis) £35

LIBERTY

In 1875 Arthur Lazenby Liberty was the manager of Farmer & Rogers, a London firm specialising in Oriental imports, when he plucked up the courage to open his own shop in Regent Street.

He commissioned works from many of the designers associated with the Arts and Crafts movement and within five years had established himself as the leading purveyor of goods in the avant garde style. His enthusiasm embraced not only furniture and fabrics but pottery, silver, pewter and jewellery.

Noted among the pewter designs are those marked TUDRIC, which date from 1902, and among the silver articles those marked CYMRIC, a range launched in 1899.

Liberty & Co. 'Tudric' pewter timepiece in almost rectangular case and with brass hands, 33.5cm. high.(Phillips) £160

Liberty & Co. two-handled silver bowl, Birmingham, 1913, 4¼oz., 14.6cm. wide. (Christie's) £150

Liberty & Co., silver and enamel frame, 29cm. high, Birmingham, 1905. (Sotheby's) £580

One of a pair of Liberty & Co. brass candlesticks, 13.5cm. high, circa 1900. (Sotheby's) £120

Liberty & Co. 'Tudric' pewter tea service by Archibald Knox. (Christie's) £220

Liberty & Co. silver stopper by Archibald Knox, Birmingham, 1906, 6.5cm. high. (Sotheby's) £143

LOCKS

Locks for doors and chests have been made in China and Egypt since early antiquity, but it wasn't until comparatively recent times that they began to lose their character and be hidden away beneath the woodwork.

What all early locks lacked in safe-keeping abilities they amply made up for in impressiveness of appearance.

Made in finely worked iron, brass, steel, bronze and ormolu many stand up as works of art on their own and are now eagerly sought after by collectors.

Louis XVI ormolu door lock. £150

17th century engraved door lock and key. £65

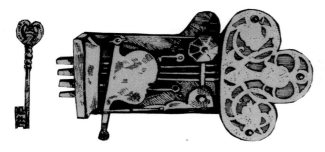

16th century steel door lock with key, from the Bohemia's Castle of Dux, where Casanova's body was finally laid to rest, 19½in. wide.£625

French steel-cased door lock with heavy ormolu trim, brass handles and escutcheon plate, circa 1790. £100

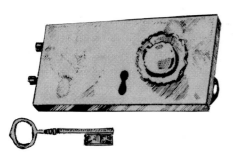

George III brass door lock, 7in. wide, with keeper and key. £60

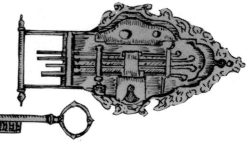

Late 17th century German door lock with brass finials. £200

MAGIC CATALOGUES

During the second half of the 19th century, with developing technology presenting a new invention or discovery almost daily, many Victorians began to think that anything might, indeed, be possible.

It is therefore, no surprise that one of the most popular music hall turns was the magician or illusionist, who achieved in their own time, the high status granted to pop stars today.

The craze swept through the Western World leaving in its wake a terrific amount of books, posters and other paraphernalia connected with magic.

A glance at one of these catalogues will explain the continuing popularity of the subject, for who could resist a descriptive list of 'new and superior wonders in the art of high grade prestidigitation, magical apparatus and necromantic mysteries'. Who indeed!

THEO. BAMBERG, NEW YORK.

former lets go the arrow which, after piercing the lady, speeds on to the target where it remains sticking. The ribbon is still attached to the arrow that has passed through the lady and the end of it now hangs down in front of her. To prove that it is really true that the ribbon is through her body she moves it backwards and forwards through her body, complete with all accessories. Price . . . See Price List

1299. THE MYSTERIOUS ESCAPE.

A gigantic set of scales are seen standing in the centre of the stage. On one side of the scales a big cage is attached, instead of the ordinary weighing pan. A lady is asked to enter the cage and is weighed, the scales being made to exactly balance by the usual weights on the other side. The curtains of the cage are now closed, a pistol is fired, and, instantaneously, the scale carrying the weights falls and the cage end rises. On drawing the curtains, it is found that the cage is empty, but the lady is seen at the same moment coming down the theatre through the audience on her way to the stage. To prove that the cage is absolutely hanging free it is swung round, so that all may see it. This is a first class illusion, and the idea is brand new. Price on application.

Theo Bamberg, 'Amateur Catalog of Magic and Novelties'; 'Illustrated Catalogue', New York. (Sotheby's) £48

Carl Willmann, Hamburg.

1279. Der indische Fakir.
The floating Ind an Fakir.   Suspension aérienne ou scéne du Fakir.

Ich bin infolge weltverzweigter Verbindungen stets vom Neuesten unterrichtet.

Carl Willmann, 4 catalogues including the 24th, 26th and 28th editions, 10 volumes in 5, Hamburg, circa 1883-1915.(Sotheby's) £260

Columbia Magic Trick Manufacturing Co.,
illustrated descriptive price list of magical
apparatus and illusions, New York, circa
1890. (Sotheby's)   £100

L. Davenport & Co., 37 catalogues, including List of Absolutely New Principles In
Magic (circa 1899); All British Catalogue
of New Magical Novelties; Illustrated Catalogue of the Latest, English, American and
Continental Magical Novelties (circa 1910).
(Sotheby's)   £170

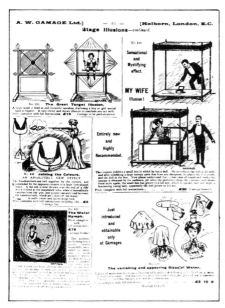

Gamages, 21 catalogues in 3 volumes with
illustrations, circa 1909-59. (Sotheby's)£170

Signor T. Somerfield, 'Descriptive Catalogue
of Entirely New And Superior Wonders in
the Art of High-Grade Prestidigitation, Magical Apparatus, Necromantic Mysteries etc.',
Paulton Bros., Wolverhampton, circa 1870.
(Sotheby's)   £170

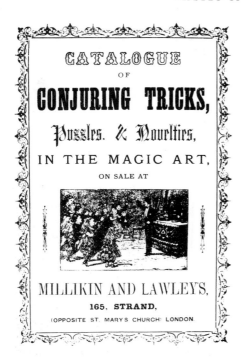

Chicago Magic Catalogue, nos. 6-10; 12 and 14-18, 2 price lists and a few other loose leaves, in 13 volumes, Chicago, 1914-41. (Sotheby's)   £50

Millikin and Lawley's, 3 catalogues, circa 1895. (Sotheby's)   £160

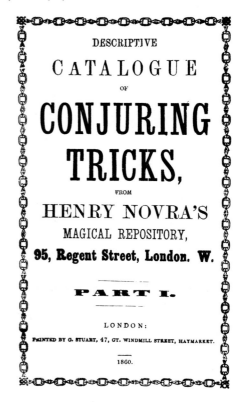

Frank Hiam, catalogues for 1881, circa 1888 and circa 1895, 4 volumes in 3 illustrations, circa 1881-95. (Sotheby's)   £160

Henry Novra, 'Descriptive Catalogue of Conjuring Tricks from Henry Novra's Magical Repository', Part I, printed by G. Stuart, 1860. (Sotheby's)   £220

MAPS

The enthusiasm shown by maps and atlas collectors has guaranteed the continuance of sales held specifically for them with the big map names of Ortelius, Speed, Jansson, Valk and Sanson well to the fore.

A travel book with maps is even more sought after than one with only prints and plates and books of maps alone can make hugh prices. A Mercator atlas worth over £150,000 turned up not long ago on a Belgium roadside bookstall.

More common maps are those produced for various religious and missionary organisations and maps made for Victorian cyclists, railway maps and even stagecoach maps. There are more of those still about than may be imagined.

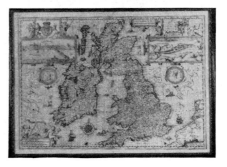

John Speed, 'Dorsetshyre', engraved map, hand-coloured in outline, 13½ x 19½in., 1614-16 Sudbury & Humble. (Christie's S. Kensington)   £170

Nicolaus Visscher, 'Atlas Minor sive totius orbis terrarum', 36 hand-coloured double page engraved maps, Amsterdam, after 1705. (Christie's)   £2,400

Hobson's 'Fox Hunting Atlas', 1880. (May Whetter & Grose)   £130

Ignace Pardies, 'Globi Coelestis . . . Opus Postumum', 2nd Edition, 6 double page star maps and large folding engraved table, French Jesuit inscription, very rare, Paris, 1693. (Sotheby's)   £650

Michael Drayton, 'Poly-Olbion, all the Tracts, Rivers, Mountains, Forests and Other Parts of Great Britain', 1st Edition, third issue, portrait of Prince Henry, 1622. (Christie's)£2,000

Noronha Freyre, 'Istoria delle Guerre del Regno del Brasilie', 2 volumes in one, 26 engraved folding maps, plans and views, Rome 1700. (Christie's) £2,000

J. Thomson, 'The Atlas of Scotland', key map, double maps of rivers and mountains, 58 fine double engraved maps, Edinburgh, 1832. (Sotheby's) £350

Claudio Duchetti, 'Majorca Insula', engraved map with attractive pictures of buildings, hills etc., Rome 1570. (Sotheby's) £180

John Knapton, 'Geographia Antiqua', maps linen backed, extra illustrations with 8 maps, Joseph Priestley's copy, 1800. (Robert W. Skinner Inc.) £310

Sebastian Munster, set of six uncoloured maps comprising three of the World and the four Continents, circa 1540. (Phillips)£1,700

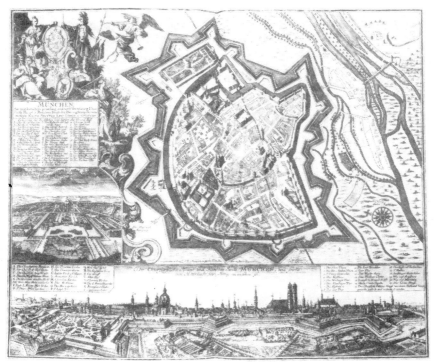

J. B. Homann, 'Atlas Novus', 3 volumes, pictorial engraved title and 367 engraved plates, Nuremberg. (Sotheby's) £38,000

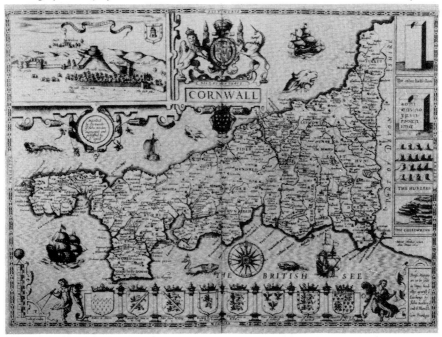

John Speed, 'The Theatre of the Empire of Great Britaine', 2nd Edition, 64 double-page maps of 67, 1614. (Sotheby's) £7,700

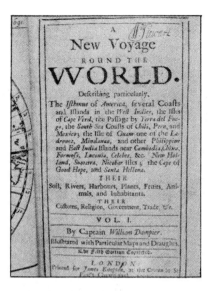

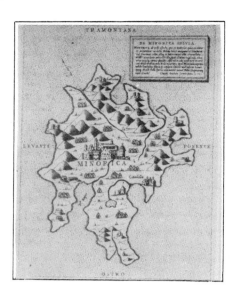

Captain William Dampier, 'A Voyage Round the World', volume 1, 2nd Edition, four maps and 'Voyages and Descriptions', volume 2, 2nd Edition, three maps, 1703 and 1700. (Allen & May)   £110

Claudio Duchetti, 'De Minorica Insula', engraved map, attractive pictures of buildings, hills etc., Rome 1570. (Sotheby's)   £210

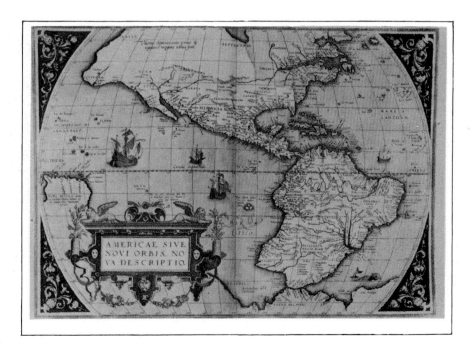

Abraham Ortelius, 'Theatrum Orbis Terrarum', 112 double-page maps, Anvers, C. Plantin, 1584. (Christie's)   £11,000

Schleswieg-Holstein, J. Majer, 'Newe Landcart von den Beiden Hertzogthumbern Schleswieg und Holstein . . . 1650, 416 x 588mm., Husum, 1650. (Sotheby's) £418

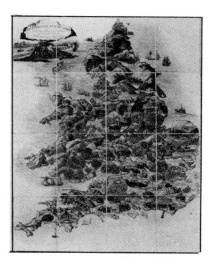

Johannes Blaeu, 'Le Grand Atlas ou Cosmographie Blaviane', 12 volumes, complete set, text in French, volumes VI and LX 1st Editions., others 2nd, 598 engraved maps, plans and plates, coloured, 1667.(Christie's)£54,000

Picturesque Round Game of the Produce and Manufactures of the Counties of England and Wales, engraved sheet mounted on linen with aquatint pictorial map, 660 x 516mm., E. Wallis, circa 1830. (Sotheby's)   £150

MASKS

Originally masks were designed to appear as ferocious as possible in order to scare the day-lights out of the enemy, and successful they must have been for all cultures abound with them.

They were also made for funeral purposes or as images of the Gods for ceremonial events. Most found today were specifically made as tourist souvenirs and originate from Africa or the Far East. Confusion arises because they are made in the traditional way and it will often take an expert to determine whether a mask is old or not. And it's the old ones that can be worth fortunes. Recently a Maori wooden head with tatoo marks made £18,000, a Tongass wooden mask from Cape Fox made £25,000 and an example from the Congo made over £30,000.

19th century Balinese mask of wood with baked on colours. £60

A Mambila wood antelope mask of helmet-like form, 20½in. high. £110

Balsa wood mask made for the 'Goelede' society, Yoruba tribe. £110

Tlingit mask representing a hawk. £650

New Guinea Sepic River wood mask, 18in. high. £75

Face mask from Baule, Ivory Coast, 32.4cm. high. £1,250

256

MARTINWARE

Robert, Walter and Edwin had all, at one time or another, worked at the Doulton factory in Lambeth but they eventually got together and opened their own workshop at Southall in 1877. It was run by the fourth brother, Charles, who also ran a retail shop in Holborn to sell the wares the brothers produced.

Most of the leering birds and other animal models were made by the eldest brother, Robert, while Walter prepared the clay and made vases, leaving the youngest brother, Edwin, to do all the fancy decoration and, doubtless, make the tea, run round the corner to get the paper and all the other things youngest brothers do. They also produced candlesticks, jugs, clock cases and goblets until the eventual close of the factory in 1914.

A Martinware jug of gourd shape, 16.5cm. high. (Christie's) £80

A Martin Brothers miniature vase incised in low relief with fish and eels, 8cm. high, circa 1900. (Sotheby's) £180

Martin Brothers stoneware double-face jug with angular strap handle, 1911, 16.5cm. high. (Christie's) £453

Martinware figure of a bird with large talons, signed on rim, 29cm. high. (Phillips) £3,000

Martinware terracotta grotesque, signed, 1898, 32cm. wide. (Phillips) £2,500

Martin Brothers vase with tapered body, dated 1-1900, 22.4cm. high. (Sotheby's) £420

MARY GREGORY

One of the most distinctive styles of glasswork is that known as Mary Gregory.

Although most of the glass in this style seen today was manufactured during the second half of the 19th century at Jablonec, Czechoslovakia, by the firm of Hahn, the original Mary Gregory worked as an enameller at the Boston & Sandwich Glass Company in the U.S.A.

There she decorated inexpensive blown and tinted glass decanters, jugs and vases with pink or opaque white figures, usually of playful children frolicking, flying kites, fishing, trundling hoops or picking flowers.

The base colours are likely to be red, green, blue, pink, amber or even turquoise, with the earlier examples tending to be slightly 'softer' than pieces made at the turn of the century.

All Mary Gregory glass however, from wherever the provenance, is now eagerly sought after for its appeal is much wider than that normally attributed to glassware.

Cranberry glass, inexpensively produced in Britain in the late 19th century, was often engraved with Mary Gregory style figures. This is a clear pinkish-red glass originally produced for use in the manufacture of chemists' bottles and then adopted in the production of vases, bowls and dishes. A characteristic of Cranberry glassware is the applied clear glass frilled rim.

Mary Gregory amber glass pin tray depicting a boy with a butterfly net. £85

Mary Gregory glass jug, 8in. high. £50

Mary Gregory green glass decanter. £30

Pair of Mary Gregory green glasses depicting a boy and girl. £60

Mary Gregory hand-painted glass cream jug. £25

Mary Gregory enamelled dish with everted rim, circa 1880, 13¼in. diam. £150

MATCH BOX LABELS

It may surprise many people to learn that matches, of a kind, were in use before postage stamps, and that collecting match box labels is at least as old as collecting stamps.

While the first match box labels only displayed instructions for using the match, the first pictorial variety, introduced by Jones around 1829 for 'Royal Patent Lucifers' carried an illustration of an Englishman and a Scotsman.

Today 'phillumeny', is a well organised world wide hobby with its own clubs, magazines and meetings. The beginner will find the range of labels infinite, amounting probably to many millions of different kinds and it need not be an expensive business. A collection can be built up from what is around, exchanging with fellow collectors and of course, from specialist dealers.

Japanese advertising label for home market. One of 100's of thousands. Nominal 2p

Packet label for Foreign made match for British market from 1958 onwards. 10p

German Export Bengal match label. Pre First World War. £1

Swedish Export label probably c. 1880. 50p

Swedish Export packet label, probably for East Indies market, c. 1913. 20p

Label obtained at a function at Buckingham Palace in 1978. Not normally available.

This label is attached to a normal box by the user himself. These labels are sometimes placed over the original label, sometimes on the reverse side to it.   20p

One of a large range of advertising and brand 'All Round The Box' labels of United Match Industries Ltd. of Bishops Stortford, Herts. Closed down in 1970.
5p

One of a range of many 1,000's of 'All Round The Box' labels, c. 1940, made by S. J. Moreland & Sons Ltd. of Gloucester. Now closed down.   25p

Old Bryant & May 'All Round The Box' label, nearly 100 years old. (Issued c. 1888.) £3

British Bookmatch Cover (non advertising) modern.
5p

From an early British Manufacturer, c. 1863/65.   £20

One of a set of Service Rank markings issued during the Second World War. Single label. 20p

An old label from a British Company no longer in existence, c. early 1920's. £20

This is an advertising box as supplied by the manufacturer to the user. Modern. 5p

Non-advertising book-match cover from France. Modern. 5p

Modern advertising cover made by Bryant & May's, who have now closed their British Book-Match Factory and supply from Canada. 5p

Book-Match cover from from U.S.S.R., an un-common country for these, which mainly uses boxes. 20p

One from a set of 48 labels (i.e. each quarter hour is shown on a label). Numerous average and minor design variations, resulting in several different sets. 10p

Finnish made advertising label for Finnish market. 5p

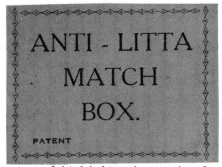

The source of this label is unknown therefore, the price is debateable — it may fetch £5 at auction.

One of a set of 40 labels issued in 1956. This is the first of a large range of Australian sets. A complete set may fetch £10.

U.S.A. advertising Book-Match cover, 1940's. 5p

Label from one of a very large range of sets that have become more and more popular in recent years. 5p

Label printed in Sweden for a Burmese maker. 10p

262

These labels are from a box supplied by the manufacturing company to the user. The user's label is placed over the supplier's label. Modern. 5p

Swedish label commemorating Children's Day. 5p

Label of one of a large range of different types of matches made by Bryant & May's over a period of well over 100 years. 50p

This label is from a type of box known as 'Pill Box'. This is cylindrical with labels round lid and box, c. 1950. Striker is at top or base of box. 20p

This label from Bryant & May's range, obtainable in numerous sizes for different boxes. This brand discontinued. 50p

Swedish Export, c. 1913. 10p

MATCH BOX LABELS

Advertising label, perhaps from Italy for Egypt or Malta, c. 1950.   5p

This label is from an advertising box, now made in enormous quantities for public houses, clubs, businesses etc., 1980. 5p

Royalty, always a popular subject in Britain, Holland and other countries, 1910.
30p

One of Bryant & May's early labels, c. 1891.   £5

'Pill Box' label c. 1950.   20p

'All Round The Box' label from a British Manufacturer no longer in existence, c. early 1900's.   £10

MATCH CASES

Matchboxes have not always been the simple card, wood or plastic containers we know today. Originally, they were known as fire boxes, match safes or safety boxes.

Owing to the fact that early matches were liable to flare into life at the slightest knock, or with exposure to not very great heat, it was felt necessary to keep them in containers which, in the event of accidental combustion, would restrict the fire.

As far as is known, the first friction matches were produced in about 1827 and were sold in a tin case to a Mr. Hixon by their maker, John Walker of Stockton-on-Tees. By 1850 the different types of fire boxes were almost limitless, often taking the form of soldiers, historical figures or animals made of iron, brass and other metals. Usually, the heads of the figures were hinged to allow matches to be stored in their hollow interiors.

Very often, there was a small hole somewhere in which a single, lit match could be placed — possibly for reasons of economy in that this allowed the full length of the wooded shaft to burn, and possibly as a means of holding the flame steady when it was being used to melt sealing wax.

In addition to the metal fire boxes, some quite beautiful examples were made of ceramics or wood. Many of these had different provisions for igniting the various kinds of matches. Some merely had roughened patches, others had two roughened discs between which the match head was sandwiched before being sharply withdrawn to effect ignition. There was also a type of match which consisted of a small wooden splint tipped with chlorate of potash. This was lit by dipping the tip into sulphuric acid. Containers for these usually took a cylindrical form, in the centre of which stood the small bottle of acid surrounded by the potash-tipped matches.

Metal match case in the form of a Gladstone bag. £50

Vesta match case advertising Otto Monsteds Margarines. £130

Oval vesta case in the form of a creel, by T. Johnson, London, 1883, 5.7cm. long. £770

French Art Nouveau silver smoker's set, circa 1900. £120

Vesta match case showing King Edward VII, 1901. £75

Silver match case with floral decoration. £35

265

MATCHSTRIKERS

Before the widespread use of matches in boxes there were numerous little containers designed to house them. Made from a variety of materials including wood, bone, glass, papier mache, Tunbridgeware, enamel, stone and china, their common feature is a lidless compartment for the matches and a grooved or roughened striking surface.

The most numerous and generally regarded as most appealing specimens are those made of porcelain by the German firm of Conte and Boehme, who were also responsible for producing most of the 'fairings' which are so eagerly sought after today.

Many bear a humorous or slightly risque inscription on the base often borrowed from a popular song of the day.

'I Am Starting For A Long Journey' and 'I Am Off With Him'.   £25–£45

' His First Love Letter'.   £25–£45

'Caught In The Act'.   £100–£150

'Cold Hands' and 'Cold Feet'.   £25–£45

MATCHSTRIKERS

'Waiting For Orders'. £25–£45

'Who Calls!' £75–£100

'Shoes'. £15–£25

'Skating Rink'. £75–£100

'A Safe Messenger'. £25–£45

'The Welsh Tea Party'.
£25–£45

'Returning From Working'
£45–£75

'I Have Had My Bath, Now Its
Your Turn'.   £25–£45

'Taking A Walk'. £25–£45

'Drummer Boy'.
£15–£25

'Elephant'.   £25–£45

'Mylord And Milady'.
£45–£75

'Peau D'Lapin Chiffons'.
£45–£75

'Any Flags, Ma'am'. £75–£100

'The Daily Telegraph'.
£75–£100

**'I Am Going A-Milking Sir,
She Said'.**   £45–£75

'Match, Sir' (also captioned
'Any Lights Sir'). £45–£75

'Present From Canterbury'.
£15–£25

'A Fresh Morning'.
£45–£75

'Announcement'. £15–£25

'Fresh Chestnuts, Sir'.
£45–£75

'A Penny Please, Sir?'
£45–£75

'Sweet Violets, Sir'. £45–£75

'A Copper Sir?'
£15–£25

'Present From Criccieth'.
£15–£25

'Good Dog'. £15–£25

'Daily News Sir'. £75–£100

MEDALS

It may surprise the uninitiated to the field of medal collecting to note the high prices currently achieved. But, for many of the thousands of people who collect, the fascination lies in the historical and personal interest. Most medals bear the name of the original owner along with that of his regiment or ship.

In this extensive field, there is ample opportunity to specialise. Some collectors buy only rare bars or medals awarded for a specific battle or campaign.

Now that medals are fetching high prices, we hear that the fakers are at work — not always successfully I am pleased to say. It may be possible to detect when a medal has been re-named for the rim is usually narrower and slightly rounded where the work has been done.

The majority of medals presented to the troops who fought in the First and Second World Wars, are unlikely ever to reach a high price for the simple reason that millions were issued.

B.S.A. Co., medal for Rhodesia 1896, no bar (engraved 3579 Pte. Frank Smith 2/W. Rid. Regt.) (Wallis & Wallis) £50

Saxe-Gotha-Altenburg Waterloo medal 1815, in bronze with some gilt highlights, as issued to officers. (Wallis & Wallis) £52

China 1900, no bar (H. J. Metters, P.O. 1 Cl., H.M.S. Aurora). (Wallis & Wallis) £65

Ashanteee War 1873-74, no bar (G. Pearson, Ord., H.M.S. Simoom, 73-74). (Wallis & Wallis) £70

China 1900, 1 bar Rel. of Pekin. (Wallis & Wallis) £78

A silver Regimental medal of The 26th Foot, dated 1823, diam. 1.7in. (Wallis & Wallis) £85

Indian Mutiny 1857-58, 2 bars, Lucknow, Central India, (impressed to Lt. R. D. Thorpe, 27th Madras N.I.). (Wallis & Wallis)£85

New Zealand 1861-66, (impressed 1415 Patk. Cassin, 2nd Bn. 14th Regt.) (Wallis & Wallis)   £95

Canada General Service Medal 1866-70, 1 bar Fenian Raid 1866, (951 Gr T. Hoare R.A.)(Wallis & Wallis)   £100

New Zealand Campaign — undated issue (253 Sjt. T. Collett Mil. Train. A.S.C.) (Wallis & Wallis)   £105

Pair: Queen's Sudan, Khedive's Sudan, 1 bar Khartoum (4577 Pte. W. Dixon 2nd Lancs. Fus.) (Wallis & Wallis)   £100

A rare Prussian 1813 Iron Cross, 2nd Class, silver arms, iron centre, in a case. (Wallis & Wallis)   £125

A rare German World War I Knight's Cross of the Iron Cross, with ribbon. (Wallis & Wallis)   £125

Q.S.A. 4 bars, C.C., Wepener, Trans., Witte (3963 Pte. G. J. Hodgkinson, Royal Scots). (Wallis & Wallis) £155

Indian Mutiny, 2 bars, Relief of Lucknow, Delhi, (Sjt. Wm. Brown, 1st Bn. 8th Regt.) (Wallis & Wallis)   £170

Punjab 1849, 2 bars, Chilianwala, Goojerat. (W. Banks, 24th Foot). £180

South Africa 1877-79, 1 bar 1877-78 (9921 Qr. Mr. Sergt. D. Bingham R.E.) £200

King's Police Medal, George V, uncrowned head, pre-1933 issue, (James Davies, Supt. Glamorgan Constab.) £220

East and West Africa 1887-1900, 2 bars Benin 1897, Sierra Leone 1898-99 (E. Talbot Ord. H.M.S. St. George). £240

Pair: South Africa, 1853, (Lt. 45th Regt.), I.G.S. 1854, 1 bar Bhootan, (Capt. W. H. Rowland, 55th Regt.). £265

N.G.S. 1793, 1 bar Navarino, (lightly impressed Benjn. Harvey). £330

Indian Mutiny 1 bar, Defence of Lucknow (F. Beagley, 90th Lt. Infy.) £360

M.G.S. 1793, 6 bars Busaco, Albuhera, Nivelle, Nive, Orthes, Toulouse, (J. P. Hely, Capt. 57th Foot). £550

Ghuznee Medal 1839 (engraved edge Major Genl Sir Robert Sale K.C.B.) £600

MEDICAL

With rapid advances in the medical profession making objects of a mere decade ago seem antiquated, it is little wonder that devices from the 19th century have such a fascination today.

Often beautifully made in fine woods such as lignum vitae or ebony they are generally embellished with a preponderance of brass, silver, ivory and tortoiseshell.

Dentistry seems particularly well blessed with spittoons, chairs, cabinets and a multitude of frightening objects. Surgery, too, has its share of fine instruments with a 16th century South German set selling recently for over £2,000.

Apothecary boxes seem to be fairly plentiful made of mahogany and having numerous glass bottles with ground glass stoppers, most date from the first half of the 19th century.

They usually contain a secret compartment often behind a sliding panel at the back where the poisons and opiates were housed.

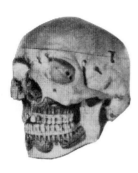

A student's demonstration human skull with hinged jaw. (Sotheby's) £99

A Czermak's demonstration laryngoscope by John Weiss & Son, circa 1870. (Sotheby's) £187

A fine toothed bone saw with steel blade and ivory handle. (Sotheby's) £286

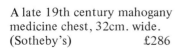

A set of thumb lancets with tortoiseshell guards, late 18th century. (Sotheby's) £176

A late 19th century mahogany medicine chest, 32cm. wide. (Sotheby's) £286

A dental spittoon in black and gilt metal, mid 19th century. (Sotheby's) £88

MINERALS

The past few years have seen a tremendous rise in popularity in collecting and polishing stones, possibly because such good results can be obtained with the simple use of a tumble polisher. Seemingly dull beach pebbles can suddenly acquire the dignity of gem stones after only a couple of weeks of revolving.

Larger crystalline formations are particularly sought after for interior decoration, those with unbroken crystals and of good colour being the most popular.

Shape can also be very important as regards value and you should be on the lookout for geodes — those stones which have been cut in half to reveal internal cavities with crystalline growth — and vugs which are similar but cut differently.

Slabs of beautifully marked agate and quartz can generally be bought for less than ten pounds, and even small examples of semi-precious stones such as garnet and amethyst can be bought for a few pounds more. Rarer minerals such as hematite, wolframite and arsenoprite are far more expensive and can cost many hundreds of pounds.

A watchful eye should always be kept for a 19th century collection of minerals. They do sometimes come on the market in the form of a simple wooden trunk full of boring looking rocks. The Victorians were, in fact, avaricious collectors, often going to great lengths in order to obtain a rare specimen, and a small fortune could well be awaiting the budding geologist prepared to do a little research. Not only can the indigenous specimens be found but often exotic finds from foreign shores; souvenirs of the Grand Tour so beloved by the Victorians.

A large group of clear quartz crystals of a slightly amethystine colour. £750

A large group of calcite crystals with natural petroleum inclusions. £75

A mass of rhodochrosite of an attractive pink colour. £80

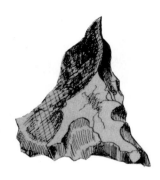

An iron meteorite from the meteor crater of Arizona. £800

An attractive specimen of Galena. £200

A brown and polished geode with blue and white agate bands and protruding quartz crystal. £140

MINIATURE FURNITURE

Miniature furniture is, as the name implies, scaled down replicas of full size pieces found in the home, and not to be confused with dolls' house furniture which is usually much smaller and designed specifically for play.

The miniature pieces were generally made by an apprentice, as perfectly as his talents would allow, as part of his final exam before graduating as a fully fledged craftsman.
Although most of the furniture found today dates from the 19th century, it is a practice which has been in operation since furniture was first made on a commercial scale, with early pieces obtaining the most money. It is a practice which would seem to have been fairly widespread for apprentice pieces can be found in all European countries as well as in America.

19th century apprentice mahogany chest of drawers, 26cm. high. (Phillips) £60

A miniature walnut oblong table of William and Mary design, 13in. long. (Vernon's) £50

Mid 19th century American miniature Empire bureau, 9in. high. (Robert W. Skinner Inc.) £140

19th century miniature gilt-wood four-poster bed, 2ft. 9in. high, with original hangings. (Christie's & Edmiston's) £360

Queen Anne walnut miniature chest of drawers, circa 1710, 1ft.3in. wide. (Sotheby's) £450

A miniature mahogany wardrobe enclosed by two doors, with carved beaded borders, 16in. high, 13in. wide. (Vernon's) £75

One of a pair of miniature corner chairs with bowed and carved crestings. (Sotheby's) £190

Fine miniature apprentice made settle, Brittany, circa 1850, in oak with hinged lid, 12¾in. long. (Christopher Sykes) £130

Mid 18th century miniature walnut bureau, 8½in. wide. (Sotheby's) £360

MINIATURES

Before the days of photography, the only way to carry a true likeness of someone was in the form of a miniature portrait; an artform which reached its peak in the last quarter of the 18th century.

Even small towns boasted their own miniaturist and fashionable resorts, such as Bath, supported whole colonies.

Their charges varied from a couple of guineas up to twenty-five guineas for the work of a master such as John Smart. Other names to look for are Richard Cosway, Henry Spicer, Horace Hone, Richard Crosse, Ozias Humphrey, Jeremiah Meyer, Charles Bestland and George Engleheart. Most miniatures from this period are painted on ivory with watercolours used to produce flesh tones and opaque colour for dress.

More reasonably priced examples can be found from the 19th century, though the skills involved seem to decline with the onset of the camera.

A gentleman wearing a black jacket and white cravat, ebonised wood frame, 7.6cm., by Thos. Richmond, circa 1800. (Sotheby's)   £270

Prince William of Orange, gouache on vellum, ebony and tortoiseshell frame, 7cm., French School, circa 1740. (Sotheby's)   £1,655

A field officer of the 42nd Royal Highlanders The Black Watch, papier mache frame, 8.2cm., attributed to George Place, circa 1785. (Sotheby's)   £2,455

A young lady wearing a tall black hat and a brown jacket over a blue and white striped dress, silver gilt frame, 5.6cm., French School, circa 1785. (Sotheby's)   £205

A gentleman wearing a plum coloured gown, signed with initials, oil on panel, 10.5cm., by Pieter Van Slingeland. (Sotheby's)   £2,860

A young girl with curling fair hair wearing a white dress with a pearl necklace, 5.1cm., attributed to Edward Nash, circa 1800. (Sotheby's) £350

MINIATURES

A young lady seated on a chair holding a book, gilt metal mount, 7cm., signed and dated 1789, by Jacques Anthoine Marie Lemoine. (Sotheby's) £1,335

A young lady with her hair falling to her shoulders, wearing a white low-cut dress, gold frame, 8.2cm., by Andrew Plimer, circa 1800. (Sotheby's) £510

A young man wearing a blue jacket, 6.5cm., signed and dated 1805, by Tonna. (Sotheby's) £190

19th century Continental School, lady wearing lace-trimmed cap, 8.2cm., painted on card. (Sotheby's) £286

Mademoiselle de Marcieux of Grenoble, giltwood frame, 9.5cm., signed and dated 1790, by Muralt. (Sotheby's) £2,385

A young girl holding a parrot, on vellum, gilt metal frame, 5.2cm., Continental School, early 17th century. (Sotheby's) £8,265

A gentleman wearing a brown jacket and striped waistcoat, gold mount, 7cm., signed, by Le Chevalier De Chateaubourg, circa 1790. (Sotheby's) £6,850

Marie De Medici kneeling in prayer before an altar, oil on copper, 12cm., Franco-Flemish School, 17th century. (Sotheby's) £765

A young lady with brown hair, wearing a white dress with lace trimmings, enamel, 8.2cm., signed and dated 1826, by Wm. Essex. (Sotheby's) £1,120

MODEL PLANES

Although Wilbur Wright and his brother Orvil are credited with making the first powered flight in December 1903, it was another American, Samuel Pierpont Langley, who actually invented the first aeroplane.

After achieving success with a model launched from the roof of a houseboat on the Potomac in 1896, he progressed to a full size machine and was ready to repeat the experiment early in 1903. Unfortunately, the starting mechanism failed and the aircraft plunged into the river. Professor Langley died in 1906 never having achieved his life's ambition.

The postscript to this story is, that in 1914, his former students fitted floats to Langley's 'curiosity' in an attempt to launch direct from the river- it flew like a bird.

Some of the early model planes now fetch amazing money and virtually any model made prior to 1940 is highly desirable and will do well.

Britain's bi-plane, complete with pilot, finished in silver, no. 1521. (Sotheby's)   £450

Scale model of The R.A.E., SE5A, frame of brass and steel, 27cm. long.(Thomas Watson & Son)   £650

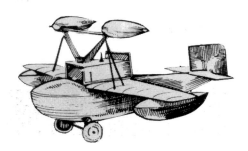

Bing tinplate monoplane, 1930's. (Christie's S. Kensington)   £100

Clockwork tinplate airliner, with lithograph detail, circa 1940. (Sotheby, King & Chasemore)   £100

Well-detailed 1in. to 1ft. scale model in wood and metal of the Bleriot Type XXVII single seater monoplane by P. Veale, 58.5cm. long. (Christie's)   £750

Model of the Bristol Scout type C, 1915.   £180

MODEL SHIPS

Many of the model ships found today could well have originated from a market stall such as that set up on the Esplanade outside Edinburgh Castle by prisoners of the Napoleonic War . They sold wonderfully detailed model ships made largely from left-over bones from the cookhouse, embellished with scraps of ivory, wood and metal bought with the proceeds of other sales. Needless to say, these model ships varied somewhat in size and skill of execution, from two foot long models of **100** gun men o' war now costing many thousands of pounds, to quite small examples.

The Victorians, too, were enthusiastic makers of model ships, particularly those which could be put into glass cases.

Shipyard model of a ship's boat with patent specification, 95cm. long. (Phillips)   £310

Marklin tinplate submarine with clockwork mechanism, circa 1935, 22in. long.(Sotheby's)   £935

Fine live steam-powered wooden model of the paddle steamer 'Brighton Queen', 47½in. long. (Christie's)   £650

Fleischmann twin-funnelled tinplate liner with clockwork mechanism, 12in. long, circa 1950. (Sotheby's)   £121

Modern English well-detailed model of the Padstow lifeboat 'Joseph Hiram Chadwick', 107cm. long. (Sotheby's)   £450

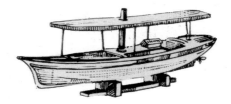

Model of the Thames steam launch 'Togo' by P. Nunn, Sevenoaks, 135cm. long. (Christie's)   £350

MODEL SHIPS

Contemporary French prisoner-of-war bone and horn model of a 112-gun man-of-war, 12in. long. (Christie's)   £5,000

Modern English model of a brig, 37cm. wide. (Sotheby's)   £250

Late 19th century English model of a steam yacht with streamlined wooden hull. (Sotheby's)   £380

Exhibition standard scale fully planked model of HMS Victory, by J. Bright, Gosport, 40in. long. (Christie's)   £1,300

Scale radio-controlled model of the salvage tug 'Lloydsman' of Hull, built by E. R. Warwick, Sevenoaks, 56in. wide. (Christie's)   £550

Finely planked and rigged 1/32nd scale model of an ocean going dhow by D. A. Brogden, Skegness, 71cm. long. (Christie's)   £550

MODEL SHIPS

Planked and framed holly and mahogany dockyard model of a 32-gun frigate, 66cm. long, circa 1830. (Christopher Sykes) £375

Fine hand made model of an early 19th century whaling boat, 33in. long, circa 1830. (Christopher Sykes) £375

French prisoner-of-war bone model of a 48-gun frigate, 19½in. long. (Christie's) £1,300

Fully rigged bone and mahogany model of a 16-gun Admiralty cutter, 16in. wide. (Christie's) £600

Accurate 1/24th scale wooden sailing model of the Thames spritsail barge 'Kathleen', 55in. long. (Christie's) £700

Exhibition standard boxwood and pine model of a single screw steam yacht, circa 1900, by W. Morrison, Saltcoats, 43in. long. (Christie's) £4,000

MODEL TRAINS

Model trains tend to fall into two distinct collecting fields. Those designed as toys, and these have been made since the last quarter of the 19th century mainly by the German firms of Bing and Marklin, and those superb scale models occasionally as large as 10ft. long, by firms such as Bassett — Lowke.

One of the most prolific British makers was Hornby and occasionally a complete set can be found in its original cardboard box. This adds greatly to the value as does the condition of the train; those with original paintwork and livery obtaining a premium.

Carriages, tenders, stations, bridges and all landscaping features are also eagerly sought after.

Marks to look for are G.B.N. for Bing, G.C. and Co. for Carette and G.M.C. for Marklin.

Cast metal 'HO' gauge 2-rail electric model of the Italian Railways Express diesel car by Conti. (Christie's)   £120

7mm. fine scale electric model of a 'Jinty' class 0-6-0 side tank locomotive, by J. S. Beeson, Ringwood, 9in. long. (Christie's) £480

Lionel tinplate gauge '0' clockwork Disney train, circa 1940, 30in. long. (Sotheby's) £308

7mm. scale electric model of a 4-2-2 locomotive and tender 'Lorna Doone', by P. G. Rose, 16in. long. (Christie's)   £950

Fine gauge 'I' live steam spirit-fired 0-2-2-0 side tank locomotive complete with pot boiler, by Bing. (Christie's)   £380

Bing gauge 'I' live steam spirit-fired 2-2-0 locomotive and tender, 39.5cm. long. (Sotheby's)   £350

3½in. gauge model of the Southern Railway 2-4-2 side tank locomotive No. 4, 66cm. long. (Christie's)   £900

5in. gauge model of the Welsh quarry 0-4-0 tank locomotive No. 1, by S. F. Price, Sheppey, 31½in. long. (Christie's) £2,400

7¼in. gauge electric display model of Delaware Lackawana & Western 4-4-0 locomotive. (Lacy Scott) £500

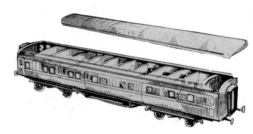

3½in. gauge model of the Hunslett narrow guage 2-6-2 side tank locomotive 'Russell', 34½in. long. (Christie's) £1,200

7mm. scale model of a London and North Eastern Railway 1st Class sleeping car, 19in. long. (Christie's) £220

Special Marklin issue locomotive, tender and carriages, 1935. (Phillips) £2,500

Fine 2½in. gauge model of Stephenson's 'Rocket', built by A. Tyrer, Hastings, 11½in. long. (Christie's) £1,500

Hornby '0' gauge clockwork train set in original cardboard box, circa 1924. (Sotheby's) £110

Cast metal 'HO' gauge 2-rail electric model of the Italian Railways three-coach train set 'Il Settebello' by Conti. (Christie's) £380

MODELS

The common theme with models, as diverse as they are, is that they are usually hand made by a skilled craftsman as opposed to being of assembly line manufacture. And that is their attraction, for each represents hundreds, if not thousands, of hours of dedicated and loving work.

They are generally found to be in good condition for they were constructed as an adult hobby and never intended for play as with a normal toy.

Engineering models of steam and traction engines tend to obtain the highest prices, but the award for charm must go to the Victorian models of butcher's shops complete with sides of mutton, ribs of beef and a rosy cheeked butcher with striped apron and boater.

Late 19th century model of a Lord Mayor's coach, 23in. long. £275

Model single horizontal cylinder bayonet frame mill engine by A. H. Allen, Keighley, 11¼in. wide. £180

American carved and painted stagecoach model and four-horse team, circa 1900, 53in. long. £300

A model butcher's shop, circa 1900, 1ft.11in. wide. £660

Early 20th century architectural model of Flaxley Abbey, 46.5cm. wide. £280

Detailed 1/8 scale wood and metal model of a gig of circa 1850, by A. Lee, Hendon, 17½in. long. £100

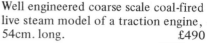

1½in. scale model of a road roller, living van and water cart, by J. McW. Morrison, Thatcham. £900

Well engineered coarse scale coal-fired live steam model of a traction engine, 54cm. long. £490

Fine model of an 1830's stagecoach in hardwood with brass fittings, modern, 16in. wide. £132

Austrian pre-World War I model Schloss. £70

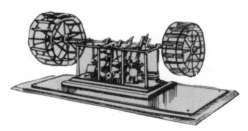

Detailed 1/12 scale model of fishermen and equipment on Worthing beach, circa 1920, by S. Bunker, 29¼in. wide. £450

Rare mid 19th century model of a twin cylinder reversing oscillating paddle steamer engine , 20½in. wide. £980

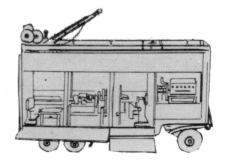

3in. scale model of a single cylinder Burrell agricultural traction engine, by K. B. Thirsk, Driffield, 1973, 45in. long. £3,400

A well-constructed six-wheeled showman's mobile workshop, trailer, 2ft.2in. wide.£155

MOTTOWARE

One day in 1867, when a certain Mr. G.P. Allen was dutifully digging in his back garden at Watcombe House, he unearthed, not gold, but what was regarded at the time as the finest red clay in England.

Recognising the potential value of his find he enlisted the aid of Charles Brock, an experienced potter from Hanley. Within two years they had established the Watcombe Pottery, engaging many imported Staffordshire craftsmen.

Most of their products were designed specifically for the souvenir trade, the most popular proving to be modest earthenware pieces with a decoration on one side and a motto on the other — now referred to as Devon motto ware.

The early mark was simply 'Watcombe Pottery' or 'Watcombe Torquay' and from 1875 incorporated a woodpecker seated upon a branch with the sea in the background.

Aller Vale Art Potteries, established in 1865, was a similar firm to Watcombe Pottery, and eventually they amalgamated in 1901. The combined factory prospered until 1962 under the trade name Royal Aller Vale and Watcombe Art Pottery.

Originally the Aller Vale pottery, situated near Newton Abbot, manufactured drain pipes and roof tiles but after the works were severely damaged by fire, John Phillips the owner re-opened and began to produce the popular Art Pottery.

The output from both firms was prolific and, because their products were bought primarily by tourists, pieces can be found in all parts of the country at moderate prices in antique shops and auctions.

A small Victorian earthenware vase, inscribed 'Never too late to mend'. £4

An Aller Vale pottery teapot bearing the legend, 'Ye may get better cheer, But no' wi' better heart'. £15

An unmarked earthenware coffee pot, the motto cut through the white slip to the brown clay. £12

An unmarked pottery hot-water jug. £12

A Watcombe pottery tile decorated with leaf and flower swirls. £12

A Dartmouth pottery jug, inscribed 'No Road is long with Good Company'. £4

MONEY BANKS

It seems ironic that old money boxes, designed as cheap receptacles for children to save their pennies for special occasions, are now nearly beyond the reach of all but the serious collector.

The scarcity (and therefore the high value) is due to the fact that most early money boxes were made of earthenware, designed to be smashed at Christmas time in order to retrieve their contents, a new one no doubt being given by the parents for the following year's efforts. They came in all shapes and sizes including pigs, hens, beehives, houses, fir cones, pillar boxes, figures and chests of drawers.

It is hardly surprising that most of those found today are of the metal variety, usually of American manufacture, often incorporating an amusing mechanical aid to coax pennies from the pocket.

Late 19th century American cast-iron 'Negro and Shack' money bank, 4¼in. long. (Sotheby's) £165

Late 19th century American 'William Tell' mechanical shooting bank, 10¼in. long. (Sotheby's) £200

Victorian varnished pine-wood child's money box, circa 1870, 6¼in. high. (Christopher Sykes) £35

American cast-iron 'Tammany' money bank, circa 1880. (Sotheby's) £110

Late 19th century American reclining 'Chinaman' cast-iron mechanical bank, 8in. long. (Sotheby's) £500

Red and black painted tin money box in the shape of a 'pillar box', circa 1930, 6½in. high. (Christopher Sykes) £30

Late 19th century American 'speaking dog' cast-iron money bank, 7¾in. long. (Sotheby's) £100

Early 20th century English 'Hoopla' cast-iron money bank, 8½in. long, by John Harper & Co. (Sotheby's) £95

19th century American cast-iron mechanical bank 'Eagle and Eaglets'. (Wm. Doyle Galleries Inc.) £80

One of a pair of German electroplated Britannia metal 'porker' money boxes, 13.7cm. long. (Sotheby's) £220

Late 19th century American cast-iron mechanical bank, 'Paddy and the Pig', 8in. high. (Sotheby's) £165

Late 19th century American 'Uncle Sam' cast-iron mechanical bank by Shepard Hardware Co., 11½in. high. (Sotheby's) £154

German tinplate 'monkey' money bank with decorated base, 6½in. high. (Sotheby's) £55

Cast-iron 'Novelty Bank' money box with hinged front, 6½in. high, American, circa 1875. (Sotheby's) £120

Unusual musical tinplate money bank, 4¾in. high, sold with another. (Sotheby's) £35

MOORCROFT POTTERY

When some bright spark at James Macintyre and Co. decided in 1913 to switch production from pottery to the new-fangled electrical goods, their pottery designer, William Moorcroft, was left a little short of work, to say the least.

So with 15 years of experience behind him, and bearing in mind that life begins at 40, he took the plunge and established his own pottery works at Cobridge, near Stoke-on-Trent, employing many of his former colleagues from Macintyres.

Without any restraints he could give full reign to his ideas leaving a legacy of distinctive pottery now eagerly sought after today.

All his products bear his signature, W. Moorcroft, usually in green until 1920 and thereafter mainly in blue, together with the impressed mark Moorcroft or Moorcroft Burslem.

Moorcroft bowl, 9in. diam., circa 1901-1913. (Sotheby's) £170

Moorcroft Hazledene biscuit jar and cover painted in moon-lit blue pattern, 17cm. high. (Christie's) £176

Moorcroft punch bowl with rolled foot, circa 1911, 14½in. wide, slightly damaged. (Robert W. Skinner Inc.) £140

A good Moorcroft Macintyre Florianware tyg, slip trailed with spiralling freesia sprays, 25.3cm. high, circa 1898. (Sotheby's) £340

Part of an eleven-piece Moorcroft coffee service in Hazledene pattern. (Sotheby, King & Chasemore) £420

One of a pair of Moorcroft Macintyre Florianware vases of double gourd shape, signed, 28cm. high. (Phillips) £180

289

MULLS

The snuff mull is a particularly Scottish container made from the 18th century to early this century, the most prevalent example of which is the baby mull, or portable version, made of a single ram's horn with a decorative silver top. Occasionally you may find one of these complete with a silver chain to which are attached a number of accoutrements, including a small spoon, a brush and a tiny mallet, all designed to lend a little extra panache to the taking of snuff.

One up from the baby mull is that made from a small antler with the hinged snuff box set on the base, the lid often enhanced with an oval agate or cairngorm.

Big daddy of them all, however, is the table mull, comprising a silver snuff box mounted on a stuffed ram's head — which comes complete with castors for easy manoeuvring.

Scottish ram's horn snuff mull. (Wallis & Wallis) £300

Silver mounted horn vinaigrette in the form of a snuff mull, Birmingham, 1885, 5.7cm. long. (Sotheby's) £95

Scottish silver mounted cow horn snuff mull, cover with central agate plaque, circa 1800, 11½in. long. (Christie's) £300

Ram's horn snuff box in the shape of a boot, circa 1790, 4in. high. (Christopher Sykes) £50

Ram's head snuff mull with silver mounts, Edinburgh, 1891, 42.5cm. long. (Sotheby's) £550

Silver and tortoiseshell snuff mull, mid 18th century, 60cm. high. (Christie's) £1,300

MUSICAL BOXES

Music in the home was as common during Victorian times as it is to-day — the difference being that, in those happy days, at least one member of most families was a more or less accomplished musician who would be happy to entertain the rest of the household at the slightest nod from Papa.

If, however, the said accomplished being was unavailable to perform, the neighbourhood would not necessarily be plunged into an abyss of silent gloom for there was a multitude of cabinets and boxes ready to spring into melodious life at the wind of a handle and the touch of a lever.

Although musical boxes had been fairly widely available during the 18th century, they had been extremely small affairs; novelties produced by ingenious clockmakers who, with wonderful precision, had fitted their tiny mechanisms into small boxes, seals, watches, and even into the handles of walking sticks.

The more widely accepted form of musical box, the antecedent, in its way, of the family record player, didn't put in an appearance until the early 19th century when it was introduced by David le Coutre.

It comprised of a clockwork mechanism powered by a coiled spring. This causes a cylinder, studded with steel pins, to rotate, the pins, pinging against a steel comb with teeth of different lengths to create the different notes.

Other still more exotic examples have drums, flutes, whistles, and even castanets to add a spot of excitement to their tunes.

Key-wound cylinder musical box by Bruguier, in plain mahogany case, circa 1845, 16¾in. wide. (Sotheby's)   £440

Nicole Freres overture cylinder musical box, circa 1860, 29in. wide. (Sotheby's)   £4,620

Nicole Freres key-wound cylinder musical box, mid 19th century, 15in. wide. (Sotheby's)
£605

291

Nicole Freres key-wound two-per-tin cylinder musical box, circa 1850, 20in. wide. (Sotheby's) £660

Late 19th century Swiss 'Overture' cylinder musical box, in rosewood case, 26in. wide. (Sotheby's) £715

Nicole Freres bells-in-sight interchangeable cylinder musical box, on stand, circa 1800, 37½in. wide. (Sotheby's) £880

Sublime Harmony cylinder musical box in walnut case, circa 1890, 23in. wide.(Sotheby's) £528

Le Coutre Freres Mandolin cylinder musical box, No. 31483, 20½in. wide, mid 19th century. (Sotheby's) £880

George Bendon bells-in-sight cylinder musical box in rosewood case, 1870-80, 21in. wide. (Sotheby's) £418

Swiss interchangeable cylinder musical box, circa 1880, 29in. wide. (Sotheby's) £990

Symphonion disc musical box in ebonised case, circa 1905, 12½in. wide. (Sotheby's) £350

Paillard Vaucher Fils bells-in-sight cylinder musical box, 25in. wide, circa 1880.(Sotheby's) £825

Large bells, drum-and-castanets-in-view cylinder musical box, 32in. wide, circa 1880. (Sotheby's) £1,100

Nicole Freres forte-piano two-per-turn cylinder musical box, 22½in. wide.(Sotheby's) £660

Symphonion rococo disc musical box, German, circa 1900, 20in. wide, in oak case. (Sotheby's) £880

MUSICAL INSTRUMENTS

When primitive man first twanged a well-tuned bow string and discovered that he could vary the note by altering the length or tension of his bow, it dawned on him that he could express himself artistically with sound — which must have made a pleasant change from churning out yards of drawings on the cave walls as a means of passing the pre-telly evenings. By biblical times, as every Cecil B. de Mille fan knows, music was everywhere, and it was played on a multitude of instruments including harps, flutes, cornets, serpents, sackbuts, and the great, grandparent of the piano — the dulcimer.

The middle ages were crowded with instruments which were plucked, banged and blown by all those strolling players and early examples, if you are lucky enough to find them, can be worth a small fortune.

Far more reasonably priced instruments come from the 19th and 20th centuries and could well form the basis of an interesting collection.

Mahogany cased silver plated cornet, 12½in. long, circa 1860.   £300

Silver bugle with single coil, St. Petersburg, circa 1905, 41cm. long.   £950

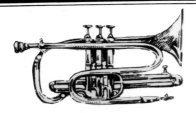

Early 19th century six-keyed pearwood bassoon by Christopher Gerock, London, 123cm. long.   £440

Late 19th century Harmonicor, Paris, 19in. long.   £150

Tanzbar accordion roller organ in black case, closed width 11in. wide.   £315

French hurdy-gurdy by Jean-Baptiste Pajot, 1795, 26¼in. long.   £1,512

Rare ivory flute by Hill, late Monzani & Co., London, with silver mounts, 23¾in. long.   £400

Unusual finely carved double flute of olive-wood, 13½in. long, circa 1820.   £48

Six-keyed boxwood clarinet in C by Goulding & Co., London, circa 1808, 59.8cm. long.£190

Early 20th century ceramic Ocarina by Meissen, 7¾in. long. £50

Mid 19th century Ophicleide, 41in. long. £200

Late 19th century Couenophone, 17½in. long, Paris. £125

Small cornet by Boosey & Co., London, circa 1880, 7½in. long. £225

Silver plated cornet by Boosey & Co., London, 15½in. long. £100

Boxwood double flageolet by William Bainbridge, London, 19½in. long, circa 1827. £450

Japanese koto, decorated in gold takamakie, of thirteen strings, the bridges absent, circa 1900. £220

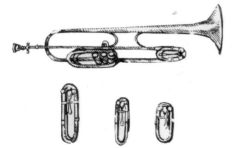

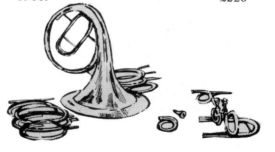

Unusual trumpet by Kohler, London, 24in. long, circa 1865. £175

Well-preserved orchestral horn by Rudall Carte & Co., London, circa 1880. £600

Fine rosewood clarinet by Jerome Thibouville Lamy, circa 1860, 22½in. long. £87

Rare Pekin glass flute (Dizi) of translucent milk-white metal, 48.9cm. £420

MUSTARD POTS

Although mustard sauce was in general use by the middle of the 18th century, it is rare to find a mustard pot from before this date.

The earliest silver mustard pots are usually of drum shape with pierced, flowing, scroll designs, which became more restrained towards the end of the century. By this time, they can be found in a variety of designs including oval and vase shaped, a style particularly popular with Hester Bateman.

Victorian mustard pots are generally much bigger. The very largest of all being the most popular for they can also be used as marmalade pots and have a far greater commercial value.

Early Victorian mustard pot by Charles Fox, London, 1837, 3in. high, 4oz.12dwt. (Sotheby's)   £170

Unusual early Victorian mustard pot by Richard Sibley, London, 1841, 4¾in. diam., 12oz. (Sotheby's)£506

Victorian mustard pot by Burrows and Pearce, London, 1841. (Sotheby's)   £150

Silver gilt mustard pot and spoon, London, and Birmingham, 1838, 5.2oz. (Sotheby's)   £473

Silver gilt mustard pot by John Bridge, 1825, 24oz. (Bruton Knowles)   .£2,450

Victorian mustard pot by R. Peppin, 1856, 8½oz. (Sotheby's)   £200

NAUTICAL ITEMS

If seafaring is your bag, then it would be easy to turn your home into a veritable nautical paradise — cash permitting.

Items you will find among the many splendid instruments of superb quality and precision are, sextants, log screws, compasses, telegraphs, octants, astrolabes, theodolites, telescopes, and nocturnal dials — any of these items will contribute to an agreeable collection. If it is possible to house something a bit larger, there are binnacles, ship's figureheads or wheels. Nautical furniture will also make an excellent theme for a collection for, almost without exception, all pieces are well proportioned and made from the finest wood set with sunken brass handles.

In fact, one of the main attributes of all nautical items is the quality of the materials used in their production for they were designed for a hard life on the high seas.

C. Gray anchor mast head lamp with conical chimney, 1950's, 18in. high. (Sotheby's) £77

Siebe, Gorman & Co. brass and copper diver's helmet with three windows, circa 1920, 19in. high. (Sotheby's) £495

Early 20th century R. C. Murray & Co. 'Not Under Command', warning lamp, 13in. high. (Sotheby's) £44

Early 20th century ship's auxiliary wheel with brass banding, 30in. diam. (Sotheby's) £150

Early 20th century Davey & Co. starboard lamp in copper casing. (Sotheby's) £44

Late 19th century oxidised brass sextant with silvered scale. (Sotheby's) £300

NAZI MEMORABILIA

When Hitler took power in 1933 he was quick to establish a distinctive Nazi image, the field grey and black uniform being a sinister replacement for the blue and silver of Bavaria and the green and gold of Saxony.

Silent factories suddenly became hives of industry manufacturing a multitude of distinctive weapons and equipment to complete the overly decorative and war-like aura.

Every department be they Luftwaffe, SS, Transport Corps, Customs Officials, Red Cross or Forestry, had their own distinctive design, which leaves a multitude of examples for today's collector.

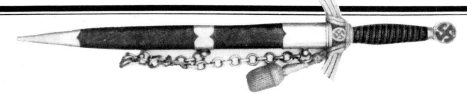

A Nazi Luftwaffe officer's 1st pattern dagger, plated blade, 12in., by 'A. W. jr.' plated mounts wirebound blue leather covered grip. (Wallis & Wallis) £90

A Nazi Visitor's Book from The Panzertruppen-Schule Wunsdorf (commencing 1.9.1940), the book with hundreds of ink signatures of visitors to the school and with watercolour scenes. The fly-leaf also with an inscription 'This Visitor's Book was Found in the Officer's Mess at 'Belsen', April '45'. (Wallis & Wallis) £510

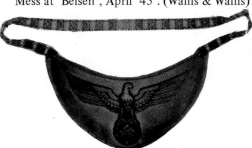

A Nazi political leader's gorget, bronzed finish, large Nazi eagle. (Wallis & Wallis) £80

A Nazi S.A. bugle of brass, with white metal mounts, the bell mouth with Nazi party eagle and swastika. (Wallis & Wallis) £105

NAZI MEMORABILIA

A Nazi painted porcelain equestrian figure of an S.S. officer on dappled grey horse, made at the S.S. Porcelain factory at Allach, overall height 12in. (Wallis & Wallis) £360

A Nazi Kriegsmarine sextant, with Nazi Eagle above 'M. 20300', graded scale, contained in its original wooden carrying case. (Wallis & Wallis) £260

An original Nazi Old Comrade's Assoc. standard bearer's shield gorget, mounted with device on brass rayed star. (Wallis & Wallis) £125

A Nazi Naval officer's sword, slightly curved, pipe-backed, clipped-back blade 29in., by W.K.C., gilt hilt with large and small folding guards. (Wallis & Wallis) £240

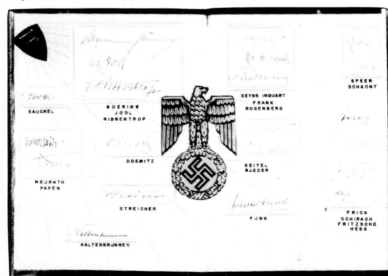

A leather bound folio size volume being the Visitor's Book of Gauleiter Dr. Friedrich Rainer. (Wallis & Wallis) £260

Nuremberg Trials: a rare collection of 21 autographs of the major Nazi defendants, obtained in Prison, 1945-6, size of double leaf 11½ x 16in. (Wallis & Wallis) £400

NETSUKE

As the traditional national costume of Japan, the kimono, didn't have pockets, objects such as an inro, purse, drinking gourd or tobacco pouch were usually hung from a cord at the waist. The cord was attached to a netsuke (pronounced netski) which was simply slipped under the sash (obi) which fastened the kimono and was held in place by pressure. Originally netsuke were simple wooden toggles but as attention was given to them they became elaborately carved reaching a sustained peak by the end of the 18th century. They were usually made of either wood or ivory but can be found of bone, rhino, buffalo and stag horn, coral, jet, turtle shell, amber or even metal. The subjects carved are more numerous than the carvers (of whom over 3000 have been identified) but two of the main groups are those depicting characters from Japanese folk history (Mukashi — Banashi) and Sugata — depictions of various craftsmen. Eroticism was also a popular subject and examples not infrequently took the form of young ladies indulging — or being indulged by — sea monsters and mythological characters.

Most netsuke originate from the large areas of population such as Osaka, Nagoya, Kyoto and Edo where the carvers could make a good living. Their popularity declined when Japan ended her seclusion with the Meija restoration in 1868 and western style dress with pockets became popular. The influx of tourists however, eager for souvenirs of old Japan became a major market for netsuke and vast numbers, of a poor quality compared to earlier ones, were exported to Europe and America.

An ivory netsuke of a group of three puppies, signed Rantei, Kyoto School, late 18th century. (Christie's) £1,188

An 18th century ivory netsuke of a crouching Karashishi, inscribed Garaku. (Christie's) £432

A wood netsuke of a peach opening to reveal a carving of Momotaro, Tokyo School. (Christie's) £900

A mid 19th century ivory netsuke of a seated tigress, signed Hakuryu. (Christie's) £3,500

An ivory netsuke of a Karako, signed Hikaku, Tokyo School. (Christie's) £183

An ivory kidney-shaped netsuke depicting a building among rocks, signed Gyokuhozan. (Christie's) £302

An ivory netsuke of a puppy pulling to pieces a Kemari, signed Kizan. (Christie's) £345

A marine ivory netsuke of one of the three mystic apes, mid 19th century. (Christie's) £259

An ivory netsuke of Kosekiko astride a horse, 18th century. (Christie's) £140

A stained ivory netsuke of a snake coiled around a loose ball. (Christie's)£702

An ivory netsuke of a recumbent dog with a ball, 18th century. (Christie's) £388

An ivory netsuke of a seated monkey picking fleas from its fur. (Christie's) £324

A fine wood netsuke of a seated Karashishi, signed Kyokuso, Tokyo School. (Christie's) £2,000

An ivory netsuke of two catfish signed Godo. (Christie's) £432

An ivory netsuke of an Oni mask with inlaid eyes, signed Kuya. (Christie's) £302

An ivory netsuke of a group of terrapins clambering over a rock. (Christie's) £280

NETSUKE

An ivory Manju netsuke decorated in Shishiaibori, signed Kikugawa. (Christie's) £259

An ivory netsuke of Raiden, the God of Thunder, signed Tomomasa. (Christie's) £226

An Okimono style ivory netsuke of an old bespectacled man, signed Tomoyuki, circa 1900. (Christie's) £270

An ivory netsuke of a priest holding a Mokugyo, inscribed Gyokuzan. (Christie's) £237

A large ivory netsuke of the Ogre King holding a gnarled staff. (Christie's) £324

An ivory netsuke of Gama Sennin leaning on his crutch. (Christie's) £237

A carved wood netsuke of a seated Karashishi signed Garaku, late 18th century. (Christie's) £1,600

An ivory netsuke of a Karashishi balancing itself on a half-hatched egg. (Christie's) £345

An ivory netsuke of a horse in a highly contorted posture, inscribed Risshisai Kangyoku. (Christie's)£518

An ivory netsuke of an eagle gripping a fox, signed Romochika. (Christie's) £432

A superb wood netsuke of a recumbent ram, Nagoya School. (Christie's) £2,200

An ivory Ryusa-style netsuke carved with various species of fish, signed Masahiro. (Christie's) £378

An ivory netsuke of a European carrying a large fish, signed Kosen. (Christie's) £324

An ivory netsuke of a standing fisherman holding a carp. (Christie's) £324

An ivory netsuke of two Buddhist guardian kings, signed Koraku. (Christie's) £270

An unusual wood netsuke of a one-eyed goblin, signed Muso, 19th century. (Christie's) £850

A wood netsuke of Futen standing on clouds signed Hokosai. (Christie's) £700

An ivory netsuke of Songoku, the monkey king, signed Gyokuzan. (Christie's) £972

An ivory Manju netsuke inlaid in Shibayama style, signed, 19th century. (Christie's) £194

A fine wood netsuke of a cockerel with head turned, signed Hojitsu. (Christie's) £1,200

A fine Kagamibuta netsuke decorated with a toad, a dragonfly, a centipede and a beetle. (Christie's) £324

A wood netsuke of a snail crawling over a bucket, signed Shigemasa.(Christie's) £1,400

A wood netsuke of a wasp on a rotten pear, signed Gekko, Nagoya School. (Christie's) £1,800

A carved wood netsuke of a snake coiled around the body of a turtle, signed Masatami. (Christie's)£900

A large ivory netsuke of Tekkai Sennin holding a gnarled staff. (Christie's) £594

A fine wood netsuke of a seated Karashishi, signed Gyokuso. (Christie's) £2,000

A wood netsuke of a recumbent ox signed Shunko, 19th century. (Christie's) £900

An unusual lacquered wood netsuke of an octopus, signed Choka. (Christie's) £900

A wood netsuke of Okame lying down and chuckling. (Christie's) £900

NUTMEG GRATERS

Early silver graters date from about 1700, a time when there was a passion for liberally spiced hot punch and mulled wine.

These little boxes generally consist of a small compartment to hold the whole nutmeg, a grater and usually incorporate a small container to catch the grated spice. Nutmeg graters are made in wood, tin, bone, ivory and silver; the latter being the most cherished by collectors.

Graters are very small for they were designed to be carried in purse or pocket so that nutmeg could be freshly grated into hot drinks. Because they were carried on the person and therefore used in company, they received a great deal of attention in design and come in a variety of inventively shaped cases.

George III silver gilt oval memorial nutmeg grater, 2in. wide, by John Reily, London, 1793.(Sotheby's) £525

Silver nutmeg grater by Elkington & Co., Birmingham, 1906, 3in. long. (Gray's Antique Market)£150

Early 19th century George III silver nutmeg grater with hinged cover by John Robins, London, 5cm. long. (Robert W. Skinner Inc.) £135

Vase-shaped nutmeg grater unmarked, circa 1800, 3½in. high. (Sotheby's) £319

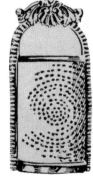

George III oblong hanging nutmeg grater by J. Reily, London, 1818, 4in. long. (Sotheby's) £352

William IV tube nutmeg grater by Rawlings & Sumner, London, 1835, 2½in. long. (Sotheby's) £352

George III oval nutmeg grater by Roger Biggs, London, 1795, 2in. wide. (Sotheby's) £275

Late 18th century egg-shaped nutmeg grater by Samuel Meriton. (Sotheby's) £200

Unusual clam-shaped nutmeg grater by Hilliard & Thomason, Birmingham, 1853, 4.7cm. wide. (Sotheby's)£396

305

PAPERWEIGHTS

Although glass paperweights are reputed to have been used in ancient Egypt, the earliest dated examples of the now familiar shape came from France and Venice in 1845.

They were developed as luxury additions to the popular writing boxes of the period, and the most sought after were produced in vast numbers by three French firms, Baccarat, Clichy and Saint Louis.

American and English glassworks such as the Boston and Sandwich Glass Co. and Bacchus and Sons followed suit a few years later, but their work is somewhat overshadowed by the charisma attached to the weights produced in the first ten years by the French firms.

While the majority of paperweights consist of a heavy clear glass dome, enclosing multi coloured glass rods designed to represent fruit or flowers, weights produced by the French glass artists such as Daum, Almeric Walter, Lalique and Baccarat are to be found in many different shapes including dragonflies, frogs, snakes, birds and nymphs.

It is worth noting that many weights are signed with an initial and a date but usually these marks are so cleverly incorporated into the design as to make them difficult to spot.

Examples by important French makers will naturally be expensive, anything from a few hundred to thousands, but a start can be made with the cheap English variety produced at the end of the 19th century. These usually depict such scenes as "The Esplanade at Hastings" simply stuck beneath a glass blob, but for all their simplicity they do have a certain charm.

Daum pate-de-verre paperweight modelled as a moth, signed, 12cm. wide.
(Christie's)   £506

Paperweight in clear and frosted glass by R. Lalique, France, 10.8cm. high.
(Christie's)   £528

Clear pale amethyst glass and grey stained paperweight by R. Lalique, 21cm. high.
(Christie's)   £880

Clear glass paperweight 'Falcon', on circular base, by R. Lalique, France, 15.6cm. high.
(Christie's)   £810

Pate-de-verre paperweight by A. Walter, 11cm. wide.
(Christie's)   £605

Unusual Lalique glass paperweight, 1920's, 12cm. wide.
(Sotheby's)   £120

306

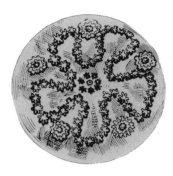

Clichy patterned millefiori weight on tossed muslin ground, 7.9cm. diam. (Sotheby's) £264

American flower weight cut with circular windows, in pink, white and green, 8.2cm. diam. (Sotheby's) £935

St. Louis dahlia paperweight, 8cm. diam. (Sotheby's) £4,000

Venetian millefiori weight by Bigaglia in red, white and turquoise, 7.8cm. diam. (Sotheby's) £374

Frosted glass paperweight 'Vitesse', moulded R. Lalique, France, 18.8cm. high. (Christie's) £972

St. Louis mushroom paper-weight of concentric canes, 8cm. diam. (Sotheby's) £286

St. Louis marble weight in alternate red and white loops, 7cm. diam. (Sotheby's) £770

Amber flashed zooglophite paperweight engraved with a stag, 8cm. (Sotheby's) £150

Clichy swirl weight in green, white and pink, 7.9cm. diam. (Sotheby's) £264

PAPERWEIGHTS

Rare Baccarat camomile and garland weight with star-cut base, 7.5cm. diam. (Sotheby's) £792

Signed St. Louis concentric millefiori weight with mauve cane, 6.3cm. diam.(Sotheby's) £638

St. Louis flat-bouquet weight of swirling latticinio threads, 7.8cm. diam. (Sotheby's) £616

Rare Baccarat snake paperweight, sides with diamond facets, 7.5cm. diam.(Phillips) £5,200

Clear and frosted glass paperweight by R. Lalique, France, 20.5cm. high. (Christie's) £660

Clichy sulphide and colourground paperweight, set with busts of Victoria and Albert, 7.3cm. diam. (Phillips) £270

Rare St. Louis colourground weight in salmon pink, green and white, 8cm. diam. (Sotheby's) £550

Baccarat butterfly and garland weight with star-cut base, 6.5cm. diam. (Sotheby's)£594

One of a rare pair of St. Louis doorknobs in the form of paperweights, 5cm. diam. (Sotheby's) £935

PARIAN

The art of parian statuary was first introduced around 1840 and almost simultaneously produced by Copeland & Garrett and Minton; followed in 1848 by Wedgwood.

Parian is a slightly translucent, silky textured, matt white porcelain bearing a strong resemblance to marble but, unlike marble which requires carving, this material could be moulded to reproduce copies of famous pieces of sculpture scaled down to a more practical size for the average home. Manufacturers also commissioned models for their statuary products.

Initially used for the manufacture of figures, groups and applied decoration, the range widened as the production process improved and includes vases, jugs, tea services and other tableware.

Large Copeland parian figure of '**Go to Sleep**', circa 1865, 17½in. high. (Sotheby's) £240

Goss parian bust of '**General Gordon**', square base titled, dated 1885, 18.5cm. high. (Sotheby's) £99

Copeland parian jug of ovoid form, circa 1872, 26.1cm. high. (Sotheby's) £200

Late 19th century Copeland parian figure of '**Corinna, the Lyric Muse**', 55cm. high, slightly cracked. (Sotheby, King & Chasemore) £120

Rare Parian group of '**Union Refugees**', 1861, 46cm. high. (Sotheby's) £280

Rare Goss parian bust of '**The Veiled Bride**', circa 1865, 26cm. high. (Sotheby's) £264

PATCH BOXES

Small patches, either round, heartshaped or in the form of a star, were originally worn by fashionable ladies to conceal blemishes on their skin; often the legacy of one of the epidemics prevalent at the time.

They soon came to be considered an essential feature of elegance and were worn by both men and women who housed their little patches in small decorative boxes.

Long after the fashion declined, the boxes continued to be made as novelties for snuff, nutmeg or to hold a sponge soaked in aromatic vinegars.

Many were of painted enamel from Battersea, Bilston, Birmingham and South Staffordshire. They were produced by fusing glass onto copper, painting the decoration by hand and firing at a high temperature to give a lasting brilliance.

Examples are also found in silver and papier mache.

Circular Birmingham patch box, circa 1760, 4.7cm. diam. £90

Silver Georgian patch box, almond-shaped and engraved with leaves and a shield enclosing the initials 'EB'. £70

Circular Bilston patch box, circa 1765, 4.5cm. diam. £380

Oval enamel patch box, the lid painted with a shepherd and shepherdess, 1¾in. wide. £150

Oval silver box having porcelain lid with picture of a lady. £60

Small Bilston enamel box, circa 1760. £225

Miniature silver patch box by Samuel Pemberton, Birmingham, 1818. £75

High quality silver box with simple design, Birmingham, 1892. £60

Oval enamel patch box, the lid painted with shipping by a quay, 2in. wide. £160

PHOTOGRAPHS

The photographs most popularly collected today fall into two main categories. Those of historical significance in the development of the art and those photographs which are the work of a recognised master. Occasionally the two are combined in one photograph.

Notables of the early days are, William Fox Talbot who patented the Calotype in 1841 and, Louis-Jacques Mande Daguerre who invented the Daguerreotype which, in its early stages of development required over thirty minutes of exposure time. Other early photographers of note are Frances Frith, J.D. Edwards, Roger Fenton, Gustave Le Gray, F.R. Pickersgill and Henry Peach Robinson.

Photographers of importance in more modern times are Man Ray, Bill Brandt and Weegee amongst others.

'City Hall and Police Office, New Orleans', by J. D. Edwards. (Sotheby's) £605

Two studies of **New Orleans**, by J. D. Edwards, numbered '85 and '87. (Sotheby's)£990

'The Mosque of Kaitbey', by Frances Frith, signed and dated 1858, 391 x 465mm. (Sotheby's)£198

One from a collection of approx. 135 nude studies, 140 x 100mm., 1880's. (Sotheby's)   £550

'I. K. Brunel', albumen print by Cundall Downes & Co., 1855/7. (Sotheby's)   £506

Portrait of '**Mrs Duckworth**', by J. M. Cameron, albumen print, 320 x 220mm., c. 1872. (Sotheby's)   £198

One of eighteen early Swiss and European views, 1850's/60's. (Sotheby's)   £638

'River Front, New Orleans', by J. D. Edwards. (Sotheby's)   £775

'Foret de Fontainebleau', albumen print, by Gustave Le Gray. (Sotheby's)   £1,760

One from an album of 35 Neapolitan Portraits, attributed to G. Sommer, 245 x 175mm., 1880's. (Sotheby's)   £550

Daguerreotype portrait of a young girl with ringlets, 1850. (Sotheby's)   £187

A good Le Blondel Freres large half-plate daguerreotype group of two young girls, 1855. (Sotheby's)   £330

A sixth-plate daguerreotype portrait of a man with a white hat and a rifle, American, 1850's. (Sotheby's)£110

'International Exhibition', albumen print, 430 x 388mm., 1862. (Sotheby's)   £286

An album of fifty-six portraits of Indian people, attributed to William Willoughby Hooper, 1860's. (Sotheby's)   £396

'Hong Kong', an album of twelve photographs attributed to John Thomson, 1860's. (Sotheby's)   £264

A group of seventeen Japanese portraits by Sohutamarko, 1870's. (Sotheby's)   £176

Group of **Ela**, **Rosamund** and **Matilda Talbot** with a seated lady, 1846-47. (Sotheby's)   £605

PHOTOGRAPHS

Miss Matilda Rigby, calotype, circa 1845.
(Sotheby's) £418

Half-plate daguerreotype portrait of a bearded gentleman, **'Vaillat 1854'**. (Sotheby's) £110

Newhaven fishwife, calotype, together with portrait of a nurse. (Sotheby's) £176

A half-plate daguerreotype portrait of prize fighter, **William Perry, 1850**.
(Sotheby's) £27

Four portraits of Chinese noblemen and women, 1860's.
(Sotheby's) £110

A rare album of thirty-two photographs taken at the **County Prison, Stafford, 1869/71**. (Sotheby's)£1,650

Study of a couple in opulent Eastern costume, albumen print, late 1850's. (Sotheby's) £220

'Melrose Abbey', salt print, signed and dated in ink 'R. Fenton 1856'. (Sotheby's) £1,045

Study of a young woman in striped Eastern costume, albumen print, late 1850's. (Sotheby's) £1,100

Still life with a basket, bottles, flask bonnet hat and dog, albumen print, 112 x 156mm., 1850's. (Sotheby's) £143

'Jackson R.R. Engine Shop', 154 x 205mm., 1850's. (Sotheby's) £715

One of a rare group of seven stereoscopic studies of **Polynesian Natives**, dated 1860. (Sotheby's) £198

A rare Mayall stereoscope, daguerreotype portrait of three girls, 1850's. (Sotheby's) £352

One from an album of 100 studies from Japan, each approx. 200 x 250mm., circa 1870. (Sotheby's) £242

The paddle steamer **'Princess'** on the New Orleans Waterfront, 156 x 206mm., 1850's, by J. D. Edwards. (Sotheby's) £880

Exterior of the **Colosseum** by Robert McPherson, 237 x 403mm.(Sotheby's)£132

One from a group of twenty-four Japanese portraits by Sohutamarko, each approx. 90 x 135mm., 1870's. (Sotheby's) £176

'Notre Dame', salt print by Ferrier, 172 x 240mm., circa 1852. (Sotheby's)   £412

'The Banks of the Seine, Paris', salt print by Ferrier, 229 x 302mm., signed and dated 1852. (Sotheby's)   £1,430

A stereoscopic daguerreotype portrait of a middle-aged lady, by T. R. Williams, circa 1855. (Sotheby's)   £286

Portrait of **Mr Brunel** by Robert Howlett and George Downes, 1857. (Sotheby's)   £506

Marilyn Monroe, silver print, by Weegee, 277 x 355mm., 1953. (Sotheby's)   £143

A half-plate daguerreotype portrait of three ladies with photographer J. G. Eynard-Lullin, passe partout, circa 1845-50. (Sotheby's)   £638

Xie Kitchin lying on a sofa with open book, albumen print by Lewis Carroll, 141 x 185mm., circa 1870. (Sotheby's)   £495

'Sleep' by John Whistler, salt print, 205 x 160mm., circa 1855. (Sotheby's)   £308

PHOTOGRAPHS

'Rest Break', silver print by Weegee, 1940's. (Sotheby's) £55

'Distortion no. 6', silver print by Andre Kertesz, 1933. (Sotheby's) £308

'Puritan' and 'Cooling Off', silver print by Weegee, 1945. (Sotheby's) £82

'Hypatia' portrait of Marie Spartali, albumen print, 300 x 345mm., circa 1870. (Sotheby's) £770

Picture of a pretty girl being shot out of a cannon, silver print by Weegee. (Sotheby's) £77

'The Flower Peddler', silver print by Weegee, circa 1940. (Sotheby's) £154

Boy seated on a bench, by J. Whistler, salt print, 259 x 217mm., circa 1855. (Sotheby's) £175

'Undine' by H. Lambert, toned silver print, 200 x 157mm. (Sotheby's) £35

Newhaven Fisherman, calotype, by R. Adamson and D. O. Hill, 155 x 116mm., circa 1845. (Sotheby's) £418

PHOTOGRAPHS

Virginia Dalrymple by O. G. Rejlander, albumen print, circa 1860. (Sotheby's) £44

A Claudet half-plate daguerreotype portrait of **A. Hewat**, after 1851. (Sotheby's) £121

Portrait of **Sir T. Phillips**, 277 x 234mm., albumen print, circa 1865. (Sotheby's) £220

Sir Henry Taylor, albumen print, 252 x 202mm., circa 1865. (Sotheby's) £770

Portrait of a woman by O. G. Rejlander, albumen print, 208 x 145mm., circa 1860. (Sotheby's) £143

One from a series of sixteen portraits of **Sporting Celebrities**, 1890. (Sotheby's) £66

Maid at the Well Dimbola Freshwater, Isle of Wight, albumen print, circa 1860. (Sotheby's) £24

Girl At A Window by Lady C. Hawarden, albumen print, 84 x 65mm., early 1860's. (Sotheby's) £3,740

Naked Wrestlers by O. G. Rejlander, albumen print, circa 1860. (Sotheby's) £90

Study of a woman in Eastern costume by Roger Fenton, late 1850's. (Sotheby's)£572

Miss Kitchin seated in profile by Lewis Carroll, 1870. (Sotheby's) £550

Miss Kitchin standing, albumen print by Lewis Carroll, circa 1870. (Sotheby's) £1,650

Xie Kitchin dressed as a mandarin, by Lewis Carroll, circa 1870. (Sotheby's) £550

Young Girl Amongst Hollyhocks, by Eva Watson Schutze, circa 1910. (Sotheby's) £154

One of three male portraits by Alois Locherer, early 1850's. (Sotheby's) £132

Architectural study attributed to Friedrich Von Martens, 1860's. (Sotheby's) £495

Portail Meridional De L'Eglise De Notre Dame, by Henri Le Seq, 1851. (Sotheby's) £495

Le Printemps, copy of Manets portrait by Chas. Cros, 1881-82. (Sotheby's) £330

PHOTOGRAPHS

Study of a child by Heinrich Kuhn, circa 1910.(Sotheby's) £396

One of three portraits by August Sander from 1906 to 1911. (Sotheby's) £264

Gerhardt Hauptman, silver print by Edward Steichen, 1932. (Sotheby's) £198

Mrs Arthur Gordon Bowman, by Edward Steichen, 1933. (Sotheby's) £467

A Reedcutter at Work, platinum print by Peter Henry Emerson, 1886. (Sotheby's) £385

The Duncan Dancers from Moscow, silver print, by Steichen, 1929. (Sotheby's) £242

Diana Wynyard in Surreal Setting, by Angus McBean, 1940's. (Sotheby's) £187

Saratoga Springs Hotel Courtyard, by Walker Evans, 1933. (Sotheby's) £242

Seated Nude, silver print, by Bill Brandt, 1950's. (Sotheby's) £220

PHOTOGRAPHS

Portrait of a young girl by Man Ray, 1930's. (Sotheby's) £88

Florence Maude and her sister posed beside a window, by Lady Clementina Hawarden. (Sotheby's) £2,420

Study of a church by Frederick Scott Archer, 1860. (Sotheby's) £286

The Himalayas, an album of forty photographs, 1820's. (Sotheby's) £154

International Exhibition, albumen print, 1862. (Sotheby's) £99

Miss Kitchin seated with a shawl over her head by Lewis Carroll, 1870. (Sotheby's) £418

Study of a gentleman in Eastern costume by Carl Haag, 1860's. (Sotheby's) £462

The Lottery Ticket, St. Louis 1952, by Weegee. (Sotheby's) £264

Study of **Carl Haag** in Eastern costume, late 1850's/early 1860's. (Sotheby's) £330

PHOTOGRAPHS

Illustrations of China, in four volumes by John Thomson, 1873. (Sotheby's) £880

Xie Kitchin in bed, albumen print by Lewis Carroll, 1870. (Sotheby's) £1,045

The photographer's son **'Hans'**, by Heinrich Kuhn, 1907. (Sotheby's) £462

Miss Kitchin standing in Grecian costume by Lewis Carroll, 1870. (Sotheby's) £660

Setting Up The Bow Nets, by P. H. Emerson, platinum print, 120 x 174mm., 1886. (Sotheby's) £242

One from an album of eight views in the **Yosemite**, by C. E. Watkins, approx. 400 x 520mm. (Sotheby's) £3,300

The Voodoo Kiss, New York, 1952, by Weegee. (Sotheby's) £121

Calcutta Exhibition, seventy-two photographs of India, 1870's. (Sotheby's) £198

A mixed album attributed to William Willoughby Hooper, 1860's. (Sotheby's) £220

PICTORIAL CHINA

Pictorial china souvenirs of Britain reached their peak of popularity in the years before the first World War in 1914 and barely a single resort, spa, city, town or even village was not represented in pictorial form on a vast range of cups, mugs, teapots, plates, etc.

The coming of the railways in the middle of the last century provided means of travel to many people who had not previously been beyond their own locality and pictorial souvenirs were eagerly sought as a gift or momento to take back to friends and relations at home.

The growing popularity of the cheaper picture postcard in the early years of this century brought about a decline in the production of pictorial souvenirs, although a few British firms continued manufacture after the first World War. Prior to 1914 most pictorial china reached us from Germany and Austria where labour was cheap and materials readily available, but the outbreak of hostilities in 1914 brought an end to this trade from which there was to be no recovery.

As with Fairings and Staffordshire figures Pictorial China pieces were intended for the markets and bazaars of the day, but some is of fine quality and despite increasing interest they are still relatively inexpensive and offer a fascinating collecting field for hobby or investment.

An added bonus is that different facets of collecting are contained within the whole; locations, type of ware or manufacturer may all be collected as a separate entity.

Cucumber dish, by P. Donath, Teifenfurt, before 1888, in white with a colour print of **Aylesbury Market Place.** £6

White cup and saucer with large black and white prints of **St. Mary's Parish Church, Rawtenstall,** no mark, English, cup 3in. high, saucer 5in. diam. £6

White, pink and green matching cream jug and sugar bowl with large black and white prints of **Rathkeale Church,** no mark, jug 3½in. high, bowl 4½in. diam. £8

Pierced pink lustre plate shading to white with colour print of **Fishponds Training College**, 8½in. diam., no mark, German. £8

Pearl lustre teapot with gilding and colour print of **The Bridge at Llangollen**, marked 'Foreign' and with retailer's name and address, 2¾in. high, x 7in. £8

Brown and cream moulded hanging plate with picture of the **Town Hall**, **Portsmouth**, 'Made in Austria', 7in. diam. £6

White, green and gilt bonbon dish with colour print of **The Leas Shelter, Folkestone**, no mark, German. £6

White mug with gilding and sepia and blue print of **Kirkby Stephen**, no mark, German, 3in. high. £5

Powder blue moulded plate, with sepia print of **Shakespeare's House, Stratford**, 'Made in Germany', 7½in. diam. £8

White Schumann ribbon plate with black and white print of **Carlisle Cathedral**, 8½in. diam. £9–£12

Orange lustre cup and saucer with colour print of the **Tea House at Glenariffe**, by Greiner & Herda, Bavaria, cup 2½in. high, saucer 5½in. diam. £5

Creamy yellow ribbon plate with colour print of **Municipal Buildings, Woolwich**, no mark, German, 7in. diam. £10

PINBOXES

These novel little porcelain boxes were designed to sit on the dressing table and, although referred to as pin boxes, they were suitable for a multitude of small things such as cuff-links, studs and buttons.

They are made of a similarly hard paste porcelain to that used in the production of fairings and match strikers and were, in fact, made by the same manufacturer, Conte & Boehme of Possneck, in Germany.

Some of the boxes are captioned and have a figure on the lid identical to those on fairings. They were clearly intended for the same market — as prizes at the hoop-la or as a cheap souvenir.

All are of fairly crude manufacture with bright enamel colouring.

'Caernarvon To Liverpool'.
£25—£45

'Cousin And Cousine'.
£150—£250

'Pins Madame?'
£25—£45

'Royal Manchester Exchange'.
£25—£45

'Love On The Tiles'.
£25—£45

'Swansea To Bristol'.
£25—£45

PINBOXES

'After The Race 1875'.
£25–£45

'A Little Turk'. £25–£45

'Champagne Charlie Is My Name'. £100–£150

'Low Life'. £15–£25

'Missus Is Master'.
£25–£45

'Lor Three Legs! I'll Charge 2d.' £25–£45

'Little John In Trouble'.
£25–£45

'The Model Of Laxey'.
£25–£45

'Anti Vivisectors'.
£25–£45

PIN-UP MAGAZINES

Pin-ups and glamour are relatively new fields of systematic collecting. As with many new collectibles, the chief appeal of these magazines lies in their nostalgia content. Compared to today's productions they represent a return to an earlier innocence.

There are four main fields of collecting. Artists/Artwork, Photographers, Specific Models and Subject Matter.

The rare, early items can be found on the shelves of antiquarian book dealers, and the middle range of 1930's American and British magazines do turn up on market stalls but can be more easily found on the sales lists of specialised dealers such as 'Yesterday's Paper'. Glamour is still an inexpensive collectible. The later magazines are still to be found from 50p. each, while the scarcest of collector's items rarely exceed £10.

As with all new fields, the time to lay the basis of a collection is now, before the prices take off.

'Beauty Parade', British Reprint of 1940's American magazine. (Yesterday's Paper) £2—£4

'Exotique' and 'Fighting Girls Monthly', 1950's fetishist magazines. (Yesterday's Paper) £3—£10

'Jane's Journal', Jane of The Daily Mirror Annual. (Yesterday's Paper)£3—£5

'Gay Book Magazine', 1930's, American. (Yesterday's Paper) £4—£8

'Dream Girl Magazine', American Star Magazines. (Yesterday's Paper) £2—£5

'Playboy', November 1968. (Yesterday's Paper) £1—£2

'Gay French Life', 1930's Spicy Stories Magazine. (Yesterday's Paper)   £2.50–£5 each

'La Belle France', French 1930's Photo Magazine. (Yesterday's Paper)   £1–£2

'Whizz' Bedtime Stories, 1950's British (mock American) Stories Magazine. (Yesterday's Paper)   £1–£2

'The New Fiesta', 1950's, British pocket-size — Monroe cover & centrefold. (Yesterday's Paper)   £2.50

'Fads & Fancies' and High-Heeled Tyrant', 1950's fetishist magazines.(Yesterday's Paper)£3–£10

'Film Fun', 1930's American. (Yesterday's Paper)   £4–£8

'French Models', 1930's American Photo magazine.(Yesterday's Paper)   £3–£10

'La Vie Parisienne', French 1911. (Yesterday's Paper)   £3–£6

'Burlesque', American 1930's, Burlesque Stars Magazine. (Yesterday's Paper)   £5

PIPES

Literally translated from the German as 'sea foam', meerschaum is in fact, a porous mineral, magnesium silicate, which is an ideal material for carving and turns mellow gold when stained with nicotine.

As the nicotine is absorbed this material gradually changes colour from a creamy white, to a pale amber then a dark brown and a skilled carver will design a pipe so that the resulting colour change both features in and, compliments his chosen subject.

Vast quantities of pipes, cigar and cigarette holders were made in this material at the end of the 19th century — the more elaborate, the higher the price.

It is worth looking out for pipe cases. The pipe smoker, then as now, often looked upon a favourite pipe, as an old and cherished friend and cases were designed to carry the pipe in safety. These may be simple containers or beautifully carved to match the pipe it protects.

Late 19th century Austrian Meerschaum pipe carved as the head of a negro boy, 17cm. long. (Sotheby's) £308

Early 20th century Austrian Meerschaum pipe, bowl carved as a hare's head, 13.3cm. long. (Sotheby's) £90

Late 19th/early 20th century Austrian Meerschaum pipe, 16.5cm. long. (Sotheby's) £286

Bizarre pipe by Charles Edwards, London, 1885, 34oz., 24cm. long. (Sotheby's) £1,000

Large Meerschaum pipe with amber mouthpiece and heavily carved bowl, early 20th century, 28.5cm. long. (Sotheby's) £1,100

Austrian Meerschaum cheroot holder, elaborately carved, 28.5cm. long, 1880's. (Sotheby's) £1,320

Late 19th century Austrian Meerschaum pipe, bowl carved as a hatching egg, 14.5cm. long. (Sotheby's) £165

Well carved Meerschaum pipe, front with nude mermaid, with silver mounted amber stem and mouthpiece, 7in. long. (Burrows & Day) £88

Carved Meerschaum in the form of a tiger and snake in combat, 6in. long. (Sotheby's) £85

Teke ceremonial pipe with faceted ivory stem and wood bowl, 13in. long. (Sotheby's) £300

One of two late 19th century German Meerschaum pipes, 9½in. long. (Robert W. Skinner Inc.) £80

Large Viennese Meerschaum bowl with silver mount, circa 1870, 20.3cm. long, in case. (Sotheby's) £2,420

Meerschaum pipe, circa 1880, with figure of a lady. (Alfie's Antique Market) £230

Edwardian pipe with silver mounts. (Sotheby's) £20

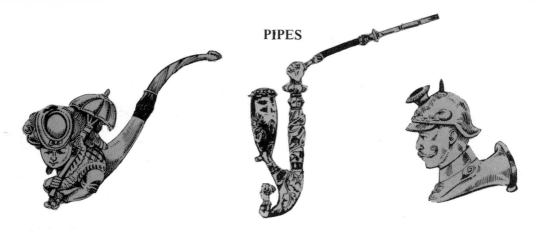

Austrian Meerschaum pipe, bowl carved as a young woman carrying a parasol, 20.3cm. long, circa 1880. (Sotheby's) £352

Austrian or Bavarian pipe with painted porcelain bowl, 1830's, 37cm. long. (Sotheby's) £360

Well carved Meerschaum cigar holder in the form of a head of a Kaiser, 3¼in. (Burrows & Day) £60

Well carved Meerschaum bowl in the shape of an Irishman's head, 6in. long. (Burrows & Day) £90

Large Meerschaum pipe, 41cm. long, carved with a figure of a mother and child, circa 1860. (Christie's S. Kensington) £3,300

Meerschaum pipe, bowl carved as a woman with a fur collar, circa 1900, 15.5cm. long, probably Austrian. (Sotheby's) £88

Meerschaum cigar holder in the form of a young boy in a skittle alley, 4in. long. (Burrows & Day) £50

Mid 19th century three-colour glass pipe with knopped stem, 482.cm. long. (Sotheby's) £176

Meerschaum pipe with bowl carved as a bearded Arab. (Christie's S. Kensington) £950

PIN CUSHIONS

Although pin cushions have been in use for over 300 years, it was not until the 19th century that they became anything more than just plain, serviceable objects.

In Victorian times, they were considered to be an essential feature of 'my ladies chamber' and were prominently displayed, decorated with colourful pins. Made in silver, pewter and brass they were produced in a variety of forms including shoes, boots, birds, hedgehogs, pigs, miniature coaches and dolls; or little round or heart-shaped beadwork cushions sometimes bearing a motto.

Anyone who collects pin cushions will, inevitably, come to collect pins for the combination makes a most attractive display.

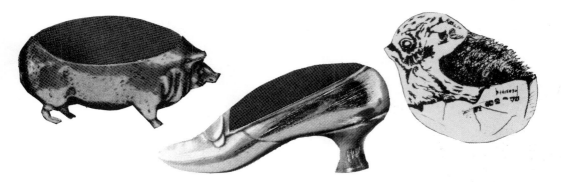

Plated brass pin cushion in the shape of a pig, circa 1895. £12

White metal shoe pin cushion, circa 1900. £10

Silver pin cushion in the shape of a chick, Chester, 1906. £50

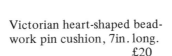

Victorian horse's hoof pin cushion with plated mounts. £10

Victorian heart-shaped beadwork pin cushion, 7in. long. £20

Late Victorian porcelain doll pin cushion. £8

PISTOLS

Antique pistols are particularly popular with collectors and investors for, as they disappear into collections, their scarcity naturally pushes the value up.

Flintlocks and percussion weapons are straightforward enough, but before purchasing those with a pinfire mechanism, check with the police as they could be regarded as firearms and then certain legislation comes into force.

Always try to buy weapons in pristine condition with no missing or replaced parts, keeping a particular eye for makers such as Nock, Manton, Twigg, Egg, Kuchenreuter and Lepage. Also be on the lookout for pairs of pistols, as they are worth at least three times that of a single — even more if they are in a box complete with accessories.

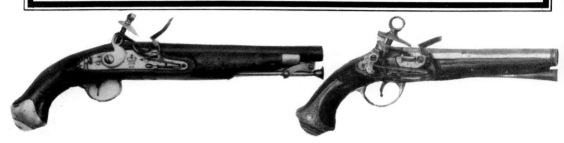

A 16-bore New Land pattern flintlock holster pistol, 15in., browned barrel 9in. (Wallis & Wallis) £280

A good rare 20-bore Spanish Ripoll miquelet flintlock belt pistol, circa 1780. (Wallis & Wallis) £280

A 24-bore percussion Police pistol of The Cheshire Constabulary for the Wirral Hundred. (Wallis & Wallis) £210

A 5-shot 120-bore Adam's patent model 1851 self-cocking percussion revolver. (Wallis & Wallis) £250

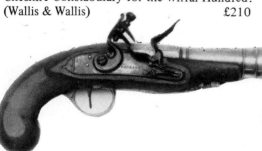

A brass barrelled flintlock blunderbuss pistol by Jackson, circa 1795. (Wallis & Wallis)£170

An interesting 5-shot .32in. extra short rim-fire Remington-Rider magazine pistol. (Wallis & Wallis) £130

A brass framed flintlock boxlock pocket pistol, 4½in., turn-off barrel 1¼in. (Wallis & Wallis) £180

A 4-shot .32in. trigger self-cocking Mariette patent percussion pepperbox revolver, 5¾in., turn-off damascus twist barrels 2in. (Wallis & Wallis) £230

A 5-shot .32in. rimfire Hopkins & Allen 'Blue Jacket No. 2' single action pocket revolver. (Wallis & Wallis) £50

A fully gold damascened 5-shot 54-bore Beaumont Adams double action percussion revolver. (Wallis & Wallis) £650

A 5-shot .31in. London Colt pocket single action percussion revolver. (Wallis & Wallis) £180

An unusual steel framed and double barrelled boxlock flintlock tap action travelling pistol. (Wallis & Wallis) £250

A .177in. pre-war air pistol, the 'Briton', overall length 8½in., barrel length 5½in. (Wallis & Wallis) £30

A double barrelled 12mm. French pinfire pistol by Pallard. (Wallis & Wallis) £100

PLATES

Specialise. There could be no better advice when it comes to collecting plates for the choice is only governed by taste and the depth of one's pocket.

A book of china marks is essential equipment as committing everything to memory is beyond the scope of most collectors but there are a few simple guidelines which may assist with dating.

Any piece bearing the words 'Bone China' or 'Made in England' suggests a product of the twentieth century. The word 'England' stamped on a piece suggests compliance with the McKinley Tariff Act of 1891. The words 'Trade Mark' can be assumed to date from the Trade Mark Act of 1862. A pattern mark or number suggests a date no earlier than about 1810 and Royal Arms incorporated into the mark indicates a date after 1800.

Late 19th century Japanese Satsuma plate, signed, 8¾in. diam. (Robert W. Skinner Inc.) £160

Chelsea plate with lobed rim, gold anchor mark, circa 1760-70, 8½in. diam. (Sotheby's) £176

Late 19th century European hand-painted porcelain plate with cobalt blue rim, 15in. diam. (Robert W. Skinner Inc.) £110

19th century Vienna porcelain cabinet plate with tooled gilt and blue border, 7¼in. diam. (Locke & England) £100

Vienna Du Paquier plate with lobed rim, circa 1730, 22cm. diam. (Christie's) £1,100

Early 18th century Castelli plate decorated with Fortitude sitting on a tomb, 19cm. diam. (Sotheby's) £902

Derby plate, decorated with a view of Worcester. (Christie's S. Kensington) £150

Late 19th century Japanese Imari charger decorated with cranes, 21in. diam. (Robert W. Skinner Inc.) £205

Very rare Leeds creamware commemorative plate, 1821, 22.7cm. diam. (Sotheby's) £396

Chelsea moulded plate painted with an exotic bird, circa 1758, 22cm. diam. (Christie's) £286

London delft plate with border pattern, 8½in. diam., circa 1710-20. (Sotheby's) £187

Bristol delft polychrome charger, cracked and riveted, circa 1710, 34cm. diam. (Christie's) £440

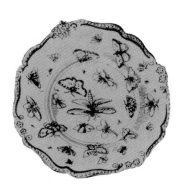

Derby plate, painted by Wm. Slater Snr., circa 1825, 23cm. diam. (Sotheby, King & Chasemore) £250

Wucai dragon and phoenix saucer dish with foot rim, 32.1cm. diam., decorated in famille verte. (Sotheby's) £2,090

One of a pair of George Jones & Sons wall plaques, signed Schenek, circa 1875. (Robert W. Skinner Inc.) £335

POLYPHONES

Polyphones are basically a development of the conventional musical box and are credited to the ingenuity of Paul Lochmann who founded the Symphonion Company in Leipzig in 1885. It was he, together with Gustav Brachhausen (founder of the Polyphon Company), who are responsible for the production of most of these delightful machines. Brachhausen in fact emigrated to America in 1894 where he started the Regina Company in New Jersey.

The music is produced by projecting pegs cut into a metal disc which ping the teeth of a steel comb as the disc revolves to produce a Gilbert and Sullivan aire or the latest singalong from the Music Hall.

The discs themselves range from 8in. on the small portable machines meant for home entertainment, to over 24in. diameter on the grander coin-operated varieties.

Polyphon disc musical box, German, in walnut veneered case, 12in. wide, circa 1910. (Sotheby's) £264

Unusual polyphon disc musical box, in oak and walnut case, circa 1900, 64in. high. (Sotheby's) £1,320

Polyphon disc musical box, Style No. 45, German, circa 1900, 21½in. wide.(Sotheby's) £1,100

Polyphon disc musical box in oak and beechwood case, circa 1895, 50in. high. (Sotheby's) £2,035

Polyphon disc musical box with coin-operated movement, German, circa 1900, 50½in. high. (Sotheby's) £950

Late 19th century German polyphon disc musical box, in coin-operated box, 34in. high. (Sotheby's) £770

POSTCARDS

The very first postcard in the world was issued in Austria in 1869 and the British G.P.O. postcard followed one year later.

At first postcards were designed to take the address only on one side and the message and illustration together on the other side. This card came complete with a printed half-penny postage stamp and it was not until 1894 that independent companies issued postcards for use with an adhesive stamp.

An Act of Parliament in 1902 allowing the message and address to be written on the same side leaving the other side free for a picture gave rise to the popular trend as we know it today.

Subjects range from scenic views to risque pin-ups and were soon eagerly collected.

Gruss Aus postcards, approximately 85 cards, circa 1900. (Sotheby's) £60

Tosca, twelve operatic chromolithographed postcards published by G. Ricordi C. Milano. (Sotheby's) £49

Pierrot, four cards, published by the Ellanbee 'Pierrot' Series, No. 115, very good condition. (Sotheby's) £27

Louis Wain, thirty cards including one advertising postcard for Jackson's Hats and Boots. (Sotheby's) £209

Mikado, by Raphael Kirchner, four cards, excellent condition. (Sotheby's) £99

Concours De Byrrh, by R. Kirchner, one card, good condition. (Sotheby's) £55

Concours De Byrrh, one of twelve postcards by B. Moloch, H. Mottel and others. (Sotheby's)   £330

Concours De Byrrh, one card by F. Vallotton, in good condition. (Sotheby's)   £50

Concours De Byrrh, one of ten cards by L. Baeyens, V. Leydet and others. (Sotheby's)   £280

Concours De Byrrh, one ten cards by H. Delaspre, C. Boulet and others. (Sotheby's)   £280

Concours De Byrrh, one card by Maurice Denis, in good condition. (Sotheby's)   £100

Concours De Byrrh, one of twelve cards by F. de Marliave, Harald D. Ponsam and others. (Sotheby's)£330

Concours De Byrrh, one of eight postcards by A. Beame-Miller, J. Hemard and others. (Sotheby's)   £220

Concours De Byrrh, one of twelve postcards by G. Trilleau, A. Brouillet and others. (Sotheby's)   £330

Concours De Byrrh, one of twelve cards by A. Edelmann, A. Foache and others. (Sotheby's)   £330

One of two decorative **Art Nouveau** cards by Eva Daniell. (Sotheby's)   £55

Sunray Girls, one of four cards showing girls with serpent and sunrays. (Sotheby's)   £198

One of 250 **Art Nouveau** and glamour postcards including novelty and photographic.(Sotheby's)   £495

One of two **Mucha** cards with Czech themes. (Sotheby's)   £60

One of twenty-one **Advertising Cards** including 'Ogden's Coolie', 'White Star Line' etc. (Sotheby's)   £200

Concours De Byrrh, one of twelve cards by Trinquier-Trianon, A. Cadiou and others. (Sotheby's)   £350

One of 250 postcard of **Children** by M. Sowerby, V. Anderson and others. (Sotheby's)   £200

One of four cards by R. Tuck, signed R. Kirchner. (Sotheby's)   £200

One of ten **Advertising Cards** including 'You Do Make Oi Laaf' and 'A Country Girl'.(Sotheby's)   £100

Viennese Fashions, four cards showing ladies in various costume, very good condition. (Sotheby's) £22

P. Raschka, **'La Guerre Amusante-Espionage'**, one card, very good condition. (Sotheby's)   £4

Father Christmas, twenty-four postcards of Father Christmas, New Year and Christmas scenes, dating from 1900. (Sotheby's)£38

Shakespeare, six chromo-lithographed postcards (Series 13). (Sotheby's)£13

Ladies with Four-Leaf Clovers, by R. Kirchner, seven cards, very good condition. (Sotheby's)£121

Clover Girls, three 'Good Luck' postcards showing ladies with clover leaves and piglets, very good condition. (Sotheby's)   £22

Art Nouveau, ladies with swans, four cards, Viennese, good condition. (Sotheby's)   £60

Hans Christiansen, Art Nouveau postcard, one card from **'Set of Paris'**, **'Cafe d'Ha'**, very good condition. (Sotheby's)   £143

Les Parfume, four cards by Raphael Kirchner, excellent condition. (Sotheby's)   £71

Jack Abeille, 1898, two cards showing **Bathing Scenes,** very good condition. (Sotheby's) £41

Concours De Byrrh, twelve postcards by J. Voloz, Louis Gardette Herbinier and others. (Sotheby's) £330

Nudes in Clouds, four cards showing ladies floating in clouds above the sea, excellent condition. (Sotheby's) £28

Art Nouveau, thirteen cards showing various Art Nouveau ladies scenes and floral pictures dating from 1899. £60

Advertising Cards, twenty-four cards for Fry's, Hudson's Soap, Ogden's, Girls' Own Paper, Castlebank Dyeworks, Wright's Shampoo Powder etc.(Sotheby's) £71

Demi-Vierge, four cards, embossed and gilded, very good condition.(Sotheby's) £33

Art Nouveau, two cards, one by Elizabeth Sonrel, the other by Hegedus Geiger, good condition. (Sotheby's) £19

Raphael Tuck **'Kings and Queens of England'**, thirty-six cards, mixed condition. (Sotheby's) £88

Av. Serail, four cards, Kirchner style, **Ladies in African/Eastern Scenes,** gold background, good condition. (Sotheby's) £60

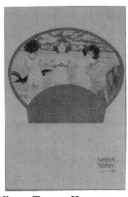

Vieux Temps II, one card by Raphael Kirchner, very good condition. (Sotheby's) £22

Fairies and Children, approx. 160 postcards by artists including M. Sowerby, Phyllis Cooper and H. Miller. (Sotheby's) £209

Ladies with Animal Friends, four cards by Raphael Kirchner, very good condition. (Sotheby's) £88

Ladies with Marionettes by Raphael Kirchner, four cards with gilded and embossed background.(Sotheby's) £77

Kunstler Postkarte Serie 197, four Kirchner cards, Christmas flavour, excellent condition. (Sotheby's) £165

Les Cigarettes Du Monde, four cards, very good to excellent condition. (Sotheby's) £88

Legendes, five cards by Raphael Kirchner, very good condition. (Sotheby's) £99

Girls with Eggs, three cards, Druck-u Verlag von D. Dondorf, very good condition. (Sotheby's) £55

Art Nouveau Ladies, four cards, R. Tuck Continental Series, Kirchner style, good condition. (Sotheby's) £55

POSTERS

Publicity posters have been collected with varying degrees of enthusiasm since they first became popular in the 1890s/1900s.

Advertising anything from theatrical works to cigarette papers, the high quality of the art work immediately aroused a passion for collecting. It is said that some eager beavers thought nothing of sneeking out, under cover of darkness, to strip a favourite subject from the billboard. Numbered copies, indicating a limited edition, were the most highly prized.

Art, probably for the first time, was being produced for 'the people' and not just for those who could afford it, and a monthly magazine 'The Poster' publishing information on how to keep abreast of the trend became a bestseller.

Unfortunately the quality of the printing varied greatly and sometimes the paper yellows and the colours fade but those lithographs printed on silk still demonstrate the richness of colour and design.

A recruiting poster 'Remember Belgium Enlist Today', pictorial – Tommy with Rifle, Poster No. 19, approx. 15 x 19½in. (Wallis & Wallis) £20

'Affiche de la Revue Blanche', by Pierre Bonnard, lithograph printed in colour on wove paper, l. 755 x 785mm., 1894. (Christie's) £2,090

'Sarah Bernhardt', lithographic poster by Paul Berthon, circa 1900, signed, 36 x 50cm. (Sotheby's Belgravia) £300

'Von Arx', World's Premier Illusionist and All American Co., coloured lithograph, 28 x 21in., circa 1910. (Sotheby's) £60

A recruiting poster 'Come Along Boys, Enlist Today', pictorial – Tommy Marching, Poster No. 22, approx. 19½ x 29½in. (Wallis & Wallis) £28

'Wallace', The Magician, The World's Greatest Illusionist, 30 x 20in., Birmingham, Moody Bros., circa 1920. (Sotheby's) £40

'Young Woman with Flowers', lithographic poster by Paul Berthon, circa 1900, 44 x 42cm. (Sotheby's) £93

Warwick Goble, 'Charming Chepstow', The New Racecourse, G.W.R. poster, 38 x 48in. (Sotheby's) £143

'Troe', The Trio, lithographed wrapper by K. Malevich, small 4to, St. Petersburg, Zhuravl, 1913. (Sotheby's) £1,320

'Palais De Glace, Champs Elysees', by Jules Cheret, lithograph printed in colour, on thin wove paper, l. 1248 x 882mm., 1893. (Christie's) £605

'Brevet De Perfectionnement, B. & D.Z.', litho poster depicting a wide variety of court cards, coloured by hand, mounted on card — 640 x 485mm., late 19th century. (Sotheby's) £65

'The Wanda's Mysterious Hand', Heads of performers on large coins, coloured lithograph, 47 x 31½in., circa 1912. (Sotheby's) £60

One from a collection of fifty-nine lithographic posters by Conrad E. Leigh, 31 x 47in. (Sotheby's) £198

'Course De Cote Chavigny-Nancy', lithographic poster by Polbor, signed and dated '32, 78 x 119cm. (Sotheby's) £46

'Princenza Wilhelmina' lithographic poster by Paul Berthon, signed, circa 1900, 39 x 36cm. (Sotheby's) £82

'Paris 1937 Expostion Internationale', lithographic poster by Paul Berthon, circa 1900, 44 x 42cm. (Sotheby's) £93

'Fap'anis' poster by Delval, depicting colourful girl holding a glass of liqueur, 62½ x 47in., circa 1920's. (Sotheby's) £55

'Austin Reed's of Regent Street', lithographic poster by Tom Purvis, signed, late 1920's, 74.3 x 49.6cm. (Sotheby's) £110

'Le Courrier Francais', French lithographic poster, signed Cheret, 31¼ x 45in. (Sotheby's) £82

'Job', by Alphonse M. Mucha, lithograph printed in colour and gold, printed by F. Champenois, Paris, l. 515 x 392mm., 1896-97. (Christie's) £4,400

'Lait pur de la Vingeanne Sterilise', by T. Alexandre, lithograph printed in colours, l. 1340 x 965mm., s. 1400 x 1000mm., 1849. (Christie's) £3,850

'Art et Decoration', lithographic poster by G. Lorin, signed and dated '98, 65.5 x 44.75cm. (Sotheby's) £220

'Chester', a G.W.R. poster by H. Russell Flint, 38 x 48in. (Sotheby's) £99

'Au Quartier Latin', small lithographic poster, 26.5 x 36cm., signed and dated '98, framed and glazed. (Sotheby's) £330

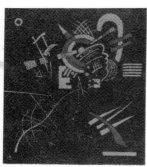

'Kleine Welten VII', by Wassily Kandinsky, lithograph printed in colour on wove paper, l. 270 x 231mm., 1922. (Christie's) £1,980

'Flirt', lithographic poster, signed, framed and glazed, 1890, 25 x 58.5cm. (Sotheby's) £495

'Sarah Bernhardt dans 'Phedre'', lithograph printed in black on wove paper, l. 341 x 238mm., 1893. (Christie's) £1,210

'Sables d'Or les Pins', large lithographic poster by C. Loupot, 1925, signed, 102 x 72.5cm. (Sotheby's) £264

'Lazenby's Specialities', framed showcard with large selection of food products, 28½ x 36½in. (Sotheby's) £71

Italian School, design for a poster announcing a street Carnival, circa 1873. (Sotheby's) £100

'Wizard of The Sphinx', head within Egyptian arch, coloured lithograph, 27 x 19in., circa 1905. (Sotheby's)£100

'The World Famed Wong Toy Sun', ink and watercolour drawing, signed Wiggin, 30 x 15in., circa 1920. (Sotheby's) £40

'Jane Avril', by Henri de Toulouse-Lautrec, lithograph printed in colour, l. 1245 x 895mm., s. 1295 x 943mm., 1893. (Christie's) £13,200

POT LIDS

In the mid 19th century many things were sold in small pots with decorative lids. One of the most notable producers of these earthenware pots was the firm F. & R. Pratt & Co., of Fenton in Staffordshire who issued well over three hundred differently decorated containers designed to hold such delights as a hair dressing of bear grease and, later, preserves.

Pots are usually circular in shape, though a few are rectangular, and consist of a shallow undecorated base made of the same material as the loose fitting lid.

In most cases it does not matter too much if the base is missing since it is the underglaze transfer printed lids which have been collected since their first appearance around 1840.

Decorative subjects range from portraits to landscapes; their current values being dictated by their rarity and condition.

Small pot lid, in good condition, showing shells. (Sotheby's)   £55

Rare medium pot lid 'The Tower of London', in good condition. (Sotheby's)   £352

Medium pot lid, 'England's Pride'. (Sotheby's)   £45

Medium pot lid 'Contrast', in good condition. (Sotheby's)   £28

Pot lid 'Our Home', one of only two known examples. (Phillips)   £2,600

Large pot lid showing the 'Exhibition Buildings, 1851', (Sotheby's)   £88

Medium sized pot lid of 'Our Pets' with registration mark. (Sotheby's)   £420

Medium small lid depicting bear hunting. (Sotheby's)   £340

Small pot lid 'Bears at School', with base. (Sotheby's)   £60

The '**Garden Terrace**', a medium-small lid with raised floral and beehive border. (Sotheby's) £260

Extra small pot lid '**Volunteers**', framed in good condition. (Phillips) £175

'**A False Move**', an unusual large pot lid in a good condition. (Sotheby's) £160

Rare lid '**Strathfield Say**', framed, in good condition. (Phillips) £230

Pot lid by Mayer Bros., circa 1850, 12.7cm. diam.(Sotheby's) £2,700

Extra small pot lid '**Old Jack**', framed. (Phillips) £220

Rare coloured pot lid '**The Matador**', by Meyer, 1850. (Phillips) £800

Medium pot lid '**The Late Prince Consort**'. (Sotheby's) £30

Rare large pot lid '**The Sea Eagle**', 1920's. (Sotheby's) £150

Large pot lid showing '**Pegwell Bay**', by S. Banger Shrimp Sauce Manufacturer. (Sotheby's) £198

Small lid with well-defined print of '**Bear, Lion and Cock**', with base.(Sotheby's) £66

Medium pot lid of '**HRH The Prince of Wales Visiting the Tomb of Washington**'. (Sotheby's) £40

POWDER FLASKS

A 17th century German powder flask made from an antler horn, the surface engraved with foliage, could cost hundreds of pounds but the metal variety by Batty, Hawkins, Ames, Dixon, or The American Flask & Cap Company among others, are fairly plentiful and therefore more reasonably priced. Most are decorated in some form, from simple fluting or basket weave designs to Coats of Arms, deer or even horrendous battle scenes. Of particular interest are the Old Colonial powder horns, which are nearly all engraved or carved by the owners themselves, often complete with personal mottos and beliefs.

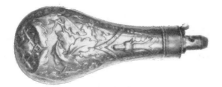

A large oak leaf embossed copper powder flask, 8in., common top graduated 2¼ to 3 drams, stamped Hawksley. (Wallis & Wallis) £54

A copper powder flask 'deer' by Hawksley, brass universal pattern, charger unit. (Wallis & Wallis) £42

A brass common topped panel type powder flask, copper body embossed with panel design, charger unit with graduated nozzle. (Wallis & Wallis) £30

An embossed gun sized copper powder flask, 8in., depicting the three horses' heads, stamped G. & J. W. Hawksley Sheffield. (Wallis & Wallis) £60

A large 19th century engraved powder flask made from the shoulder blades of an ox, 16in. overall, probably by Ernst Schmidt of Munich. (Wallis & Wallis) £510

A Scottish silver mounted dress powder horn, circa 1850, 15in., oval Cairngorm stone mounted in thistle embossed silver cap. (Wallis & Wallis) £170

PRAMS

Victorian middle class families usually worked to a fairly disciplined daily routine which started in the nursery and extended throughout the household.

After morning prayers, the youngest members would be wheeled out in their perambulators for their 'daily dose of God's rich air', though, in reality, the exercise was more for the benefit of the nannies who enjoyed exchanging the latest chit chat.

Most early prams are very narrow, (swaddling being the order of the day), have iron wheels and a wooden handle both in front and behind.

Some prams were made in wickerwork and some even came complete with a wooden horse jogging in front to keep the young charge amused.

Towards the end of the century they were designed to resemble the carriages of the day, becoming large coach built affairs with well sprung frames.

Early 20th century American wicker baby carriage with parasol, 56½in. high. £125

English/American wickerwork pram, 4ft.4in. long, 1930's. £30

Edwardian painted wood doll's pushchair with folding hood. £145

International Baby Carriage Store child's pushchair, circa 1900, 48in. long. £130

Victorian pram with folding hood and brass fittings. £45

Edwardian doll's perambulator with folding hood and boat-shaped body. £150

PRATTWARE

The term Prattware is generally associated with the transfer printed pot lids of the Victorian period manufactured by F. & R. Pratt & Co., of Fenton.

Much of the success of this firm was due to their engraver Jesse Austin who was a master of the art of transferring the works of Landseer, Gainsborough and Mulready onto lids, plates and other tableware, using a multi colour printing process made up of small dots.

Many of his engraved plates were rediscovered and subsequently revived at the turn of this century. Articles from this period often bear fine cracks all over the glaze, a process known as crazing.

An earlier member of the Pratt family however, also shares the term Prattware for his Toby jugs, some bearing the portraits of Nelson or Admiral Vernon. He also made a variety of figures and a distinctive type of earthenware of Italian influence, with either orange, green, blue or yellow panels.

Comport from an eleven-piece Prattware part dessert service printed with Tyrolean views. (Sotheby's) £198

A Prattware tea caddy depicting George III, 6¼in. high, 1780-90. (Sotheby's) £300

Late 18th/early 19th century Pratt type cow creamer and cover, 14cm. high. (Sotheby's) £160

Rare Prattware Toby jug, circa 1780-90, 10in. high. (Sotheby's) £240

Early 19th century rare Prattware cradle of oval form, 30.5cm. long, cracked. (Sotheby, King & Chasemore) £420

Prattware cockerel standing 10in. tall. (Sotheby's) £430

PUB SIGNS

All types of old advertising boards are now appreciated to an extent which would bring smiles of amused pride to the faces of the old sign-writers who made·them.

Unfortunately, most artists of merit consider it beneath them to devote their talents to such commercial subjects, which is a shame, considering that such notables as Toulouse Lautrec and Alphonse Mucha regarded signs and playbills as worthy fields for their not inconsiderable abilities.

One of the last remaining bastions of this art form is the Pub sign which, thanks to many large breweries, is at present undergoing a healthy revival. Sadly, much of value was destroyed during the fifties and sixties when Victorian pubs were frequently gutted without thought or sentiment (or, possibly, with thought, which is far worse) and masses of tasteless, sad plastic substituted.

With the revival of interest on the part of the breweries, of course, the old pub paraphernalia can rarely now be begged from the demolition men but some of it is still to be found on the market from time to time.

The art of painting a good pub sign lay in the ability on the part of the artist to create a design which would be visually arresting from a distance, even though it hung twenty feet in the air, and which was painstakingly researched and attractively rendered. The latter qualities, of course, are important to those who intend using their pub sign as a feature of interior decoration.

'The Waggon & Horses', double sided, iron banded woodboard Tavern sign.   £250

Old sheet iron Tavern sign from the 'Elephant and Castle', 41in. high, 36in. wide.   £350

Old English Tavern sign 'Fox and Hounds', 42 x 39½in.   £200

Old English double sided Inn sign, **'Rose & Crown'** 4ft.8½in. £95

An amusing and colourful Inn sign **'The Three Frogs'**, 47 x 47in. £275

Old hand-painted pub sign **'The Bell'**, on solid wood frame, 34in. wide. £95

19th century double sided sheet iron Tavern sign **'The Prince of Orange'**. £250

Trumans enamelled pub sign **'The Flying Eagle'**, circa 1945, 3ft.6in. high. £20

Hodges Inn sign with oval shield, **'Vermont'**, circa 1790, 31¾in. wide. (Robert W. Skinner Inc.) £2,715

Double sided Tavern sign **'The Bell'**, 40 x 31in. £150

Double sided iron Tavern sign the **'White Hart'**. £250

A finely painted double sided Tavern sign, **'The Falcon'**, 42 x 33in. £250

PURSES

Throughout the 19th century purses and other small bags designed to hold money, spectacles and a variety of necessary bits and bobs, acquired the status of a high fashion accessory. A lot of attention was given to detail particularly in the working of the clasps, mounts and hinges which were often made of silver or gold but more commonly of tortoiseshell.

The body of the purse or pouch was produced in many materials including beadwork, tapestry, leather, embroidered silks and a chain mail of silver or steel links.

A purse collection would be an excellent project for a new collector as there are many inexpensive and appealing examples around.

Art Nouveau silver purse, 1908. (Alfie's Antique Market) £90

14ct. yellow gold mesh purse with engraved frame, cabochon garnet clasp and a pencil attached to side. (Robert W. Skinner Inc.) £435

Late 19th century purse with mother-of-pearl flowers and gilt clasp. (Alfie's Antique Market) £35

Stylish German silver mesh evening purse, circa 1910, 18cm. long. (Sotheby's)£66

18th century gentleman's knitted green wool purse with diamond pattern. (Sotheby's) £60

Late 19th century purse made from Victorian beadwork. (Robert W. Skinner Inc.) £355

QUILTS

Quilting has a longer history in America than in Britain but the art was soon mastered by women particularly in the North of England and South Wales.

Designed to keep out the cold, bedcovers were made from two thicknesses of cloth with padding sewn between and more often than not the thrifty sempster used odd scraps of cloth to form a patchwork overlay. This developed into an art and before long we had the richly decorated quilts so highly prized by collectors.

Traditional patterns evolved but there are many individualistic designs and all are extremely attractive. It is interesting to note that sometimes old quilt patterns, cut from documents, were sewn in along with the quilt pieces and may reveal dates and names which, apart from adding interest, may help to date the quilt.

An Ohio pieced quilt of 'Flower Basket' pattern, circa 1860. (Sotheby's)   £400

A pieced and applique quilt of 'Star and Diamond' pattern, circa 1900. (Sotheby's) £250

A pieced quilt of 'Washington Sidewalk' pattern, 1860-70. (Sotheby's)   £300

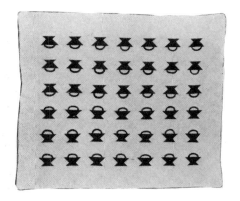

A Maryland pieced applique quilt of 'Basket' pattern, circa 1860. (Sotheby's)   £450

A Cumberland County, Pennsylvania, pieced and applique quilt, circa 1830. (Sotheby's) £600

An Ohio pieced quilt of 'Tracks' pattern, circa 1870. (Sotheby's) £350

New England, applique coverlet, mid 19th century, 92in. square. (Robert W. Skinner Inc.) £250

Early 19th century pieced and appliqued quilt, New England, 72 x 72in. (Robert W. Skinner Inc.) £300

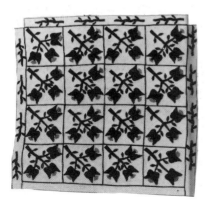

A pieced and applique quilt of 'Pennsylvania Tulip' pattern, 1860-70. (Sotheby's) £700

19th century American pieced and appliqued quilt, 84 x 84in. (Robert W. Skinner Inc.)£245

QUILTS

An Amish pieced quilt of **'Monkey Wrench'** pattern, circa 1870. (Sotheby's) £600

Civil War patriotic quilt dated 1864, 68 x 88in. (Robert W. Skinner Inc.) £245

An Ohio pieced quilt of **'Star'** pattern in red and white cottons, 1860-70. (Sotheby's) £350

An Ohio pieced quilt of **'Monkey Wrench'** pattern, 1840-60. (Sotheby's) £300

A Pennsylvania child's floral applique quilt, 1840-60, 34 x 35in. (Sotheby's) £350

A Pennsylvania pieced quilt of **'Spider's Web'** pattern, 1860-70. (Sotheby's) £385

RADIOS

Put an old 78 record on an old wind up gramophone and the atmosphere of a bygone era bursts forth from the elegant horn. It therefore comes as something of a surprise, to find todays 'Six o'clock news' emitting from a 30's bakelite radio, when '2LO calling' might be more appropriate.

Radios have come a long way since Mr. Marconi harnessed the transmission of electro magnetic waves back in 1894 and this is the fascination for collectors.
From Catswhisker and crystal to three valve battery sets in kit form, the plug in coils, grid leaks and flexi valve holders, hold all the magic of a pioneer world in which the reward is a signal from far away places — if assembled in the right order.

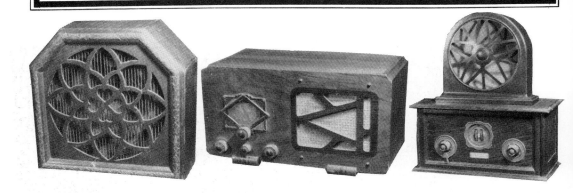

'Celestion' Speaker, wood cabinet 1928. (Capricorn Curios) £25

'Vulcan' All Battery Set SG3, J.G. Graves 1935. (Capricorn Curios) £25

'Kolster Brandes' Straight 3 1928. (Capricorn Curios) £25

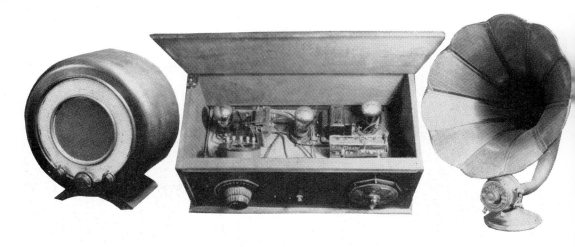

'Ekco' AC Mains model A22 round, bakelite 1938. (Capricorn Curios) £80

Early Kit Constructed Straight 3 Valve Battery Set 1929. (Capricorn Curios) £20

'Amplion' Moving iron speaker, wood petal horn, brass base, 1927. (Capricorn Curios) £50

RADIOS

'Freed Eiseman' Junior Bedside AC-DC U.S.A. Line Cord Set 1935. (Capricorn Curios) £35

Crystal Set with Earphones 1922. (Capricorn Curios) £25

'Bestone' Clock Radio, U.S.A., oak cabinet 1934. (Capricorn Curios) £45

'Fellophone' Super 3 Bright Emitter Battery Set 1922-24. (Capricorn Curios) £120

'Phillips' Mains AC "Super Inductance" model 830A 1932. (Capricorn Curios) £100

'Ultra' AC Mains '3', wood cabinet 1932. (Capricorn Curios) £35

'Ekco' AC Mains model AC74 bakelite 1939. (Capricorn Curios) £50

'Gecophone' 3 Valve All Battery Set 1928. (Capricorn Curios) £35

'Ekco' Mains AC Radio model 830A bakelite 1932. (Capricorn Curios) £35

RAILWAY TICKETS

Railway tickets have been collected since the earliest days of the railway system. Traditionally collectors have built up their collections by exchange, but in recent years several large collections of tickets have been auctioned and many more offered for sale by collectors. This has enabled a price to be placed on certain of the rarer items. A few examples are shown below. The value placed on any particular ticket is dependant on several factors, such as the age, condition and the station or company of issue.

Platform tickets are also a popular item with many collectors who aim to get one from as many different stations as possible.

Issued by the Somerset & Dorset Joint Railway in 1899. This line has always been popular with collectors and such a ticket would fetch about £20.

Issued by London & North Western Railway at Loudon Road station which was closed in 1917 it re-opened in 1922 as South Hampstead. £20

A Midland Railway ticket issued at Highgate Road Station would be sought after by collectors specialising in station names as it was only open for eighteen years, closing in 1918. £20

Issued at Junction Road on the Tottenham & Hampstead Joint Line in 1942. This is the only known example of a platform ticket issued by this station and could well fetch a price approaching £100.

Special ticket issued for one day only to view locomotives at Waterloo Station — not of great value as almost all the tickets issued were kept as souvenirs. £5

This very early issue from the Dumbarton & Balloch Joint Line dates from the 1860's but is worth much less than would be expected as it comes from a large lot found during the rebuilding of Glasgow (Queen Street) Station one hundred years later. £5

This platform ticket from Edinburgh has a misprint, the words 'leaving platform' appear as 'yeaving jjijtform'. Many collectors keep these misprints as an interesting sideline. Their value is not very high as hundreds of each type usually exist. 15p

At first sight this appears to be for a return trip to Clapham Junction from Worcester — for 35p? This is in fact a misprint for Worcester Park. 5p

These two half tickets are interesting as they give a glimpse of railway history. The L.B.S.C.R. ticket to Crystal Palace includes admission to the Palace. The S.E.C.R. ticket is available only on the special cheap trains for the working class. £1 each

RAILWAYANA

One of the beneficial effects of the savage cuts administered by Dr. Beeching was that Railway buffs could graduate from trainspotting to collecting. They bought parts of trains, even whole trains and for the real fanatic the purchase of an actual station or signal box became a reality.

Of the many fields of collecting, Railwayana is one of the most enthusiastically subscribed, with magazines, museums, clubs and even societies running their own railways — often with great success.

The field is vast, for absolutely everything connected with the railway is collectible, from station signs, lamps, clocks, tickets to even the locks of the loo doors.

In fact, so valuable have some of the locomotive nameplates and numberplates become, that many of those displayed on trains are replicas. The real plates are locked away in a safe place.

Hunslet Engine Co. Ltd., Leeds, No. 1451, Holly Bank No. 3, brass nameplate, 40in. long. (Sotheby's) £88

Brass locomotive number plate, 1448, with black background, orange lining and green border. (Sotheby's) £77

Unlined cast iron number plate, 4101. (Sotheby's) £44

'Campbell', one of a pair of locomotive nameplates in cast brass, 35¾in. long. (Sotheby's) £800

Cast iron plate, 2254, with green outer border. (Sotheby's) £55

Cast iron number plate with black border, 3840. (Sotheby's) £44

Brass industrial locomotive nameplate, Atlas No. 17, 38in. long. (Sotheby's) £66

Cast iron 5613 plate, in black with green border. (Sotheby's) £49

Cast iron plate with orange lining, No. 6374. (Sotheby's) £44

'The Middleton', cast brass locomotive nameplate , named after the Fox Hunt, circa 1932, 35in. long. (Sotheby's) £935

Cast iron number plate, 5242, repaired. (Sotheby's) £22

Cast iron number plate with black border, 5506. (Sotheby's) £49

A1 Class brass locomotive nameplate 'Holyrood', 50in. long. (Sotheby's) £715

RATTLES

Most silver rattles to be found today, date from the 19th century, and often come complete with an ivory or coral teething ring.

Unfortunately, many were abused, and condition is an important factor with those surviving examples. Those with a full compliment of bells, good makers mark and date letters will always obtain good prices.

Silver rattles from the 18th century, and earlier, are rare and will make prices far exceeding their merits as examples of the silversmith's art.

The most highly prized however, are those of American Indian origin which can obtain truly amazing money. They are generally made of carved wood and designed for ceremonial purposes rather than pacifying the offspring.

A baby's Victorian silver rattle, unmarked, with whistle and carved ivory handle. £150

Collector's example of a baby's Georgian silver rattle and comforter, Sheffield, 1818, 5in. long. £125

Victorian silver rattle dated 1886. £35

Early 18th century child's silver rattle, 5¼in. long, circa 1700. £360

North American Indian carved wooden rattle, 1ft. long. £3,400

17th century child's rattle bearing the Edinburgh date letter for 1681. £1,250

Victorian silver rattle with ivory teether and whistle. £90

18th century child's rattle and whistle by Shem Drowne, Boston, 1749. £220

RAZORS

Razor collecting is still a fairly new field and exceptionally fancy specimens can still be bought.

The vast majority of plain black and white handled cut-throat razors are too plain and recent to interest many collectors and these are worth less than one pound each.

Items at a premium are; perfect pearl-handled razors, preferably Sheffield, with carved pearl panels — £15-£20; and Sterling silver handled razors, preferably solid and engraved, though silver on ivory are also desirable at £20-£30.

Good, uncracked 1800 period razors with straight handles are generally more collectible than later items and German razor sets, and imitation ivory sets are always worth less than the equivalent Sheffield made ivory sets.

1800 period razor with straight ivory handles and wedge blade. £6—£10

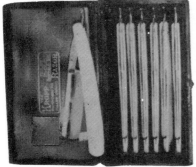

Matched pair of ivory-handled, wedge bladed razors by Thomas Turner, Sheffield, in oak casket. £7—£10

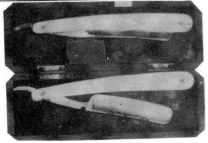

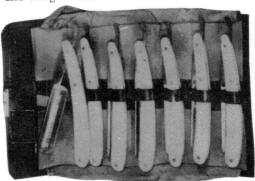

Imitation ivory seven-day set of razors by Tennis, Germany, in morocco leather case. £15—£25

Ivory-handled seven-day set of razors by Kropp, Sheffield. £30—£45

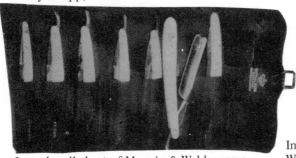

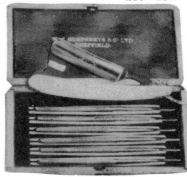

Ivory-handled set of Mappin & Webb razors, in silk-lined suede roll-up case. £12—£15

Imitation ivory seven-day set of razors by W. R. Humphreys, Sheffield, in oak box. £25—£35

ROBERTSON'S GOLLY BADGES

It was just before the First World War, whilst on a visit to the 'backwoods' of North America, that a son of James Robertson, the founder, noticed a large number of young children playing with little black rag dolls with white eyes made from their mothers' discarded black skirts and white blouses.

The young Mr Robertson was so intrigued by the popularity of the small 'Golly' (the name being the children's interpretation of Dolly) that he thought it would make an appealing mascot and trade mark for the Robertson's range of products.

The first golly badge Robertsons produced was in 1930 commencing with the Golly Golfer. Four years later a series of fruit badges were produced with a Golly head superimposed into the berries. In 1937 came a Union Jack waistcoated Golly with it's arm raised in formal salute and Cricketers with County names printed on them. These early pre war Gollies had pale yellow waistcoats with Golden Shred printed on them.

The scheme was discontinued during the war because of the metal shortage but in 1946 a further series of Gollies were introduced with white waistcoats and the words Golden Shred — sportsmen, scout, standard walking Golly, bagpiper and guitarist.

About 1960 the golly changed, his eyes now looked to the left, hair became wavy and the words Golden Shred removed from his bright yellow waistcoat.

In 1977 came the skateboard and the motorcycle brooches and in the same years a series of 15 woven Golly jeans patches were designed which have become as popular as the brooches.

Post 1960 Gollies with bright yellow waistcoats.   75p—£1

366

ROBERTSON'S GOLLY BADGES

Post War 'Golden Shred' white waistcoated Gollies. £1.50—£2

Pre War 'Golden Shred' pale yellow waistcoated Gollies. £2—£2.50

Post War fruit badges without Golly heads.
£1.50—£2

Pre War fruit badges with Golly heads.
£2.50—£3.50

ROCK 'N ROLL

At first thought to be 'just a flash in the pan' the market in rock & roll memorabilia is now well established.

Anything to do with the early stars, no matter how tenuous the connection, is being collected but it is the items more personally identified with our idols that really fetch money. For example a piano, once the property of Paul McCartney, sold for £9,900. This is perhaps a more obvious treasure but early photographs of John & Paul on stage can fetch upwards of £100 and all promotional material such as Elvis Presley film posters or concert programmes is also readily saleable.

One of eight Jimi Hendrix photographs, together with twenty-two negatives and eleven colour transparencies, sold with copyright. (Sotheby's) £440

A radio telephone, once the property of Elvis Presley, contained in a leather briefcase with initials E.A.P. beneath carrying handle. (Sotheby's) £660

Elvis Presley, a portrait of the singer executed in black ballpoint pen, signed and dated 24 December 1973. (Sotheby's) £495

Four photographs, negatives and copyright of the Beatles on the day they were voted top group by the Mersey Beat, 1961. (Sotheby's) £572

Bruce Welch's electric guitar, a Fender Strat Anniversary, with letter of authenticity signed by Bruce Welch. (Sotheby's) £385

Eight photographs of the Beatles performing in Aldershot in 1961, sold with negatives. (Sotheby's) £1,210

The Who gold disc for 'Who Are You' on MCA records for 500,000 copies sold. (Sotheby's) £330

A rare photograph sold with copyright and negative of the Beatles and NME Poll Winners Trophy, Wembley 1964. (Sotheby's) £550

John Lennon, a photograph sold with copyright and negative. (Sotheby's) £352

'Our First Four', first four 45 r.p.m. singles produced by Apple Records Ltd. comprising the Beatles, Black Dyke Mills Band, Mary Hopkin and Jackie Lomax. (Sotheby's) £385

A set of seven Beatles Fan Club Christmas records, dating from 1963. (Sotheby's) £385

Eric Clapton platinum disc for 'Backless' presented by RSO Records Inc. for the sale of one million copies, circa 1978. (Sotheby's) £770

Three early Beatles posters for Merseyside venues, 1962. (Sotheby's) £528

'Meet The Beat', Polydor J 74557, with the Beatles, Tony Sheridan and the Beat Brothers. (Sotheby's) £220

An autographed Cavern Club membership book for 1961, containing the signatures of Pete Best, Johnny Lennon, George Harrison and Paul McCartney, 1961.(Sotheby's) £462

Cliff Richard in 1958, contemplating his rise to top of the bill at Chiswick Empire. (Sotheby's)   £77

Buddy Holly and the Crickets, photographed in England during 1958. (Sotheby's)   £88

Mitch Mitchell's twelve-piece drum kit with accessories and spares. (Sotheby's)   £242

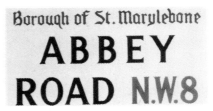

Abbey Road, The Borough of St. Marylebone, enamelled street sign, 30 x 18in. (Sotheby's)
£640

A Raleigh Super 50 Moped once owned by John Lennon, complete with registration book, 69in. long, c. 1965. (Sotheby's)
£2,860

The Beatles Royal Variety Performance programme, signed, 11¾ x 8¼in. (Sotheby's)
£1,155

An Audiotek/Cadec mixing console used by John Lennon to record the 'Imagine' album, together with a letter of authenticity, circa 1970. (Sotheby's)   £6,050

An Elvis Presley wrist-watch, by M. Tissot, 'Elvis Presley' in raised letters, c. 1970. (Sotheby's)   £2,090

A pair of Beatle woven nylon stockings printed with caricatures of the Beatles, c. 1965.
(Sotheby's)   £280

The Beatles for their fans — a handout leaf-
let — 6 x 9in., c. 1961. (Sotheby's)   £242

Eddie Cochrane and Gene Vincent photographed in 1960 on a British tour.
(Sotheby's)   £99

Introducing Elvis Presley in 'Love Me Tender'
Film Poster, 30 x 40in. (Sotheby's)   £35

Dire Straits, gold disc for the LP 'Making
Movies', with presentation, 16 x 14in.,
1981. (Sotheby's)   £462

A bronzed bust of Elvis Presley, by J. Douglas,
8½in. high, English, 1976. (Sotheby's)   £60

John Lennon, a pen and ink self-portrait,
seated within a circle, 3¾in. (Sotheby's) £8,800

Paul McCartney's Chappell & Co. Ltd. upright
piano, 50 x 50 x 24½in., English, c. 1902.
(Sotheby's)   £9,900

Paul McCartney gold disc for ½ million copies of 'London Town' sold on Capitol Records, 1978. (Sotheby's) £770

A Beatles gold disc for the LP 'Sgt. Peppers Lonely Hearts Club Band', presented to the Beatles by EMI, dated 1967. (Sotheby's) £14,300

A gold Beatles disc for 'The Beatles Story' on Capitol, circa 1964. (Sotheby's) £1,870

Two original contracts for the Beatles relating to a concert at the Wimbledon Palais De Danse on 14th December 1963. (Sotheby's) £220

An autographed Beatles concert programme signed on the front by all four members of the group, Blackpool, 1964. (Sotheby's) £352

George Harrison letters to a fan, a handwritten letter encouraging the fan to buy 'From Me To You', dated 1963. (Sotheby's) £198

An unusual paper collage by John Lennon in the form of cuttings from newspapers and magazines, 1966. (Sotheby's) £3,300

The Beatles LP, VJ 1092, the first LP released in the United States. (Sotheby's) £44

1963 Royal Variety Performance autographed programme signed by four members of the Beatles and others. (Sotheby's) £286

An acetate of John Lennon unreleased composition, 'God Save Oz', on Apple label, 1971. (Sotheby's) £660

The Beatles in Mathew Street, a bronze by A. Curran, 1978, 32in. high. (Sotheby's) £1,540

John Lennon original drawing in black felt-tip pen on yellow lined foolscap paper. (Sotheby's) £1,430

John and Yoko, twenty-eight black and white prints of the Montreal Hotel 'Bed-In', 1969. (Sotheby's) £440

Ringo Starr's stage suit with plum coloured lining and no plectrum pocket, 1966. (Sotheby's) £275

John Lennon 'Starting Over', the paper sleeve to the single bearing signatures of John Lennon and Yoko Ono. (Sotheby's) £385

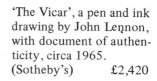

'The Vicar', a pen and ink drawing by John Lennon, with document of authenticity, circa 1965. (Sotheby's) £2,420

A pen and ink drawing, probably by John Lennon, of a nude with a tea-cup, on Bag Production notepaper. (Sotheby's) £605

Official documents relating to John Lennon in Hamburg, 1960/63. (Sotheby's) £1,100

A good bronze bust of John Lennon by K. Carter, 15½in. high. (Sotheby's) £3,080

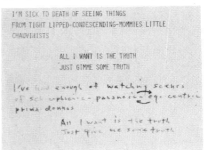

John Lennon, a photocopy of the lyrics of four verses of 'Gimme Some Truth' with alterations and additions in Lennon's hand, circa 1961. (Sotheby's) £1,650

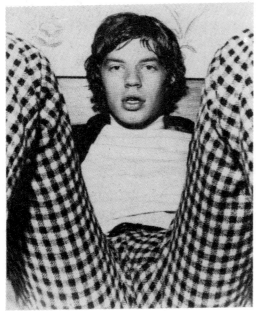

Series of twenty-four photographs of The Rolling Stones in the early stages of their career. (Sotheby's) £385

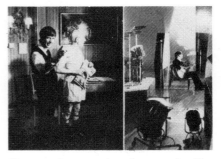

Sixteen photographs taken on the film set of 'A Hard Day's Night', sold with negatives and copyright. (Sotheby's) £1,100

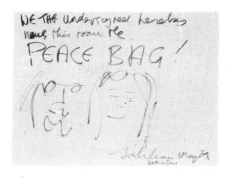

John Lennon, an original drawing in black felt-tip pen of portraits of John and Yoko entitled, 'We The Undersigned Hereby Name This Room Peace Bag'. (Sotheby's)   £2,200

'The Motley Bunch', a pen and ink drawing by John Lennon, circa 1965. (Sotheby's) £2,420

An autographed 'Help' premiere programme signed by Ringo Starr, John Lennon, Paul McCartney, Jane Asher, George Harrison and Pattie Boyd. (Sotheby's)   £605

Seven concert programmes relating to the Beatles, 1962-65. (Sotheby's)   £638

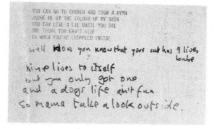

John Lennon, detail from hand-drawn Christmas card in wax crayon, 1968. (Sotheby's)   £2,200

John Lennon, a photocopy of the three first verses of 'One Thing You Can't Hide' with added fourth verse in Lennon's hand, 1971. (Sotheby's)   £770

The Beatles 1962, copyright Harry Hammond, mounted on card. (Sotheby's) £242

Paul McCartney's drum kit with letter of authenticity from Mike McCartney. (Sotheby's) £1,320

An autographed Beatle concert programme for the 1964 Tour, signed by the four members of the group. (Sotheby's) £462

The Beatles by James Hall Thomson, four caricature pen and ink drawings used in the Melody Maker newspaper. (Sotheby's) £308

John Lennon's two-piece suit with velvet collar, three buttons and single vent, 1966. (Sotheby's) £220

The Beatles, Chris Montez and Tommy Roe, copyright Harry Hammond, 1963. (Sotheby's) £82

John Lennon's film suit for 'A Hard Day's Night', with blue lining, 1966. (Sotheby's) £220

ROYAL DUX

This most distinctive porcelain was produced at the Royal Dux factory established in 1860, in Dux, Bohemia.

The factory quickly gained a reputation for beautifully fashioned portrait busts and ornate vases but the most sought after pieces around today are the scantily clad nymphs of flowing form, more often than not seductively draped around shell-shaped bowls or curved mirror frames.

The most noticeable characteristic of this unglazed porcelain is the colour tones of soft pastel beige, pink and green.

Marks include an embossed pink triangle stamped Royal Dux Bohemia or E (proprietor: E. Eichler) in an oval surrounded by Royal Dux Bohemia.

Dux figures were exported in considerable quantities to America and Australia establishing a lasting international popularity.

Royal Dux centrepiece of a bowl in the form of a shell with two nymphs at one end, 43cm. high, circa 1910. (Sotheby's) £400

Unusual pair of Royal Dux 'clown' figures, 23.4cm. high, circa 1910. (Sotheby's) £190

Royal Dux figure group of a family, circa 1880, 25in. high. (Robert W. Skinner Inc.) £210

20th century Royal Dux mirror frame, 53cm. high, applied and impressed pink triangle. (Sotheby's) £330

Royal Dux camel group, applied pink triangle, circa 1910, 45.5cm. high. (Sotheby's) £418

20th century pair of Royal Dux figures 'Farmer's Boy' and 'Farmer's Girl', 16½in. high. £330

RUSKIN POTTERY

The Ruskin pottery illustrated is the work of William Howson Taylor (1876-1935). In 1898, Mr. Taylor took over premises at Smethwick and went into commercial production of this quite novel and highly colourful pottery. The variety of objects produced range from vases and bowls to eggcups, even hatpins, and the colours and glazing techniques employed in their decoration seem endless.

The skill of this highly personalised craft was known only to Taylor who, unfortunately, destroyed his worknotes. His wares are usually dated and the mark is composed of the name Ruskin, the monogram W.H.T. and scratched or painted scissors.

A Ruskin high-fired vase with finely mottled plum, lavender and mauve glaze, 23.5cm. high, dated 1912. (Sotheby's)   £110

Ruskin high-fired porcelain shallow bowl and stand, 26cm. diam. (Phillips)   £200

Ruskin high-fired porcelain vase of baluster form, dated 1928, 36cm. high. (Phillips)   £300

Ruskin high-fired vase with shouldered globular body, dated 1925, 17.5cm. high. (Sotheby's)   £150

Ruskin high-fired vase with slender bulbous body dated 1925, 18.5cm. high. (Sotheby's)   £150

Ruskin high-fired cylindrical vase in mottled purple and blue glaze, 19cm. high, 1907. (Christie's)   £150

SAMPLERS

Samplers were produced from early in the 18th century right through until after the First World War as a means of showing how adept a young girl could be at the useful art of embroidery, as well as knowing her alphabet.

A variety of coloured silks were worked, most popularly in cross-stitch, on a canvas backing to incorporate the name and age of the exponent, the date, numbers one to ten together with the alphabet, a hymn or a poem and a multitude of designs depending on how clever our young needlewoman was.

Examples include such worthy subjects as a documented family register but, above all, these charming pieces reflect a refreshing simplicity of style.

An early 19th century needlework sampler by Selina Doughty, 1835. (Phillips)£140

An embroidered band sampler by Elizabeth Woodworth, 1758. (Sotheby's) £374

A sampler by Emma Toogood finished June 28th, early 19th century. (Sotheby's) £143

A fine spot motif sampler, the ivory linen ground with geometric samples, circa 1630. (Sotheby's) £990

'Life of a Man' needlework sampler, early 19th century, American. (Robert W. Skinner Inc.) £2,000

Spot motif sampler with geometric panels in a variety of stitches, circa 1630. (Sotheby's) £880

A late 18th century needlework sampler designed with a house and peacock. (Phillips) £180

Sampler by Sarah Ann Hunt, aged 12, 1839, 24½ x 20in. (Sotheby's) £143

Needlework sampler 'Ann Major her work 1812', Philadelphia School. (Robert W. Skinner Inc.) £2,500

Needlework sampler in circular reserve on linen ground, 1817, by Jane Simmons. (Robert W. Skinner Inc.) £705

Mid 19th century wool worked picture of a mother and child. (Phillips) £80

Needlework sampler with wide floral border by Betsey Duncan, circa 1825. (Robert W. Skinner Inc.) £190

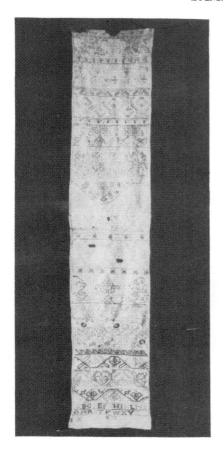

17th century needlework sampler worked mainly in cross stitch. (Phillips) £270

Mid 19th century needlework sampler by Ann Rebecca Willingham, aged 13, 1842. (Phillips) £150

Sampler by Mabia Wade Bliss, together with portrait, American, circa 1830. (Robert W. Skinner Inc.) £1,500

Needlework sampler by Elizabeth Drew, aged 13, Plymouth, Massachusetts. (Robert W. Skinner Inc.) £1,250

Needlwork sampler by Joanna Emersons, A.D. 1812, New Hampshire School. (Robert W. Skinner Inc.) £900

SCENT BOTTLES

Scent bottles can be found made in a number of materials including, silver, gold, enamel and porcelain, but the vast majority are made of glass with a variety of decorations. Throughout the 18th and 19th centuries, it was customary to carry a container of insoluble crystal salts blended with aromatic essence purchased from a chemist or perfumier.

It was not until the 20th century that perfume was sold in ready filled bottles, and of these, the bottles made by Lalique for Coty and Nina Ricci are particularly sought after. Examples by Daum, Galle and Webb also fetch good prices but a start can be made with Victorian overlay scent bottles, often double ended, and far more reasonably priced.

Silver gilt mounted double overlay scent bottle, interior stamped S. Mordan & Co., London, 1850's, 9.2cm. high. (Sotheby's) £104

Lalique glass perfume bottle and stopper in original box, 1920's, 13.5cm. high. (Sotheby's) £410

Wiener Werkstatte cut glass globular bottle with electroplated bottle top, circa 1910. (Sotheby's) £1,000

Unusual Daum cameo glass perfume bottle and stopper, signed, 13.5cm. high. (Phillips) £360

Lalique glass perfume bottle and stopper for Worth's 'Dans la Nuit', 1920's, 10cm. high. (Sotheby's) £140

Late 19th century moulded overlay scent bottle shaped as a perching owl, 11.5cm. high.(Sotheby's) £23

Cylindrical scent bottle of clear glass with frosted top and stopper, 4¼in. high, marked R. Lalique, France. (Lawrence Fine Art) £110

Guerlain 'Mitsouko' glass scent bottle of Art Nouveau shape. (Christie's) £25

Silver mounted and tortoiseshell veneered scent bottle case complete with silver mounted scent bottle, London, 1910. (Sotheby's) £242

French parcel gilt silver mounted clear glass scent flask, circa 1844, 11.4cm. high. (Sotheby's) £352

Unusual silver gilt mounted enamel scent flask in the form of an egg, 8.6cm. high, London, 1882. (Sotheby's) £550

Cameo glass silver mounted scent bottle of teardrop form, circa 1885, 11cm. long. (Christie's) £280

Late 19th century unfinished cameo glass scent bottle, 6.5cm. (Sotheby's) £44

One of a pair of French 19th century lime green opaline glass square-shaped scent bottles, 4¾in. high. (Geering & Colyer) £140

Lalique turquoise glass perfume bottle, moulded with triangular leaves, circa 1925, 9cm. high. (Sotheby's) £495

SCRIMSHAW

Scrimshaw work was a popular pastime for sailors aboard the big whaling ships of the 19th century. The work can best be described as extremely fine engraving on bone or ivory, the incised detail darkened down with black ink or soot.

Usually working on a whale's tooth, though sometimes on whalebone, the sailors most commonly chose a theme relating to life at sea but, just occasionally, one may come across a mildly erotic design.

Scrimshaw work is often mounted for display or used to embellish objects such as gongs, inkstands and a variety of small boxes.

Late 19th century whale's tooth scrimshaw, 16cm. high. (Sotheby's)   £150

Early 19th century American scrimshaw jagging wheel in the form of a horse's head, 6in. long. (Robert .W. Skinner Inc.) £300

Silver mounted whale's tooth scrimshaw, Birmingham, by Hilliard & Thomason, 16cm. long. (Sotheby's)   £320

Mid 19th century American pair of whale's tooth scrimshaw, mounted on wooden plinths, 14.5cm. high. (Sotheby's)   £100

19th century engraved scrimshaw whale's tooth, 7in. high. (Robert W. Skinner Inc.) £165

Late 19th century pair of whale's tooth scrimshaw, one entitled 'Jane' the other 'Eliza', 12cm. high. (Sotheby's)   £200

A scrimshaw cow horn beaker, incised with a picture of four horses, pulling a mail coach, circa 1820 (Vernon's)   £80

Unusually large example of scrimshaw ware, engraved on whale bone, circa 1815, 8in. tall, 15¾in. wide. (Sotheby's)   £700

Late 19th century whale's tooth scrimshaw, 16.5cm. high. (Sotheby's)   £95

SEALS

There are three main types of seal. A desk seal, a fob seal and a seal, or signet, ring.

Early desk seals of the late 17th and early 18th centuries were shaped rather like a mushroom, with a bulbous wooden handle, and a carved silver seal set into the end of the stem. Over the years the shape was modified to slimmer proportions and the handles made of precious materials set with stones.

Fob seals were made of gold, silver and silver gilt, with ornate handles and seal matrices cut in gemstones, steel and a variety of materials. Around the middle of the eighteenth century it was considered fashionable to wear not one, but a cluster of fobs, hanging from the fob pocket of the breeches.

Although designs are numerous and elaborate it may still be possible to identify and date a sealing instrument from the print. Many bore coats of arms, self portraits or initials.

From 1791 the law required gold and silver seals to be hall-marked.

English gold, hardstone, mother-of-pearl triple seal, circa 1835, 6cm. high. (Sotheby's) £360

French gold mounted rock crystal desk seal, 5.4cm. high, circa 1910. (Sotheby's) £440

Mid 19th century French parcel gilt silver desk seal, 6.9cm. high. (Sotheby's) £180

English gold fob seal with domed fluted base and flower-chased border, circa 1830, 3.5cm. high. (Sotheby's) £270

Mid 19th century gold and hardstone swivel desk seal, 3.5cm. high. (Sotheby's) £620

19th century gold fob seal with urn-shaped handle, 3.8cm. high. (Sotheby's) £230

Gold and turquoise desk seal, circa 1840, 8.5cm. high. (Sotheby's) £800

Ivory seal carved with a squirrel on a grapevine, circa 1900, 7.5cm. high. (Sotheby's) £38

Mid 19th century Italian gold and hardstone desk seal, 8.3cm. high.(Sotheby's) £682

385

SHELLS

Unfortunately, the shores of Britain don't seem to harbour much in the way of excitement for shell-collectors, but for the last 150 years generations of expatriate beachcombers have sent home an abundance of beautiful examples from warmer climates which can be found almost anywhere if you keep your eyes open.

Good examples of the abalone (mother-of-pearl) shell or the Queen Conch can be bought for a few pounds, but rare examples like the Conus Gloriamarus (the glory of the seas) can cost hundreds of pounds.

Of particular interest to serious collectors are series of the same shell in progressively larger sizes showing the growth development.

A fine golden cowrie shell from the Fiji Islands.£240

A magnificently engraved nautilus shell, 7in. across.   £700

Ammonite, the fossilised shell of large size, 1ft.2in. wide.   £50

A late 19th century carved cameo shell.   £40

The infernal harp shell from the Fringing Reef, Mauritius.   £125

A replica of an example of scrimshaw presented to Queen Victoria on the launching of 'The Great Britain', 21.5cm. long.£700

SHOES

In the past, collectors have followed the history of footwear through collections of highly detailed replica boots and shoes originally designed as containers and made of silver, pewter, brass, porcelain and glass.

Today they are looking for the 'real thing'. Early or unusual examples are being snapped up at auction sales and more antique shops are making space to display footwear from all periods up to the 1940's.

Prices range from a few pounds to a thousand and more, depending on the appeal, rarity and condition of the goods. Late Victorian shoes and little satin low heeled slippers are fairly common and will cost about £25, and Edwardian leather strap shoes about £15.

Pair of small leather clogs with brass buckles. £15

Pair of late 18th/early 19th century gent's black leather riding boots, now used as an umbrella stand. £250

Pair of American Plains Indian hide and quill-work moccasins, 9½in. long. £1,300

Rare pair of shoes made in 1780. £125

Pair of leather postillion rider's coaching boots with copper and wrought iron hanging plates, 21in. high, circa 1710. £250

Pair of very decorative pierced leather boots, 11in. long. £75

SHOP SIGNS

Stand in any main shopping centre today and one is confronted with the familiar shop signs of the multiple stores. Which is a shame, for shops are becoming so impersonal these days with individuality being a thing of the past.

Town planning is partly responsible for it has stifled the use of elaborate shop signs which used to boldly display the interests of the shopkeeper. Literacy is more the cause of their demise however, for graphic signs were often the only way many people could identify the trade.

Tobacconist shops seem particulary well endowed with signs, from magnificent life size blackamoors and Red Indians to a multitude of smaller figures and animals of carved wood.

19th century American moulded copper fish sign, gold leafed, 36in. long. £620

19th century Victorian butcher's shop sign of a carved bull's head, 13in. high, made of oak. £285

Antique carved walnut tobacconist's sign modelled as a rotund Turk, 22in. high. £560

Shop window sign of a monkey, made entirely of French pipe briar-wood, 27in. wide, circa 1850. £165

American kettle advertising sign in metal with iron handle, 22½in. high. £220

Gargantuan-sized carved wood Hessian Boot covered with gold leaf, circa 1760, originally a boot shop sign, 39¼in. high. £280

SIGNED PHOTOGRAPHS

The value of a signed photograph is more likely to be determined by the rarity of an example rather than the popularity of the subject.

Efficient Press Officers often issue many thousands of signed photographs on behalf of important and popular personalities and the sheer volume of material available reduces the desirability and value to a collector.

Recent developments now make it possible to produce a machine signed photograph with all the attributes of the real thing so, even authentic looking examples of modern personalities should be treated with a degree of scepticism.
It is often an advantage to have some historical background to establish provenance.

Laurel and Hardy, good photograph of them in characteristic pose signed by both, 5 x 7in. (Sotheby's) £80

Pablo Picasso, full length photograph of Picasso in bathing trunks, signed in ballpoint, 7¼ x 5in. (Sotheby's) £150

Virginia Woolf, leaf extracted from her passport bearing her photo and signature, both overstamped by the Foreign Office, 18th April, 1933. (Sotheby's) £170

Elvis Presley, Photograph of Presley in military uniform in a car, signed in blue ballpoint, with another, 5½ x 3½in. (Sotheby's) £110

389

Charles Chaplin, good photograph in black and white, signed in black ink, 10 x 8in. (Sotheby's) £140

Mae West, photograph signed, inscribed 'To John Best Wishes Mae West', 10 x 8in. (Lawrence Fine Art) £19

Ronald Reagan, 40th President of the U.S.A., Photograph of Reagan when a film star, signed and inscribed 'Good Luck', postcard 5½ x 3½in. (Sotheby's) £55

Piotr Ilyich Tchaikovsky, 1840-93, fine photograph, signed and inscribed by the composer in ink, in Russian, to the pianist Anna Alexandrovna Essipova-Leschetizky, and dated 2 May 1885, 159 x 102mm. (Christie's) £1,100

SIGNED PHOTOGRAPHS

Johann Strauss, The Younger, carte de visite photograph, signed with an autograph musical quotation of four bars from 'The Blue Danube', framed and glazed. (Sotheby's) **£825**

Sir Winston Churchill, fine photograph of the young Churchill, signed on mount, 9 x 7½in. (Sotheby's)   **£250**

Leo Tolstoy, postcard photograph signed in black ink in English script. (Sotheby's)**£200**

Victoria, the official Diamond Jubilee photograph, signed and dated by the Queen, inscribed on reverse by her private secretary, Sir Arthur Bigge, to the photographer Downey, 13 x 7½in., April 1897. (Sotheby's)   **£620**

SLAG GLASS

Although examples of pressed glass have been attributed to the Romans it wasn't until the Americans perfected the mass production process in the 1820's that the public at large could fill their homes with the stuff as a substitute for the blown and cut glass bought by the wealthy.

It still required, however, at least seven people to operate each machine: a presser, a melter, four lads (whose duties are not defined) and, most important of all, a gatherer, whose skill was to place exactly the right amount of molten glass into the gunmetal mould.

By mid century one or two factories were producing coloured glass in their moulds, which prompted J. G. Sowerby of the Ellison Glass Works of Gateshead to experiment by mixing the scum from the top of molten metal, from the nearby iron and steel works, with his glass to give it a purpled marble finish. He referred to his wares as vitro porcelain and went on to introduce a variety of hues including turquoise, green, white, black, yellow and occasionally orange.

The mark he used was that of a peacock's head moulded in relief while other manufacturers of note like George Davidson of the Teams Glass Works also in Gateshead used a lion rampant emerging from a castle turret. The other main manufacturer was Greener & Co. of the Wear Glass Works of Sunderland whose mark was a lion rampant holding an axe. Most slag, however, was unmarked but is usually of the same quality as that of the well-known firms.

Articles embellished with nursery rhymes or shell motifs often command a premium.

Victorian purple slag glass tea caddy of sarcophagus form.   £75

Newcastle slag glass tumbler in purple and white.   £15

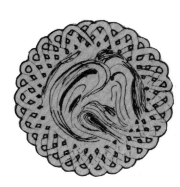

19th century purple slag glass candlestick.   £20

19th century light blue slag glass plate with basket weave edge. £12

Victorian white slag glass jug with thistle decoration.   £15

Victorian white slag glass bowl with thistle decoration.   £15

SNUFF BOTTLES

Chinese snuff bottles usually resemble small vases about 6cm. (2½in.) high, and are made of a variety of materials including porcelain, ivory, jade, cloisonne, horn, agate, glass and bronze. Most sought after, and therefore most expensive are those made of porcelain from the late 17th and early 18th century, closely followed by carved hardstone such as agate, quartz and amethyst. A guide to quality, although it is not infallible, is the size of the hole in the neck (the smaller the better) and the degree of hollowing out — those with a large interior being the best. This also applies to glass bottles which were generally carved out of a solid piece as opposed to being blown.

A glass overlay snuff bottle with a fan tailed carp on each side, 1800/1860. (Sotheby's)   £176

A glass overlay snuff bottle overlaid in green with a fan tailed carp. (Sotheby's)   £286

A fine glass overlay snuff bottle overlaid in white with two fan tailed carp. (Sotheby's)   £1,430

A glass overlay snuff bottle overlaid with a swooping bat, 1750/1850. (Sotheby's)   £715

18th century glass overlay snuff bottle with a fan tailed carp flanked with stylised cloud scrolls. (Sotheby's)   £682

A glass overlay snuff bottle of slender pear shape, 1800/1860. (Sotheby's)   £176

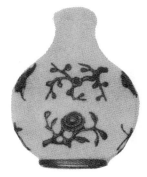

A rare overlay glass snuff bottle with a frieze of crested birds in flight. (Sotheby's) £1,540

A glass overlay snuff bottle with a parrot chained to a perch. (Sotheby's) £88

A glass overlay snuff bottle overlaid in black with sprays of prunus. (Sotheby's) £121

Glass snuff bottle overlaid in high relief with five bats. (Sotheby's) £352

Glass overlay snuff bottle with a panel enclosing a farmer. (Sotheby's) £462

Glass snuff bottle overlaid with a crab on a lotus leaf. (Sotheby's) £132

Glass snuff bottle with a well carved stylised chilong on each side. (Sotheby's) £154

Glass snuff bottle overlaid with precious objects on the sides. (Sotheby's) £121

Overlay snuff bottle with a bear snarling up at an eagle. (Sotheby's) £352

A five colour glass overlay snuff bottle depicting a yellow dog playing with a butterfly. (Sotheby's) £1,045

A rare glass snuff bottle with a continuous design of lily sprays, 1780/1850. (Sotheby's) £2,310

Glass overlay snuff bottle carved with the eight Buddhist Emblems. (Sotheby's) £1,430

A fine 18th century snuff bottle overlaid with two windswept fishermen. (Sotheby's) £2,640

A rare carved glass snuff bottle overlaid with the Immortal Lan Caihe. (Sotheby's) £1,760

Glass snuff bottle with fan tailed sea dragon emerging from the waves. (Sotheby's) £1,375

18th century overlay snuff bottle with a powerful leaping dragon with forked tail. (Sotheby's) £792

Overlay snuff bottle with archaistic dragons encompassing a Shou medallion. (Sotheby's) £792

Glass snuff bottle of clear bubble-suffused body overlaid in pale amber. (Sotheby's) £814

A Pekin glass snuff bottle of amber coloured metal, 18th century. (Sotheby's)   £286

Amethystine quartz snuff bottle carved as a melon with a bat to one side. (Sotheby's)   £60

Pekin glass snuff bottle moulded in the form of a melon, 1750/1850. (Sotheby's) £374

Pekin glass snuff bottle of slender pear shaped body. (Sotheby's)   £66

A silhouette agate snuff bottle of flattened form depicting a farmer approaching a horse. (Sotheby's)   £396

Porcelain snuff bottle of double gourd shape decorated in famille rose enamels. (Sotheby's)   £297

A chalcedony snuff bottle of pear shape in honey-coloured stone.(Sotheby's)   £198

An unusual chalcedony snuff bottle carved with a seated sage. (Sotheby's)   £396

A silhouette agate snuff bottle depicting a bearded and hatted figure. (Sotheby's)   £110

An aquamarine snuff bottle carved from a natural crystal. (Sotheby's) £176

A rare inkstone snuff bottle of disc shape, 18th century. (Sotheby's) £198

An amethystine quartz snuff bottle carved as a fruit enveloped by pods. (Sotheby's) £60

A good puddingstone snuff bottle of cylindrical form. (Sotheby's) £330

A lacquered burgaute snuff bottle of flattened disc shape, Japanese. (Sotheby's) £82

A porcelain figure subject snuff bottle moulded as Liu Hai. (Sotheby's) £638

A shadow agate snuff bottle, the sides with mark and ring handles. (Sotheby's)£55

Pekin glass snuff bottle of flattened slender baluster form, 1780/1880. (Sotheby's) £264

Rare porcelain snuff bottle of pear shape moulded with a coiled dragon. (Sotheby's) £704

SNUFF BOXES

For many hundreds of years people have been taking snuff and, an indication of the popularity of this habit can be seen in the abundance of delightful snuff boxes we have to choose from.

They come in all shapes and sizes and made from many materials including gold, silver, tortoiseshell, papier mache, and enamel ware. Like the vinaigrette, many have gilt interiors. Generally the lids are decorated and here the variety is infinite. They may be painted, inset with semi-precious stones or inlaid with contrasting materials. Those ornamented with representations of the famous castles, 'castle-tops', are particularly desirable boxes, notably that of Windsor Castle by Nathaniel Mills.

Unusual examples have two compartments so that snuff can be separated into grades and a most uncommon box may have a watch inset in one section.

Mother-of-pearl and gilt metal snuff box, 7.2cm. wide, circa 1760. (Sotheby's) £150

Copenhagen snuff box and cover modelled as the head of a dog, circa 1793, 6.5cm. wide. (Christie's) £350

18th century English snuff box with portrait of Frederick the Great. (Woolley & Wallis)£900

Rectangular silver gilt snuff box by Ledsham Vale & Wheeler, Birmingham, 1827, 77mm. long. (Christie's)£600

Rare Bilston enamel snuff box formed as a woman's head, circa 1765, 7.5cm. high. (Christie's) £680

Rectangular silver and elephant's tooth snuff box by Joseph Willmore, Birmingham, 1834, 9cm. wide. (Sotheby's) £220

French Vernis Martin snuff box, lid painted with flowers, circa 1755, 8.5cm. diam. (Sotheby's) £400

Louis XV painted oval silver snuff box, Paris, 1763, 90mm. long. (Christie's) £750

Mid 18th century English silver and hardstone snuff box of cartouche form, 6.5cm. wide. (Sotheby's) £180

George III Irish oval snuff box by Alexander Ticknell, Dublin, 1795, 3¼in. long. (Sotheby's)   £400

Silver gilt mounted horn snuff box with hinged lid, London, 1880. (Sotheby's)   £143

Mid 18th century circular English gilt metal snuff box, 7cm. diam. (Sotheby's)   £180

Heart-shaped silver and enamel snuff box, 6.8cm. high, 1722-1726. (Sotheby's)   £650

Rectangular silver snuff box, lid inset with an unusual medal, by Norbert Roettier. (Woolley & Wallis)   £240

Nymphenburg snuff box with shaped oval body moulded with basketwork, circa 1755-65, 6.5cm. wide. (Sotheby's)   £462

Russian silver snuff box, Moscow, 1838, 3in. long, 2.5 troy oz. (Robert W. Skinner Inc.)   £160

Early 19th century coquilla nut snuff box of boat form and with silver gilt thumbpiece, 3½in. long. (Christie's)   £160

German oval silver and tortoiseshell snuff box, 1750, 7.7cm. wide. (Sotheby's)   £176

Silver and tortoiseshell pique snuff box, lid decorated with a figure, circa 1710, 8.5cm. long. (Sotheby's)   £396

Silver gilt double opening snuff box, one side with a verge watch by Iohan Georg Gugel of Brin, 91mm. diam., circa 1720. (Sotheby's)   £2,800

Circular silver snuff box, hinged lid set with tortoiseshell portrait of Charles I, 2½in. diam. (Woolley & Wallis) £260

SPOONS

Seventeenth century silver is extremely rare, can cost a small fortune and is usually kept under lock and key. However, early silver spoons can still be found and their value will increase at a greater rate than later examples.

Their survival could possibly be attributed to the fact that they are not worth a great deal as scrap and, if a household did possess a few silver spoons, they were likely to be handed down from generation to generation and so they gained a sentimental value.

Most sought after are the seal top spoons, including apostle spoons. The finials of these are usually cast and fitted into the flattened stems with a 'V' joint. The trefid spoon is more common and these have a 'rat tail' continuing from the stem down the back of the bowl. Good examples have a lace pattern. The bowls of these spoons should be quite large in proportion to the handle and quite thick at the edge.

It will add interest to a collection if it also includes spoons designed for a particular function eg. a mote spoon. In the early days, loose tea was produced with a much bigger leaf than we are now accustomed to. This resulted in 'fat gentlemen' floating around on the surface and the spout of the teapot becoming bunged up. The mote spoon was designed to cope with this, once could scoop up the floating debris with the bowl of the spoon and use the spiked end for unblocking.

Small silver spoons are often worth only a few pounds but, be on the lookout when sifting through boxes of cutlery for silver tea caddy spoons. There are many made up of a large plain bowl with a short handle worth about £20 each but, if you are lucky enough to find an unusually shaped one, say in the form of an acorn or eagle, or one by a notable maker such as Hester Bateman, it could be worth over £100.

Gibson-patent type castor oil spoon by Henry Flavelle, Dublin, circa 1835, 5½in. long. £1,000

Heavy Edwardian fiddle and thread silver serving spoon, by W. Hutton, London, 1903, 6oz., 13in. long. £55

Early Charles II silver spoon, York, 1661. £840

Electroplated dessert spoon designed by Charles Rennie Mackintosh, circa 1903, 15.5cm. long. £850

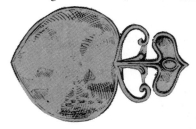

Arts & Crafts silver caddy spoon, Birmingham, 1919, 9.5cm. long, handle set in mother-of-pearl. £75

16th century seal top spoon probably by John Quycke, Barnstaple, circa 1590. £330

Russian silver and enamel decorated serving piece with scalloped lip, 15cm. long.   £130

Guild of Handicrafts Ltd. silver teaspoon by C. R. Ashbee, London, 1907.   £240

Silver tablespoon by Ebenezer Coker.   £25

Gibson-patent type castor oil spoon, circa 1800, 2oz., 5¼in. long.   £176

A caddy spoon with fiddle pattern engraved bowl, 1835, London.   £60

Silver apostle spoon showing St. Philip and enlarged London hallmark for 1490. £6,800

George III jockey cap caddy spoon by Joseph Taylor, Birmingham, 1798.   £165

Charles I apostle spoon by Ralph Herman, Exeter, circa 1630.   £990

A Victorian caddy spoon with a waisted bowl and engraved handle, circa 1860.   £50

Guild of Handicrafts Ltd. silver spoon designed by C. R. Ashbee, London, 1905, 19.3cm. long.   £320

20th century Liberty 'Cymric' spoon with enamelled bowl by Archibald Knox. £200

Scandinavian plique a jour silver spoon.   £85

SPORTING MEMORABILIA

There is always a ready market for any sporting paraphernalia, be it the actual items connected with a certain sport, or articles commemorating certain events or personalities. Golfing items have a particularly strong following for it is a sport with international appeal and early golf balls and clubs will often obtain hundreds of pounds at auction.

Cricket, horseracing and tennis are also keenly collected with angling, boxing and to a lesser degree football and rugby also having their disciples.
Porcelain manufacturers have always been quick to take advantage of a market and, Doulton and Staffordshire in particular, have produced some delightful sporting momentoes.

Doulton stoneware cricketing tyg, 1884, 6¼in. high. £120

Pair of early 19th century Staffordshire figures of Tom Cribb and Molineaux, 21.5cm. high. £800

Staffordshire silver lustre jug transfer-printed in black with the Molineaux/Cribb fight, circa 1810, 14.5cm. high. £170

Doulton stoneware beaker, showing golfers, circa 1900, 4¾in. high. £99

Doulton stoneware cricketing jug, circa 1900, 10¼in. high. £120

Cast metal clock showing a racing cyclist, circa 1900, 18cm. high. £65

Doulton stoneware loving cup with cricketing subject, 1882, 6in. high.£462

Mid 18th century cricket bat, 105cm. long.   £580

Earthenware mug with black transfer of a cricketer, dated 1924-25.   £40

Early Bow coffee pot and cover of the 'Golfer and Caddy' pattern, circa 1752-55, 9in. high, slightly cracked.   £1,650

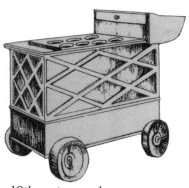

19th century mahogany cricket bat trolley.£250

Early 20th century cast metal clock showing footballers, 18cm.   £75

Enamelled silver flint lighter, 2in. high.£90

Rare pair of Staffordshire figures of cricketers of about 1865.   £400

Golfer match box by Sampson Morden & Co., 1891.   £235

STAFFORDSHIRE FIGURES

Vast quantities of these earthenware figures were produced from around 1850 right up until the First World War. They are referred to as Staffordshire figures although many were produced at factories in the north of England and in Scotland.

Known as flatbacks because the back of the ornament was left flat and undecorated, they are of extremely simple and unsophisticated design.

The figures were press moulded and decorated usually in two underglaze colours, blue and black, often with touches of colour in overglaze enamel and gilding.

Again rarity dictates value and those either of a limited edition or signed S. Smith are the ones to look for.

The saltglaze Staffordshire figures made prior to the flatbacks are, naturally, more desirable and valuable collectors items.

Brightly coloured Staffordshire '**Alliance**' group, circa 1854, 12in. high.(Sotheby's) £100

Rare Staffordshire equestrian figure of '**Lady Godiva**', circa 1870, 25.5cm. high. (Sotheby, King & Chasemore) £460

Staffordshire figure of '**The Allied Powers**', circa 1854, 11¾in. high. (Sotheby's) £360

Rare Staffordshire figure of '**Rev. C. H. Spurgeon**'. (Christie's S. Kensington) £480

Rare pair of figures of a stag and hind at lodge, circa 1750-55, 17cm. wide. (Sotheby, King & Chasemore) £500

Early Staffordshire figure of a shepherdess, circa 1800, 13.5cm. high. (Phillips) £28

Early 19th century Staffordshire pearlware pointer by Wood & Caldwell, 11.5cm. wide. (Sotheby, King & Chasemore) £65

Cottage pastille burner, 11cm. high, circa 1840. (Sotheby, King & Chasemore) £190

Staffordshire pearlware cowcreamer group with brown hide, circa 1780, 16.5cm. wide. (Christie's) £150

Rare Staffordshire porcelain figure of 'Van Amburgh', 15.5cm. high. (Sotheby, King & Chasemore) £1,600

Staffordshire group of 'The Elephant of Siam and Mr Hemming as Prince Almansor', 15.7cm. high, circa 1840-50. (Sotheby, King & Chasemore) £170

Staffordshire group of 'The Victory', modelled as an English sailor and a Turkish and French soldier. (Christie's S. Kensington) £950

Staffordshire figure of 'Princess', circa 1853, 10in. high. (Sotheby's) £55

Staffordshire portrait of 'George Washington', 21cm. high. (Sotheby, King & Chasemore) £260

Pre-Victorian Staffordshire figure of 'Moses', 11in. high, with bocage base. (Phillips) £95

When the government of 1860 removed the ban on imported silk goods, it had a disastrous effect on the weavers of Coventry, forcing many of them out of business. It did, however, spur on a certain Thomas Stevens to try out some of his new ideas. By adapting his looms to weave small, multi-coloured pictures and bookmarks instead of the traditional ribbons, he found instant, overwhelming success. He also produced Christmas, birthday and Valentine cards, plus calendars, sashes and badges, all of which were offered to a totally new market, since they were sold through booksellers and fancy goods shops.

Stevens travelled to trade fairs all over Britain, Europe and America taking along with him portable looms so that visitors could watch the production at first hand and buy whatever took their fancy. The response in America was so favourable that he went on to export great quantities of pictures which explains why there are so many excellent collections in that country today.

Although a variety of woven silk pictures can be found, those by Stevens usually bear the inscription 'woven in pure silk by Thomas Stevens, Coventry' printed on the front of the mount.

Thomas Stevens died in 1888, leaving the business to his two sons. Their products continued to be popular until the outbreak of the First World War but, although they continued to turn out a few portraits after that time, main production became geared to the manufacture of hatbands and the like. The firm survived until 1940, when the factory was completely demolished in the blitz.

'The Last Lap', pennyfarthing race, yellow axles, original mount. (Sotheby's)   £71

'The Present Time 60 Miles An Hour', with two carriages. (Sotheby's)   £25

'The Present Time', train emerging from tunnel, original mounts. (Sotheby's)   £41

'The Death Of Nelson', deck of the Victory, remounted and framed. (Sotheby's)   £24

'**The Lady Godiva Procession**', original mount, framed and glazed. (Sotheby's) £60

'**Windsor Castle**', a view of the castle with the Thames in the foreground. (Sotheby's) £40

'**The Forth Bridge**', a view of the bridge under construction. (Sotheby's) £60

'**Called To The Rescue**', original mount, framed and glazed. (Sotheby's) £24

'**A Present From Blackpool**', a view of the town and piers. (Sotheby's) £60

'**Dick Turpin's Ride To York On His Bonnie Black Bess**', original mounts. (Sotheby's) £29

'**The Good Old Days**', original mount, framed and glazed. (Sotheby's) £35

'**Are Your Ready**', Boat Race, original mount, framed and glazed. (Sotheby's) £60

'Charles Stewart Parnell M.P.', with yellow harp and clover leaves below portrait. (Sotheby's)£35

'Crystal Palace', woven in brown and white, mounted framed and glazed. (Sotheby's) £27

'F. Barratt', with black hat and sleeves. (Sotheby's) £30

'H.R.H. Prince of Wales', facing left with flags below. (Sotheby's) £45

'Field Marshal Sir John French'. (Sotheby's) £45

'Rt. Hon. W. E. Gladstone MP', looking ahead with sprays of thistles and roses. (Sotheby's) £20

'General Georges Boulanger'. (Sotheby's) £50

'Roberts F.M.', with small signature. (Sotheby's)£20

'Marquis of Salisbury, K.G.', with roses below portrait. (Sotheby's) £20

'Her Majesty Queen Alexandra', with the crests of England, Scotland and Ireland below portrait. (Sotheby's) £25

'Leda', a study of Leda and the swan. (Sotheby's) £70

'Jake Kilrain', study of notable American boxer. (Sotheby's) £40

'A Gentleman In Khaki', depicting a wounded soldier with rifle raised. (Sotheby's) £20

'The Late Earl Of Beaconsfield', with black and white portrait facing left. (Sotheby's) £20

'Kitchener of Khartoum', with head and shoulders above a Union Jack. (Sotheby's) £22

'Ye Peeping Tom of Coventry', with brown window surround. (Sotheby's) £40

'Sergt. G. H. Bates', the American Standard Bearer. (Sotheby's) £60

'Her Majesty Queen Victoria', Queen of a an Empire on Which the Sun Never Sets. (Sotheby's) £20

TEA CADDIES

Of all boxes, chests, caskets and other assorted containers, tea caddies must surely be the most numerous and the most varied with regard to shape and style.

One reason for this is that tea has been drunk in Britain for some three hundred years, at prices ranging from £10 per lb. (at the beginning of the 17th century) down. Naturally, a commodity as expensive as this was neither served direct from the packet nor dumped in just any can on the kitchen shelf.

Early (i.e. 17th century) containers were usually of pottery or porcelain. As the cult of tea-drinking became more widespread during the 18th century, tea-containers of gold and silver began to appear, and these were housed in lockable chests or caddies (the word caddy is derived from the Malay "kati", a measure of tea weighing about 1¼lb.) The more widespread the tea-drinking habit became, the greater the variety of caddies to cater for the demand.

Chippendale, Sheraton and all the other designers and cabinet makers of note produced caddies in their characteristic styles, and ornamentation varied from the simplest, most elegant inlay work to encrustations of brass, ormolu, coloured straw, curled paperwork and every other possible decorative device.

Not too many years ago, it would have been easy to start a collection, for caddies could be picked up almost anywhere for only a few pounds — none but the very best reaching double figures. Nowadays, they are just as ubiquitous but the prices must warm the cockles of any heart who got a collection together at the right time.

They are to be found in a number of materials, including wood, ivory, papier mache, silver, copper, tortoiseshell, china, straw work, Tunbridgeware and with painted decoration.

Blue-ground French enamel caddy, circa 1900, 10cm. high. (Sotheby's) £180

George II embroidered tea caddy of hexagonal shape, circa 1775, 7½in. wide. (Sotheby's) £165

Regency mother-of-pearl inlaid tortoiseshell veneered tea caddy, circa 1820, 6¾in. wide. (Sotheby's) £231

Birmingham fine enamel tea caddy of oval form, circa 1765, 4¾in. wide. (Christie's) £3,300

Bristol delft tea caddy of octagonal form, circa 1760-70, 4¼in. high. (Sotheby's) £935

George III ivory veneered tea caddy of oval shape, lid with pineapple finial, circa 1790. (Sotheby, King & Chasemore) £190

TEA CADDIES

Small Victorian rosewood tea caddy, inlaid with mother-of-pearl. (Alfie's Antique Market)   £45

Regency rosewood tea caddy, with mother-of-pearl inlaid lid, 35cm. wide. (Sotheby's)   £40

Early 19th century tortoise-shell tea caddy, inlaid with mother-of-pearl. (Gray's Antique Market)   £200

Georgian satinwood inlaid tea caddy. (Christie's S. Kensington)   £100

Rare George II japanned tea caddy, circa 1740, 10¼in. wide. (Sotheby's)   £390

Meissen arched rectangular tea caddy and cover, circa 1740-50, 13cm. high. (Christie's)   £240

Rare George III maplewood and tortoiseshell tea caddy, 6in. wide, circa 1780. (Sotheby's)   £440

Red tole painted tea caddy and writing box, circa 1790, 8in. wide. (Robert W. Skinner Inc.)   £165

Early 19th century covered oval quill work box with ivory finial, 5½in. long. (Robert W. Skinner Inc.)   £90

TEAPOTS

Teapots dating from early in the 18th century will always command high prices for at first the famous leaf was an incredibly expensive luxury supped only by the very wealthy. Teapots of this period are accordingly very rare and of a high quality.

The duty on tea was reduced dramatically midway through the 18th century, considerably increasing its popularity which continued, unabated, throughout the 19th century.

Teapots have therefore been made in every conceivable shape, style and material for a very long time and as a result any would-be collector will need to be pretty discriminating, sticking strictly to a chosen type — be it Staffordshire barge teapots at under £100 to early saltglaze examples costing over £1,000.

Whieldon oviform teapot and cover with crabstock spout and handle, circa 1755, 19cm. wide. (Christie's)   £352

Large Staffordshire coffee pot, circa 1825, 11in. high, with C-scrolled handle. (Robert W. Skinner Inc.)   £435

Ludwigsburg porcelain teapot, spherical shaped tapering to base, circa 1755, 4¾in. high. (Robert W. Skinner Inc.)   £475

Spode's Imperial covered teapot with gadrooned and leaf mouldings, circa 1810. (John Hogbin & Son)   £20

Rare Ludwigsburg teapot and cover supported on three twig feet, 13cm. high, circa 1770. (Sotheby's)   £1,600

Wedgwood Whieldon teapot and cover moulded with fruits and foliage, circa 1760-65, 5¼in. high. (Sotheby's)   £160

Kinkozan earthenware teapot and cover, painted and gilt, circa 1900, 12.5cm. high. (Sotheby's) £85

Superb Rockingham rococo-shaped porcelain teapot and cover, circa 1830. (John Hogbin & Son) £55

Staffordshire saltglaze polychrome Jacobite teapot and cover, circa 1745, 12.5cm. high. (Christie's) £300

Sevres pink-ground cylindrical miniature teapot and cover, circa 1775, 9.5cm. high. (Christie's) £130

19th century Staffordshire 'barge' teapot, 13in. high. (J. M. Welch & Son) £90

Early 19th century New Hall teapot from a thirty-three-piece tea and coffee service. (H. C. Chapman & Son) £210

Rare Bottger/early Meissen teapot and cover, 11cm. high, circa 1730.(Sotheby's) £3,800

19th century Satsuma decorated teapot, 7½in. high. (J. M. Welch & Son) £180

Worcester teapot, circa 1758-60, 4in. high, in underglaze blue. (Sotheby's) £260

TELEPHONES

Hailed at the time as the Greatest Miracle of Human Achievement, early examples of the humble telephone are now ringing up good prices.

Although Alexander Graham Bell is credited with the invention of the telephone, an American, Elisha Grey, actually filed a patent on a similar machine exactly the same day as Bell but, unfortunately for him, a few hours later, so he lost his claim in an ensuing Supreme Court action. Surprisingly, the first telephonic contrivance was actually made 16 years before either Bell or Grey, by Professor Philip Reis of Friedrichsdorf. For the microphone, our ingenious friend hollowed out the bung of a beer barrel which he then covered with the skin of a German sausage to make a diaphragm. To this he attached a strip of platinum which vibrated with the diaphragm to form a make-and-break electrical circuit. Then he took a knitting needle surrounded with a coil of wire, which he attached to a violin to act as a sound box. This, unbelievably, reproduced the sound received by the bung covered with sausage skin — and gave rise to the first telephone.

Most of the older telephones found today are of the Ericsson type and eminate from Sweden, Denmark, France, Germany or Britain. There are particularly fine examples among these with their polished mahogany and walnut stands and brass and copper fittings.

Apart from those of a domestic nature there is also a ready market for military field telephones from both wars and also for the old red G.P.O. telephone boxes themselves — ideal for their original purpose or even as a novel shower unit.

An Ericsson table telephone with hand-set supported above a column on a circular metal base, French, circa 1920, 9in. high.   £49

A Purcell Nobbs table telephone with Ericsson-type hand-set supported in a cradle, English, circa 1920, 13in. high. (Sotheby's)   £200

A table telephone with black metal case, plaque initialled K.T.A.S., with magneto handle at side, 13in. high. (Sotheby's)   £140

THIMBLES

Thimbles date back to Roman times and have been made in gold, silver, bronze, brass, pewter, iron, porcelain, enamel, ivory, bone, wood and leather.

Very early thimbles are rare and valuable and few on the market today date from earlier than the turn of the 18th/19th century. Between 1739 and 1790 silver thimbles were not hall-marked but, it may be useful for identification purposes to note that, before the middle of the eighteenth century, thimbles were hand punched and show irregularity in the indentations.

The growing interest in thimbles has led to an escalation of current values but, condition is all important if a high price is to be fetched. If the tops are perished to any extent this will detract from the value.

Chinese ivory thimble, about 1920. £5

Chelsea thimble in hinged silver filigree case, circa 1700, 2cm. high. £1,200

Meissen thimble decorated with fruit and inscription 'J' y pense', 2cm. high. £600

Art Nouveau style silver thimble. £8

Seven silver thimbles engraved with the names of the Lost Boys from 'Peter Pan'. £150

Meissen thimble, decorated in schwarzlot and gold by I. Preissler, 2.4cm. high. £4,250

Victorian silver thimble in a real leather case. £10

German, Meissen, porcelain thimble decorated in schwarzlot and gold, by I. Preissler, early 18th century, 2.4cm. high. £4,000

Victorian silver thimble in a mother-of-pearl case. £20

TILES

Although decorative tiles had been made way back in the 16th century, it wasn't until the 19th century that they achieved widespread popularity. Minton's were one of the first firms to start manufacturing again (in about 1830) with just about all the other major ceramics firms following suit as demand grew. They were used in bathrooms, kitchens, for fireplace surrounds, splashbacks, table tops, washstands, or simply framed.

Designs vary enormously from blue and white delft-ware varieties depicting canalside scenes and windmills, to stylised Art Nouveau flowers in vigorous colours made at the end of the century.

Occasionally one can still find a whole shop decorated with the most superb tiled scenes stretching right along the front, or a pub that some far-sighted licensee has had the foresight to leave tiled.

Bristol delft polychrome tile, circa 1760, 13cm. square, slightly chipped. (Christie's) £110

Late 16th/early 17th century stove tile showing Emperor Rudolph II, 11in. high. (Whiteheads) £780

Mid 17th century Dutch Delft tile, one of a set of four, slightly damaged. (Sotheby's) £140

One of ten rare Minton tiles from the Elfin series, 15.5cm. square. (Phillips) £115

18th century Italian pottery tile, painted in polychrome enamels, 11½in. high.(Robert W. Skinner Inc.) £150

Unusual De Morgan lustre tile, 9in. square, circa 1888-1897. (Sotheby's) £140

TOBACCO TINS

Cigarette and tobacco tin collecting has become very popular not only in Britain but also abroad, with collectors in America, Australia, and New Zealand. As a result, the varied and beautifully designed early tins, in good condition, are becoming increasingly scarce and consequently rising in price.

1880-1930 was probably the golden age for pictorial tins, as this period saw many tobacco companies, large and small, competing with one another in the tobacconist's window, trying to catch the eye of the smoker with their colourful tins; a pretty girl, a man about town image or more popularly a naval theme.

Sadly most of these early tobacco companies have gone, never the less, the tins can still be found and what a thrill for the collector to spot a tin bearing the name of Taddy, Lusby or Kriegsfeld.

Hignett's **'Cavalier Bright Flake'**, circa 1900-20. £10–£15

Gallaher's **'Rich Dark Honeydew'**, circa 1900-20. £15–£20

Lambert & Butler **'Log Cabin'**, circa 1900-20. £10

'Sweet Leaf' smoking mixture, circa 1900. £20

Hignetts **'Pilot Flake'**, circa 1900-20. £15–£20

Carroll's **'Mick McQuaid'** cut plug, circa 1900-10. £20

TOOLS

Medical, nautical and draughtsman's instruments have always been recognised as precision made tools worthy of the attention of collectors.

Now the old tools of all professions, vocations and crafts are appreciated for their beautiful workmanship and charm.

Those particularly sought after are, the carpenter's mortice gauges and brace and bits made of ebony and brass, also butcher's cleavers and bone saws. Woodworking chisels will form a splendid collection on their own as will the infinite variety of different sized wood-working planes.

Apart from the tools of the trade, furniture fittings and embellishments are also worthy of note. Handles, casters, hinges, and key escutcheons make an interesting collection particularly if they are chosen to show the changing styles throughout the ages.

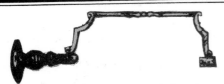

17th/18th century surgeon's iron brace with turned head, 8½in. long. (Christie's S. Kensington)					£1,080

Rare late 18th century London pattern cabinet maker's screwdriver with pinewood handle, 17in. long. (Christopher Sykes)			£24

Steel framed wheelbrace with revolving handle in beechwood, 11in. long. (Christopher Sykes)					£28

Rare lignum vitae and brass folding parallel rule and sighting instrument, circa 1900, 12in. long. (Christopher Sykes)			£75

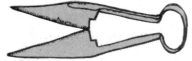

A large pair of 19th century sheep shears. (Vernon's)					£8

19th century butcher's cleaver. (Vernon's)					£25

Ebony and brass cabinet maker's mortice gauge, 7½in. long, circa 1850. (Christopher Sykes)					£25

19th century butcher's bone cutting saw with beechwood handle, circa 1860. (Christopher Sykes)					£34

A butcher's small 19th century cleaver in steel with oak handle, 13in. long. (Christopher Sykes)					£18

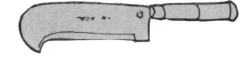

Small, Victorian butcher's cleaver. (Vernon's)					£9

Mid 19th century plumber's soldering iron, 16in. long, with turned ashwood handle. (Christopher Sykes)   £28

Copper soldering bit with wooden handle, 15in. long. (Christopher Sykes)   £18

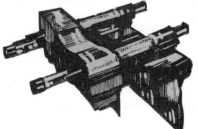

Beechwood and brass plough plane by J. Mosele, Bloomsbury, London. (Vernon's)   £25

Brass cased set of three steel fleams, circa 1820, 3½in. long. (Christopher Sykes)£28

Mid 18th century South German or Austrian gunmaker's mainspring cramp, 5in. long. (Sotheby's)   £500

Beechwood and brass plated brace by Henry Dixon, Sheffield. (Christopher Sykes)   £60

Rosewood, brass and steel cabinet maker's set square stamped 'A. Surridge', 7¾in. long, circa 1860. (Christopher Sykes)   £14

Rare circular plane by Stanley Rule & Level Co., 1877, 10¼in. long. (Christopher Sykes)   £80

Steel Scotch pattern brace by F. Soakes. (Christopher Sykes)   £50

Rare East Anglian haybond twister made from wood. (Vernon's)   £10

Antique beechwood cabinet maker's smoothing plane, circa 1850, 6¾in. long. (Christopher Sykes)   £28

Brass protractor by Godelar of Paris, 4in. diam. (Christie's)   £25

TOYS

Throughout the 19th century children were generally left to make their own entertainment with only rarely an outing to the seaside or zoo.

They certainly did not lack for toys with which to amuse themselves however, for, apart from the familiar stuffed animals or wooden playthings, there was a multitude of the new optical and mechanical devices to arouse great wonder.

Zeotropes, kaleidoscopes, phenakistiscopes, stereoscopes, magic lanterns and thaumatropes, all products of the new age of inventions. There were board games, jigsaw puzzles and model theatres for rainy days, and tops, kites, hoops and skipping ropes for sunny weather.

From Germany, there were mechanical toys galore, simply waiting to be wound up; model trains, lead soldiers, doll's houses and, standing proudly aloof, the elegant Victorian rocking horse.

Gun mounted on a tank chassis by Britain. (Phillips) £115

Early 19th century child's three-wheeled carriage. (Sotheby's) £435

French chamois-covered pig automaton, probably by Decamps, circa 1910, 10¼in. long. (Sotheby's) £88

Schoenhut 'Barney Goggle' and 'Spark Plug', Pennsylvania, circa 1924, 6in. and 7in. high. (Robert W. Skinner Inc.) £355

Late 19th century English carved wood rocking horse with horsehair mane and leather saddlery, 54in. long. (Sotheby's) £286

German hand-enamelled tinplate duck in original cardboard box, circa 1905, 7in. long. (Sotheby's) £45

French 'walking griffon' automaton, circa 1920, 14in. long. (Sotheby's) £176

Rare 1930's model of a police car by Britain, in original box. (Phillips) £240

German tin auto by Whitan Co., circa 1925, 13½in. long. (Robert W. Skinner Inc.) £95

Child's American pedal car, circa 1925, by Steelcraft, 36in. long. (Robert W. Skinner Inc.) £185

Philip Vielmetter tinplate drawing clown, 5in. wide, circa 1905, with six metal cams. (Sotheby's) £350

Bing tinplate tram with clockwork mechanism, circa 1920, 7in. long, slightly rusted. (Sotheby's) £275

Large hand-enamelled tinplate limousine, probably by Carette, circa 1911, 16½in. long. (Sotheby's) £700

Child's French tinplate cooking stove complete with utensils, circa 1900, 17½in. wide. (Sotheby's) £165

Early 20th century pull-along barking dog, English, 1ft.2in. high.(Sotheby's) £125

Child's French 'galloper' tricycle with applied mane, tail and saddlery, circa 1880, 29in. long. (Sotheby's) £528

Clockwork model, a 'Zilotone', by Wolverine Supply & Manufacturing Co., circa 1930. (Sotheby, King & Chasemore) £170

Distler clockwork organ grinder, circa 1923, German, 7in. high. (Sotheby's) £455

Early 20th century German clockwork clown toy, 9in. high. (Sotheby's) £50

Early German hand-enamelled tinplate carousel, 15¼in. high, circa 1895. (Sotheby's) £495

French clockwork tricyclist, circa 1870, with bisque head and original clothes.(Phillips) £520

German Arnold tinplate motorcycle, 8in. long, circa 1950. (Sotheby's) £110

German tinplate clockwork 'Jolly Sambo', 6¾in. high, circa 1920. (Sotheby's) £135

There are a multitude of interesting vehicles about just waiting to be welcomed into a good home.

Some of the Brougham coaches, spider phaetons or governess carts are a little on the large size but a start can be made with something smaller such as a knifegrinder's cart or that from a baker's roundsman or ice cream seller.

You have to have the room of course, or the reason, before you start buying Romany Vardos or Model T Fords but over the years they have proved to be a sound investment. The beauty is that most vehicles will be your ticket to attend innumerable annual gatherings of like minded people who have also bought a wheeled extravaganza.

19th century horse-drawn hearse. £1,500

Late 19th century Russian painted wooden sledge.   £500

French pastry cook's van, circa 1900. £1,000

Late 18th century hard-topped Surrey with iron-rimmed wheels.   £3,000

Wooden Victorian dogcart. £300

A Victorian upholstered bathchair. £150

Beautifully restored Romany Vardo. £4,000

19th century hand milk float of iron and wood, 61in. high. £200

Governess cart by Wade of Norwich, circa 1900, 10ft. long overall. £700

1924 Model T Ford with original engine and bread van body. £3,000

TREEN

Treen, according to the dictionary, means "of a tree". It is also used as a collective term for innumerable wooden articles, usually turned on a lathe, which were in everyday use in the home, as well as by trades-people, farmers and the professions, particularly apothecaries.

The variety of objects embraced by the term is endless and includes bowls, spoons, goblets, coasters, moulds, napkin rings, egg-cups, mortars, boxes and boot trees — in fact just about everything was made of wood if it could fulfil its function adequately, for it was the cheapest available material.

Articles used "below stairs" were often left quite plain but those elevated to drawing-room status, such as seal boxes, chess sets and watch stands, were usually inlaid with ivory, mother-of-pearl or various coloured woods. More exotic pieces were painted and lacquered or even inlaid with coloured glass, which doubles or even trebles their value.

Late 18th century lignum vitae coffee mill, 9in. high. (Sotheby's) £130

18th century squat fruitwood mortar, 3in. high, sold with another. (Sotheby's) £60

18th century turned cherry-wood tobacco jar, 5½in. high. (Sotheby's) £80

Lignum vitae apothecary's mortar, 5¼in. high, circa 1800, sold with another. (Sotheby's) £60

Large 18th century lignum vitae cup, 19in. high. (Butler & Hatch Waterman) £400

18th century English yew-wood rushlight nip, 11½in. high. (Sotheby's) £280

TSUBAS

Tsubas (hand protectors from a Japanese sword) are usually about 2in. across, are made of iron, brass or copper — occasionally with gold or silver decoration — and have a wedge-shaped hole in the centre for the blade (tang). There are usually other openings for the sword knife (kogatawa) and skewer (kogai).

Some are simply patterned while others bear decoration, either inlaid or applied, depicting a variety of subjects including landscapes, animals, historical events and folklore. Later examples were sometimes decorated with cloisonne or Champleve enamel.

At first they were made by the swordsmith but as they became more important armourers took over their production until finally specialist craftsmen emerged who made nothing but tsubas.

Higo school tsuba of circular form, 7.3cm. high, unsigned. (Sotheby's) £60

Iron Choshu tsuba carved and pierced as a carp, signed Choshu Hagi Ju Toyoaki Saku. (Sotheby's) £190

Soten school tsuba of circular form, pierced within the rim, unsigned, 8.3cm. high. (Sotheby's) £132

Tsuba formed of red copper and sentoku plate, signed Tshiguro Masatsune, 9cm. (Sotheby's) £2,100

Shibuichi tsuba by Seiryoken Katsuhira featuring the three Sake tasters. (Sotheby's) £5,000

Solid silver tsuba carved over both surfaces, 7.2cm. (Sotheby's) £210

Iron tsuba of the Hiragiya school. (Sotheby's) £600

One of three 19th century Japanese cut-out iron tsubas of round shape, signed. (Robert W. Skinner Inc.) £95

Oval tsuba applied in silver, gold and coloured enamels, unsigned, 7.9cm. long. (Sotheby's) £374

426

TSUBAS

Large armourer's tsuba by Hamano Noriyuki. (Sotheby's) £1,000

Kinai school tsuba of mokko form, pierced with a rain dragon, eye in gold, 8.1cm. high, signed Echizen ju Kinai saku. (Sotheby's) £66

Tsuba of mokko form, by Mikami Yoshihide, 6.4cm. high. (Sotheby's) £750

19th century unsigned Shakudo mokko tsuba decorated with a dragon, 8cm. high. (Christie's) £240

Iron Migaki-Ji tsuba, unsigned, Shoami School, 8.2cm. high. (Christie's) £160

Rare copper tsuba decorated in katakiri with a pair of Sumo wrestlers. (Sotheby's) £1,200

Shakudo Nanako tsuba by Yanagawa Naomasa. (Sotheby's) £1,600

Iron tsuba, 7.7cm., signed Sunagawa Masayoshi. (Sotheby's) £320

Shakudo tsuba decorated in relief, silver and copper inlay, 6.7cm., signed Juryusai Yoshinari. (Sotheby's) £600

Circular tsuba, pierced and applied in relief, 8.2cm. long, signed Tetsugendo. (Sotheby's) £319

Tsuba of mokko form applied with two spiders, details in silver and gold nunome, 7.9cm. high, signed Chikatoshi. (Sotheby's) £187

Sukashi tsuba of oval form, details in gold nunome and copper, 7.9cm. high, unsigned. (Sotheby's) £110

TUNBRIDGEWARE

In the 17th century, visitors flocked to take the waters at the spa town of Tunbridge Wells in Kent. Local craftsmen, eager to meet the demands of a growing souvenir trade, developed a method of producing thin sheets of patterned veneer known as Tunbridgeware or 'English mosaic'. Thin strips of different woods in a variety of colours, were set in an arranged pattern then stuck together to form a block from which thin sheets could be cut. This way the pattern could be repeated over and over again. The decorative veneer was applied to a great variety of objects and in particular to boxes.

The earliest pattern was made up of cube shapes and later veneers show a great number of intricate designs including flowers, birds and landscapes.

The popularity of Tunbridgeware continued throughout the 18th and 19th centuries and it is from this period that most examples originate; the last firm in production was Boyce, Brown and Kemp 1837-1927.

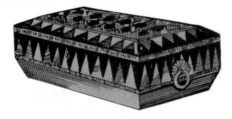

Regency Tunbridgeware box inlaid with cube pattern, circa 1820, 12in. wide. (Sotheby's) £170

Tunbridgeware rosewood bookstand with serpentine support, 14in. wide, circa 1860. (Sotheby's) £140

Tunbridgeware coromandel box by Thos. Barton, circa 1870, 9½in. wide. (Sotheby's) £250

Mid 19th century Tunbridgeware coromandel box by Thos. Barton, enclosing three graduated drawers, 8in. wide. (Sotheby's) £65

Adjustable Tunbridgeware bookshelf with two arched ends, circa 1870, 11½in. wide, closed. (Sotheby's) £130

Rosewood Tunbridgeware writing slope with a view of Hever Castle, circa 1870, 12in. wide. (Sotheby's) £270

TYPEWRITERS

Many 19th century typewriters had a double keyboard with one key for each capital together with one for each of the small letters and the major disadvantage of most was that it was impossible to read the typed sheet until after the work had been completed.

The breakthrough came with a machine, based on a design by Sholes, incorporating the shift key mechanism — very much on the same principal as modern manual machines.

In the first ten years of manufacture **50,000** were sold by Remington, Oliver, Smith, Underwood and Yost; names still well to the fore in typewriter manufacture today.

Interest in these early machines has increased considerably and the trends of the last few years, points to a worthwhile investment.

Rare Merritt typewriter, linear index mechanism, with plunger selector, circa 1895, 12¼in. wide. (Sotheby's)   £715

Williams No. 2 typewriter with grasshopper action type bars, length of platen 8¼in., circa 1893. (Sotheby's)   £352

Williams No. 3 typewriter with grasshopper action type bars, circa 1895, length of platen 13in. (Sotheby's)   £352

Rare Corona special folding typewriter in red lacquer body, circa 1910, 12¼in. wide. (Sotheby's)   £220

American Columbia typewriter No. 2, with circular letter index, 9¾in. wide, circa 1890. (Sotheby's)   £440

Rare Hammond No. 1 typewriter with swinging sector mechanism, circa 1886, 14in. wide. (Sotheby's)   £660

VALENTINE CARDS

Some of the prettiest Valentine cards come from the Victorian period and many display a profusion of ribbon, gilding, tiny metal mirrors and an intriguing series of paper lace lift-up flaps concealing a motto or love poem. The notion of the lift-up flap was introduced by an American, Miss Howland, who produced Valentine cards between 1849-1881 in Worcester, Massachusetts.

A fruitful source of material can often be found in old scrapbooks, where the treasured card was placed for safe keeping — and to be shown off.

Condition is important, with pristine examples obtaining tens of pounds rather than two or three.

'Pop-Up' Valentine card, circa 1920. £2

Embossed Valentine card 'My Comfort and My Joy', late 19th century. £3

Embossed Valentine card 'My Darling Still', with verse by J. T. Wood. £4

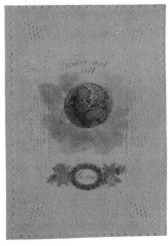

Lace paper Valentine card 'Thou art all the world to me', late 19th century. £4

Lace paper Valentine card 'Like an Oyster in Love'. £7

Mid 19th century lace paper Valentine card 'When you can still the rolling sea'. £5

Comic Valentine card 'To Arms, to Arms, ye British brave'. £10

Mid 19th century lace paper Valentine card 'Can you tell me how to build a happy home'. £10

VINAIGRETTES

There were many thousands of small useful boxes and among the most precious — and the smallest — are those known by the unlikely name of 'vinaigrettes'.

Descendants of the pomander and, before that, the pomme d'ambre, vinaigrettes began to appear towards the end of the 18th century. Their function was to contain, under a pierced grille, a small piece of sponge or wadding soaked in aromatic oils and 'vinegars' whose vapours were thought to ward off disease and could be sniffed to counteract the less pleasant effluvia not uncommonly encountered in the days before efficient municipal refuse collection.

These little boxes were carried either in a pocket, muff or purse or, were worn suspended from a chain on a chatelaine or pocket watch and some have little fixing rings attached. The inside was almost invariably gilded to avoid corrosion.

Occasionally made of gold but more commonly of silver, pinchbeck, glass or porcelain and sometimes inset with precious stones, vinaigrettes have the advantage over many collectible items in that they are usually particularly beautifully made and, being so often constructed of precious metals, they are fairly certain to resist those fluctuations of fashion which can so easily undermine the investment potential of less stable items.

Prices and values naturally vary according to the maker, quality, material, age and condition of the pieces. Vinaigrettes by Nathaniel Mills are particularly desirable, especially those with embossed scenic views on the lid.

William IV silver gilt vinaigrette of oblong form, by Nathaniel Mills, Birmingham, 1835, 2in. long. (Sotheby's)   £187

Large rectangular vinaigrette by Francis Clark, Birmingham, 1845, 5.1cm. long. (Sotheby's)   £572

George III silver articulated fish vinaigrette, Birmingham, 1817. (Bonham's)   £265

Rectangular silver gilt vinaigrette with view, by Taylor & Perry, Birmingham, 1836, 5cm. long. (Sotheby's)   £462

VINAIGRETTES

Silver vinaigrette as a purse by L. & C., Birmingham, 1817. (Sotheby's) £225

Turquoise set oval vinaigrette in gold coloured metal. (Sotheby's) £300

Unusual vinaigrette in gold colour with aventurine cover and base, circa 1820. (Sotheby's) £235

George IV silver gilt vinaigrette by Nathaniel Mills, Birmingham, 1827, 1½in. long. (Sotheby's) £154

Good silver gilt vinaigrette posy holder with red hardstone cap, by Thos. Wm. Dee, London, 1866, 155gm. (Sotheby's) £950

Victorian shaped rectangular vinaigrette by Yapp & Woodward, Birmingham, 1845, 1¾in. wide. (Lawrence Fine Art) £80

Small shaped rectangular vinaigrette by Edward Smith, Birmingham, 1855, 2.6cm. long. (Sotheby's) £65

Silver vinaigrette in the form of a watch by J. Lilly, Birmingham, 1815. (Sotheby's) £280

George IV silver gilt vinaigrette, by W. S., Birmingham, 1825, 1½in. wide. (Lawrence Fine Art) £120

George III purse-shaped vinaigrette by John Shaw, Birmingham, 1819, 1¼in. wide. (Sotheby's) £255

Silver gilt vinaigrette in the form of a lamp, by H. W. & L. Dee, London, 1870, 3.4cm. high. (Sotheby's) £462

George IV vinaigrette in the form of a flower-filled basket, by John Shaw, Birmingham, 1820, 1in. long. (Sotheby's) £418

WALKING STICKS

The walking stick, an indispensable accessory for the 17th/18th century man-about-town, was fashioned in a limitless variety of designs, the least important feature being that of a support or aid to walking.

Some of the most popular materials used include cane, rosewood, fruitwoods, ebony or ash, decorated with ivory, bone, shark's vertebrae or rhinotail with the cane handles designed in an almost inexhaustible variety of shapes. (See Cane Handles).

Canes may cleverly disguise anything from a gun to a sword the mechanism activated by a carefully hidden control incorporated into the decoration.

Collectors tend to form real attachments towards their sticks; the ultimate being a famous Victorian politician who had such a high regard for his collection that, upon choosing a stick to take on an outing, he apologised in turn to each of those left behind.

A Georgian blue and gilt bladed swordstick, double edged slender blade 27in., with short slender fuller, cane scabbard, overall length 36in. (Wallis & Wallis)   £80

An unusual cellarman's combinate walking stick and barrel measure, 37in. overall, with brass ferrule and turned ebony top unscrewing to reveal 36in. wooden measure graduated in gallons, stamped 'Cook Maker to the Honble. Board of Excise, Late Wellington Crown Court Soho London'. (Wallis & Wallis)   £65

A late Victorian walking cane with concealed horse measuring instrument, 37in. overall, the gnarled handle pulls away from silver ferrule to reveal a calibrated boxwood measure in hands, inches and metres with folding brass pointer, total capability, 5ft.6½in. (16 hands 2½). (Wallis & Wallis)   £30

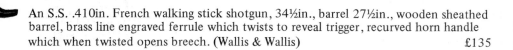

An S.S. .410in. French walking stick shotgun, 34½in., barrel 27½in., wooden sheathed barrel, brass line engraved ferrule which twists to reveal trigger, recurved horn handle which when twisted opens breech. (Wallis & Wallis)   £135

A Victorian artist's walking cane, 35in., unscrews in four sections with silvered copper fittings to reveal glass lined ink well, pen, pencil and ruling sections. (Wallis & Wallis) £65

WATCHSTANDS

Watchstands have been in use for some **400** years but, as with most other antique objects, the largest numbers of surviving (and, for the average collector, the only realistically priced) specimens date from the 19th century.

Early 19th century examples are typically of the one-pillar type, usually of wood but not uncommonly of brass, agate or marble. Some were of rigid construction, but better examples often contained a pivot which allowed the watch to be tilted to a convenient viewing angle. Because of the materials used in their construction, and because of their rudimentary design, watchstands of this type are placed at the lower end of the scale.

The "wellhead" design consists of two pillars joined at the top by an arch from which the watch was suspended. Another two-pillar design encloses a pivoted holder for the watch, and sometimes has a short, central pillar on which might be a small mirror or pin cushion. Others, without the central pillar, are usually dished to take rings, studs and other trinkets.

A third variety, known as the "triangular prismatic watchstand" from its shape, is usually of hard wood, often beautifully inlaid, and quite commonly has a small door at the back giving access to the velvet-lined interior. A variant on the same theme has opening front and back panels, the watch being safely contained inside for travelling.

Purpose-built travelling watchstands were made to several designs, usually with some souvenir-type decoration. Some have hinged lids which, in the in-use position, are propped open by a flap pivoted from the front of the piece and fitted with a stud or hook from which the watch hangs against its dished backing. These pieces are usually beautifully made, often with locks embellished with ivory, bone or brass escutcheons.

20th century American ebony and ivory watchstand, 6¼in. high. £150

A French Napoleonic prisoner-of-war carved bone watchstand, in the form of a classical arch supported by two Roman soldiers, height 8¾in., width 6in. £180

German porcelain watch holder entitled 'Gravelotte'. £150

WATCHES

Although watches with single hands were made in the 17th century it wasn't until the 18th century that the need for an accurate timepiece was required specifically as an aid to navigation aboard ship.

This prompted a number of significant developments such as, the lever and cylinder escapement and established a wealth of watchmakers whose work is most sought after today. Among them are Mudge, Tompion, Graham, Quare, Frodsham, Breguet, Leroux, Barraud and Ellicott.

Watches were originally carried in the 'fob pocket' in the waistband of the trousers only moving up to the waistcoat pocket in the 19th century. Wrist watches are basically a product of the 20th century.

Recent manufacturers to look for are Rolex, Movado, Piquet and Cartier.

An unusual gold plated calendar wrist watch by Brevet, the movement with compensation balance. (Sotheby's) £165

A wrist watch by Movado, the lever movement with compensation balance. (Sotheby's) £572

Gold plated calendar wrist watch, the dial signed Bavet, Swiss made. (Sotheby's) £110

A good and rare mysterieuse wrist watch by Vacheron & Constantin, Geneve. (Sotheby's) £1,430

An 18 carat gold turnover wrist watch by Lisica S.A. (Sotheby's) £627

An unusual gold automatic wrist watch by Jaeger Le Coultre. (Sotheby's) £330

A 9 carat gold automatic wrist watch by Rolls, the self-winding movement with various numbers. (Sotheby's) £286

A steel digital wrist watch stamped Brevet, the seconds dial rotating within the minute dial. (Sotheby's) £82

18 carat gold lady's digital wrist watch, the sixteen jewel movement with compensation balance. (Sotheby's) £264

A gold plated centre seconds calendar wrist watch signed Pierpont. (Sotheby's) £132

A calendar wrist watch by Universal, Geneve, with compensation balance. (Sotheby's) £319

A gold plated calendar wrist watch by Record Watch Co., Geneva. (Sotheby's) £88

An automatic alarm wrist watch by Jaeger Le Coultre, circa 1950. (Sotheby's)£440

A Prinz wrist watch by Rolex, the fifteen jewel movement with compensation balance. (Sotheby's) £880

A calendar chronograph wrist watch by Universal, Geneva, circa 1945. (Sotheby's) £935

WATCHES

A fine calendar wrist watch by Audemars Piquet with compensation balance. (Sotheby's) £2,090

An automatic wrist watch by Harwood, the self-winding lever movement with compensation balance. (Sotheby's) £363

A calendar wrist watch by Omega, the seventeen jewel movement with compensation balance. (Sotheby's) £1,100

A 9 carat gold wrist watch signed Kendal & Dent, Birmingham, 1940. (Sotheby's) £121

A chronograph wrist watch with exposed steel chronograph mechanism. (Sotheby's) £297

Lady's wrist watch by Cartier, the movement stamped European Watch & Clock Co. (Sotheby's) £660

A wrist watch by Hamilton, U.S.A., inscribed Glenn Miller. (Sotheby's) £440

A gold plated calendar wrist watch by Record Watch Co., Geneve. (Sotheby's) £115

An unusual silver self-winding wrist watch, the movement on a sliding platform. (Sotheby's) £385

A good and rare automatic perpetual calendar chronometer wrist watch by Rolex. (Sotheby's) £3,300

A gold digital wrist watch by Movado, the fifteen jewel movement with compensation balance. (Sotheby's) £616

A good and fine oyster perpetual calendar wrist watch by Rolex. (Sotheby's) £3,740

An enamelled lady's wrist watch by Optima, circa 1925. (Sotheby's) £115

A good 18 carat yellow and white gold Rolex Prince wrist watch. (Sotheby's) £1,760

A gold plated chronograph wrist watch, the lever movement with compensation balance. (Sotheby's) £77

A gold plated calendar chronograph wrist watch, stamped Buttes Watch Co. (Sotheby's) £88

A gold plated wrist watch by Vacheron & Constantin. (Sotheby's) £99

A gold chronograph wrist watch signed Exactus, Swiss made. (Sotheby's) £110

WEATHERVANES

If there was any doubt that collecting weathervanes is a subject for serious investment, it was dispelled recently in America when an entire auction was devoted to the sale of just one weathervane with historical connections to the patriot Paul Revere.

Weathervanes have also been disappearing mysteriously from atop some of the highest churches in New York State as the result of daring helicopter raids at dawn, no less. A sure indication of their worth.

American weathervanes tend to be more adventurous in their design than their British counterpart and feature running horses, Red Indians, stagecoaches, sailing ships and butterflies as well as the universal cockerel.

Late 19th century American gilded stage-coach weathervane on modern tripod base, 34½in. long. (Robert W. Skinner Inc.) £230

19th century copper eagle weathervane from Massachusetts, 30in. long. (Robert W. Skinner Inc.) £330

20th century wrought iron and copper pea fowl weathervane, American, 30½in. wide. (Robert W. Skinner Inc.) £380

Mid 19th century American metal rooster weathervane, 24in. high. (Robert W. Skinner Inc.) £695

Late 19th century sheet metal butterfly weathervane, American, in copper. (Robert W. Skinner Inc.) £605

Copper running horse weathervane with hollow body, 23½in. high. (C. G. Sloan & Co. Inc.) £200

WHISTLES

New collectors tend to gather these little whistles without much system or discrimination then, realising that there are so many different types and styles, they quickly start to specialise.

Dog whistles and those in the form of a dog are particularly attractive, especially those made of porcelain by the Derby factory.

Others collect just military or police whistles including the bosun's call which is often made of silver and has a special fascination all of its own.

There are whistles for train guards and whistles for referees but most interesting of all are those disguised within the form of another object, such as, a penknife, spoon, peeper, pencil, or tape measure.

Materials will include silver, gold, jet, agate, brass, porcelain, wood and ivory.

Victorian silver whistle and penknife, London 1879.   £175

Silver police whistle, dated 1888.   £60

Victorian carved jet whistle.   £50

George III silver bosun's call.   £140

Bulbous-shaped whistle in chased silver, 1901.   £60

Early 19th century Derby whistle, 4.5cm. wide.   £200

Victorian army officer's silver whistle. £80

Good quality silver military whistle and case with Tudor rose deocration.   £250

WOOD

Prior to the 18th century, the average piece of English pottery was a pretty crude affair but, with the discovery of a hard white stoneware suitable for more delicate modelling, a new era dawned.

Part of the glazing process involved throwing common salt on the pottery while it was still in the kiln, the heat causing it to combine with the surface of the object to form a vitreous coating — hence the term "saltglaze". Figures glazed in this way were extensively made in Staffordshire, notably by Wedgwood and Astbury, and later by the Wood family throughout the 18th and early 19th century.

Ralph Wood, Senior (1715–72) and his brother Aaron (1717–85), sons of a Chedleton miller, developed a unique style for their productions, perpetuated by their respective sons, Ralph Jr. (1748–95) and Enoch (1759–1840). Their products were particularly noted for their delicate colouring and fine design but Aaron's son, Enoch, was later tempted by the prospect of increased production, as a result of the industrial revolution, and a good deal of the quality associated with the family was lost in the process.

All of their wares are clearly marked. The rarest of these takes the form of an impressed 'R. Wood', which although taken to be the work of Ralph Wood Senior has been recorded as late as 1794; 22 years after his death.

Enoch Wood started his own factory in 1784 and later, in 1790, went into a partnership with James Caldwell which continued trading successfully until 1818. During this time they shipped vast quantities of their tableware to America marked 'Wood & Caldwell' impressed around an American eagle.

Ralph Wood figure of a recumbent goat, horns and ears restored, circa 1780, 18cm. wide. (Christie's) £380

Ralph Wood figure of a squirrel seated on his haunches, circa 1775, 18.5cm. high. (Christie's) £1,000

Ralph Wood group of St. George and the Dragon, circa 1700, restored, 10¾in. high. (Sotheby's) £506

Ralph Wood Toby jug, seated, wearing a reddish-brown coat and yellow breeches, 25cm. high high. (H. Spencer & Sons Ltd.) £450

An interesting marked Ralph Wood mask-jug with a satyr's smiling face, 8½in. high, circa 1770. (Christie's) £480

An inscribed and dated Ralph Wood jug of large size, modelled by Jean Voyez, 9½in. high, 1788. (Sotheby's) £440

INDEX

Aberdeen Banking Co. 49
Academy 221
A Cat, A Cat 193
Actors 115
Adam's 68, 332
Adamson R. & D. O. Hill 316
Adolphus Won't Tell Papa 193
Adventure 135
Advertising Signs 11-15
Aeolian Vocalion 216, 222
Aeroplane Markings 113
After Marriage 192
After The Race 1875 325
After You 196
Ahrens 25
Air Raid Precautions 112, 115
A.L. 240
Alexander, Madame 180, 181
Alexandre, T. 345
Allen, A. H. 284
Aller Vale 286
All Gay 124
All Over 196
Amio 126
Am I Right. . .? 196
Amplion 358
Amusement Machines 22-25
Andersen, Hans C. 106
Anderson, V. 339
Animalia 26, 27
A Nip On The Sly 194
Anti Vivisectors 325
Apache 17, 18, 19, 20
A Pastoral Visit 194
Apple Blossom 123
Applied Electricity 117
Arcadian China 155
Archer, Frederick Scott 320
Ark Royal 125
Armour 28, 29
Arms & Armour 115
Army Signs 114, 115
Arnold 422
Arthurs Silver Steel 219
Arts & Crafts 400
Ashbee, C. R. 401
A Spicey Bit 193
Association Cup Winners 115
Astrophilogeon 101
At Ease 124
Athenaeum Fire Office 201
Attack 197
Auden, W. H. 34
Audiotek/Cadec 370
Ault, N. & L. 107
Autograph Letters 30-37
Automatons 38-40

Automobilia 41-43
Aylesbury Market Place 322
Aynsley China 155

Baby's First Step 196
Baccarat 308
Bach, Carl 36
Badges 44-46
Baeyens, L. 338
Bainbridge, Wm. 295
Bakst, Leon 150, 151, 153
Balmoral China 155
Bandit 127
Bandmaster 126
Banger, S. 348
Bank of England 47, 50
Bank of Poyais 47
Bank of Scotland 48, 49, 50
Barbedienne 26
Barker, Susannah 91
Barlow, F. 185
Barlow, H. & E. E.
    Stormer 185
Barn Owl 65
Barrel Bitters 79
Barton, Thos. 428
Barye, Antoine Louis 80, 81
Bateman, Hester 400
Bathing Machine 155
Bath Fire Office 203
Bath Sun Fire 202
Batman Annual 108
Battie, Wm. 73
Bavet 436
Bazu Band 29
B.D.V. Sports 125
Beales 63
Beame-Miller, A. 338
Beano, The 132
Beaton, Cecil 151, 152, 153
Beaumont,Adams 333
Bebe 40
Beer Bottle Labels 53-57
Beeson, J. S. 282
Beethoven, Ludwig Van 35
Begay, Harrison 21
Beilby, W. & M. 159
Belcher, Jonathan 30
Belleek 58
Belliene 93
Bell Punch Co. Ltd. 84
Bells 59
Beltona 218
Ben Akiba 96

Bendon, George 292
Benois, Alex. 150-153
Bentivoglio, Cardinal 35
Berlin 158, 239
Berliner 222
Berlin Woolwork 60
Bersaglieri 51
Berthon, Paul 343-345
Bestone 359
Beware of a Collision 194
Bibber, O. S. 161
Bible Boxes 61
Bicycles 62, 63
Biggs, Roger 305
Bilikin 156
Bilinsky, B. 151
Billiards 115
Bilston 189, 190,
    310, 398
Bing 278, 282, 421
Bird Cages 64
Bird In Hand 126
Birds 65
Birds & Eggs 113
Birds Eggs 117
Birmingham 189, 310, 410
Biscuit Tins 66
Bizarre 130
Black-Bellied Plover 162, 163,
    165
Black Duck 162, 163
Blaeu, Johannes 255
Bleriot 43
Bligh, William 72
Bonaparte, Napoleon 34
Boneshaker 63
Bonnard, Pierre 343
Bonsa 144
Bontems 39
Books 69-75
Boosey & Co. 295
Bosco 93
Bottger 413
Bottles 76-79
Boucher 189
Boulet, C. 338
Bourgoin 180
Bovril 76
Bow 403
Bowick, T. 104
Boy Scouts 114, 117
Boys Dream, The 135
Boxers 119
Brandt, Bill 319
Brant 163
Breast Plate 28, 29
Brevet 436, 437

Bridge at Llangollen 323
Bridge, John 296
Bright, J. 280
Bristol 103, 335, 410, 416
Bristol Crown Fire Office 202
Britain's 244, 245, 278, 421
British Birds 115
British Linen Co. 48
British Warriors 119
Britannia (Minerva) 217
Broadbill Drake 162, 163
Broadbill Hen 164, 165
Broadcasting 118
Brogden, D. A. 280
Bronze Animals 80
Brooke Bond Tea 11
Brooks, John 67
Brouillet, A. 338
Brown Bear 26
Brown, Lancelot 33
Bruguier 291
Bru Jeune 179
Brunswick 52
Bryant & May 260, 261, 263,
    264
Buckland-Wright, John 71
Buckles 82, 83
Buffalo 27
Bull, John 15
Bulldog 156
Bunker, S. 285
Burglar, The 22
Burnet, Gilbert 31
Burrows & Pearce 296
Bus Tickets 84-89
Butler, Frank A. 185
Butter Stamps 90
Buttes Watch Co. 439
Buttons 91
Byron, Lord 30
By The Roadside 114

Cadbury's 15
Cadiou, A. 399
Caernarvon to Liverpool 324
Caille 22, 25
Cake Walk, The 153
Calcutta Exhibition 321
Caldecott, Randolph 104
Caledonian Banking Co. 47
Cameras 92-95
Cameron, J. M. 311
Canada Goose 162, 163
Cane Handles 96
Canon 94

Canvasback Drake 165
Canvasback Hen 164
Capitol 372
Capitoline Wolf 81
Car Mascots 97
Card Cases 98
Cards 99-101
Carette 421
Carlisle Cathedral 323
Carnival Glass 122
Caroline 136, 138
Carroll, Lewis 315, 318, 320
Carroll's 419
Carter, K. 374
Cartier 83, 438
Castelli 334
Castrol 15
Cathedrals 119
Cathedrals & Abbeys 115
Caughley 67, 68
Cavalcade 122
Cayman 27
Celestion 358
Central Insurance Co. 202
Chad Valley 179
Chagall, Marc 30
Chait, Nat 122
Chamber Pots 103
Champagne Charlie 325
Champenios, F. 345
Champion, The 135
Champions of 1936 112
Chaucer, Geoffrey 72
Chanel 145, 147-149
Chantilly 145
Chapbooks 104, 106
Chappell 219
Chappell & Co. Ltd. 371
Charles II 35
Charles V 33
Chawner & Co. 227
Chelsea 334, 335, 415
Cheret, Jules 344, 345
Cheruit 145, 146
Chicago Magic 250
Children Playing 154
Children's Books 104-109
Children's Meeting 196
Chippendale 30
Chippewa 20
Choctaw 18
Choka 304
Choshu 426
Christiansen, Hans 340
Chromo 12
Cigar Bands 110
Cigarette Cards 112-119
Cigarette Cases 120, 121
Cigarette Packets 122-129
Cino Chevaux 97
Clarice Cliff 419
Clark, Francis 432
Clarkes 78
Clichy 307, 308
Clipper 128
Cloisonne 131
Clowns & Circus Artistes 114
Coal Trade 137
Cochran, Dave 163
Codd, Hiram 76, 77, 79
Coker, Ebenezer 401
Coleman 236
Columbia 249, 429
Columbia De Luxe 217
Columbia Duragold 217
Columbia Superbe 217
Columbia Triple Tin 216
Comics 132-135
Commemorative China 136-138
Companie Des Indes 68
Comyns, William 82, 83

Conklin, Hurley 163, 165
Conti 282, 283
Cooper, Phyllis 342
Cooper's Sheep Dip 13
Coot 161
Copeland 309
Copenhagen 398
Cope's Golfers 119
Copper & Brass 139-141
Corkscrews 142-144
Cornstalk 127
Corona 14, 429
Coronation Day 137
Costume 145-149
Costume Designs 150-153
Coultre, Jaeger Le 436, 437
Cousin & Cousine 324
Cowan's Whisky 14
Cowham, Hilda 105
Coxe, Alban 36
Crayol 129
Cree 21
Crested China 154-156
Cros, Chas. 318
Cross, Wm. & Sons 236
Crouch, S. 75
Crowell, A. Elmer 162-164,
  166
Crowley & Co. 184
Cruikshank 104
Crusoe, Robinson 112
Crystal Palace 64
Cundall, Dowes & Co. 311
Cups & Saucers 157, 158
Curran, A. 373
Curtis, Edward 21
Cymric 82
Czech Air Force 45

Dallmeyer 92, 95
Dampier, Capt. Wm. 254
Dandy, The 132
Dandy Dan 127
Daniell, Eva 339
Dartmouth 286
Daum 306, 382
Davey & Co. 297
Davenport, L. & Co. 249
Davies, M. 185
Dean's Rag Book Ltd. 174
Death Dive 24
Decamps 39, 420
Decanter Labels 160
Decanters 159
Decca 218, 219
Decoys 161-166
Dee, H. W. & L. 433
Dee, Thos. Wm. 433
Delamain 67
Delaspre, H. 338
Delval 345
De Morgan 167, 416
Denis, Maurice 338
Derby 158, 335, 442
Derbyshire Regt. 45
Detmold, E. H. 104
Diamond Navy Cut 129
Dick Whittington 196
Dillens, Julien 238
Dinky Toys 168-170
Dior 145, 147, 148
Disneyana 171-174
Distler 171 422
Dixon, Henry 419
Do You Know 116
Doboujinsky, Matislav 150
Dobson, Austen 104
Dogs 116
Dolls 175-181

Dolls' Houses 182, 183
Don, The 124
Donath, P. 324
Donkey 154
Donnington Castle 36
Door Stops 184
Dorsetshire Regt. 44
Doughty, Selina 379
Douglas, J. 371
Doulton 185, 186, 402, 403
Dowitcher 162
Doyle, Arthur Conan 30
Drayton, Michael 252
Dresden 157
Drew, Elixabeth 381
Drowne, Shem 364
Drunkard's Dream, The 22
Duchetti, Claudio 252, 254
Dulcken, H. W. 107
Dumfries 137
Duncan, Betsey 380
Dundee Banking Co. 49
Duplex 89
Dursley-Pederson 63
Dutch Delft 416
D.W. 204

Eared Grebe 161
East Surrey Regt. 46
Eaton, Arthur Charles 186
Eaton, Wm. 59
Edelmann, A. 338
Edison 211-223
Edison Amberola 221, 223
Edison Bell 217, 220
Edmonson 86
Edwards, Charles 328
Edwards, J. D. 311, 314
Effanbee 175
Egg Cups 187
Einstein, Albert 36
Ekco 385, 359
Electric Light Bulbs 188
Eliot, George 35
Elizabeth I 36
Elkington & Co. 305
Elliston, Robert 164
EMI 372
Email Belg 13
Embassy 218
Embassy 'Gramotube' 216
Emerson, Peter Henry 321
Emerson, Ralph 35
Emersons, Joanna 381
Emes, R. & E. Barnard 187
Empire Exhibition 113
Enamel 189
Enfield 52
English Neutrality 195
Ensign Tropical 94
Ericsson 414
Erte 151
Essex, Wm. 277
Esso Man 97
Etuis 190
Eugene of Savoy 32
European Watch & Clock Co.
  438
Evans, Walker 319
Exactus 439
Excelsior Lever 143
Exter, Alexandra 153
Eynard-Lullin, J. G. 315

Faberge 121
Fables & Their Morals 113
Facey, Mrs. 33
Fahrner 239
Fahrner, Theodor 82
Fairground Gallopers 191
Fairings 192-197

Famous Jockeys 114
Famous Scots 117
Fans 198-200
Fantastic Four, The 109
Farmers Insurance Co. 201
Fellophone 359
Fenton, R. 313, 318
Ferrier 315
F. G. 180
Film Fun 132
Film, Stage & Radio Stars 114
Fire & Life Assurance Co. 203
Firemarks 201-203
Fish & Bait 113
Fisher 207
Fishing Reels 204
Fishponds Training College 323
Five Win 23
Flags 205
Flags & Funnels 116
Flavelle, Henry 400
Fleischmann 279
Flint, H. Russell 345
Foache, A. 338
Fonteyn, Margot 153
Football, 22-Man 25
Footballers In Action 112
Forbes, William 50
Ford 424
Forth Bridge 154
Fortuny 145, 149
Fox, Charles 296
Franklins 67
Freed Eiseman 359
Frennet, J. 95
Frith, Francis 311
Fry's Chocolate 43
Furstenberg 190

Gainsborough 125
Gallaher 417
Gamage, W. 206
Gamages 249
Games 206-208
Gardening Hints 117
Garden Life 117
Gaufridy 37
Gauntlet 28-29
Gecophone 359
Gekko 304
Genco 24
Gerock 294
Gibson 84, 85
Gill, Eric 72, 73
Ginori 158
Gleason, Ken 165
Glengarry Badge 44, 45
Gloves 209
Godelar 419
Godiva, Lady 155
God Save The Queen 195
Golden Cockerel Press 70, 74
Goldeneye Drake 161, 164,
  165
Goldeneye Hen 165
Golden Pyramid 220
Golden Shred 14
Gold Flake 123
Goldscheider 210
Goldscheider, Friedrich 210
Goss 211-215, 309
Gottlieb 24
Gould, John 72
Goulding & Co. 295
Gramophone Co. Ltd. 221-223
Gramophone Needle Tins 216-
  220
Gramophone & Typewriter
  Ltd. 223
Gramophones & Phonographs
  221-223

Grand Parade 128
Gray, C. 297
Gray, Gustave Le 311
Great Auk 65
Great Blue Heron 165
Greater Yellowlegs 165
Great Race 25
Greenaway, Kate 104
Greenock Bank Co. 48
Greenwing Teal Drake 165
Greenwood, James 106
Greinder & Herda 325
Greyfriars Herald 135
Greys, The 126
Guangxu 238
Guerlain 383
Gugel, Iohan Georg 399
Guild of Handicrafts Ltd. 401
Gwatkin, Theophila 34
Gwin, James & Simon-
   Francois 160
Gyokukozan 301, 303

Haag, Carl 320
Haertel, Harold 161
Haida 16-18, 20
Hair Combs 224
Hakuryu 300
Hall, Wm. Snooke 160
Hamilton, Lady Emma 33
Hamilton, U.S.A. 438
Hammond 429
Hans 321
Hants, Sussex & Dorset
   Security 201
Happy Father What Two? 195
Hardy Bros. 204
Harmonicor 294
Harper, John & Co. 288
Harradine, L. 186
Harrow Rifles, The 45
Hart, W. 72
Hartford Militia 46
Harwood 438
Hassall, John 104
Hat Pins 225
Hats 226
Haunted Churchyard 24
Haunted House 22
Hauptman, Gerhardt 319
Hawarden, Lady C. 317, 320
Hawksley 349
Hawksley, G. & J. W. 349
Hays Decoy Co. 162
Heart's Delight 126
Heath Robinson, W. 105
Hedgehog 27
Heemkerk, Willem Van 76
Heideloff, N. 75
Hemard, J. 338
Henry VIII 30
Herbinier, Louis G. 341
Herman, Ralph 401
Heroes 119
Heron, Douglas 50
Herouard 108
Herring Gull 164, 165
Hertfordshire Regt. 44
Heubach 177, 178, 180
Hewat, A. 317
Hiam, Frank 250
Hidden Beauties 116
Hignett 417
Higo 426
Hill 294
Hilliard & Thomason 98, 305,
   384
Hiragiya 426
His First Pair 195
His Master's Voice 217
Hit Him Hard 197

HMV 220
Hobson, H. 83
Hobson's 251
Hodgesinn 353
Hojitsu 304
Hokosai 303
Hollie Point 242
Holmes, Ben 161
Homann, J. B. 253
Hooper, Wm. Willoughby 312,
   319, 321
Hopkins & Allen 333
Horn 227
Horse Brasses 228
Horsfall, J. B. 33
Household Hints 119
How to Swim 117
Howitt, Samuel 70
Howlett, Robt. & G. Downes
   315
Hudsonian Curlew 164
Humphreys, W. R. 365
Hunslet Engine Co. Ltd. 362
Hunt, Sara Ann 380
Hunter, James 50
Huntingdonshire Regt. 46
Huntley & Palmers 13, 66
Huret 181
Hutton, W. 400

Icons 229-232
Ideal Novlety & Toy Co. 172
I'm First Sir 192
Imari 335
Indianware 16-21
Inros 233-235
International Baby Carriage
   Store 350
International Reel Co. 25
Irons 236
Ironsides 126
Iroquois 19
Island Queen 128
Ivory 237, 238

Jackson 332
Jacobs 52, 66
Jacobs Sc., F. M. 237
Jacquet-Droz 38
Jelly Mould 140
Jennens & Bettridge 207
Jeu Des Drapeaux 101
Jewellery 239, 240
Jivaro 17
Joan of Arc 101
Johilco 245
Johnson, Lloyd J. 166
Johnson, T. 265
Johnson, Thomas W. 32
Jokasai 233
Jolly Sailor 127
Jones, E. D. 78
Jones, George & Sons 335
Jumeau 39, 40, 176
Jumeau, Emile 177, 179-181
Junior Monarch 222
Juster, Joe 167

Kajikawa 235
Kammer & Reinhardt 179
Kandinsky, Wassily 346
Karashishi 301 302 304
Keats, John 71, 74
Kendal & Dent 438
Kennedy 99
Kenrick 236
Kensitas 129
Kenzan 235
Kertesz, Andre 316
Kestner 177, 178
Kestner, J. D. 176, 177, 179

Keys 241
Kikugawa 302
Kilner, Dorothy 104
Kinai 427
Kinema, The 135
King of Abyssinia 103
King, Jessie M. 104
King, Joe 166
King Midas 124
King of the Road 42, 43
Kings College 98
King's Own Borderers 45, 46
Kings of Speed 119
Kinkozan 413
Kirkby Stephen 323
Kirchner, Raphael 337, 339,
   340-342
Kisan 301
Kitchin, Miss 318, 320, 321
Kitchin, Xie 318, 321
Knapton, John 252
Knockout 133
Knox, Archibald 246, 401
Kodak 94
Kohler 295
Kolster Brandes 358
Koma Koryu 233, 234
Koma Kyuhaku 235
Koraku 303
Koryusai 233
Kosen 303
Krauss-Zeiss 93
Kropp, Sheffield 365
Kuhn, Heinrich 319, 321
Kwakiuth 16
Kyprinos Cyprus 128

L. & C. 433
Lace 242
Lafayette 67
Lalique 159, 239, 382, 383
Lalique, R. 306-308, 383
Lambert 39, 40
Lambert, H. 316
Lambert & Butler 417
Lamy, Jerome T. 295
Lancashire Clog 156
Lane Fox 188
Lang, Andrew 104, 105
Laughing Sailor 23
Lawn Tennis Strokes 119
Lawrance, A. C. 94
Lawson, Oliver 163
Leach 243
Leach, Bernard 243
Lead Soldiers 244, 245
Lear, Edward 32, 74, 104
Leas Shelter, The 323
Lecoultre 291
Lecoultre Freres 292
Ledsham Vale & Wheeler 398
Lee, A. 284
Leeds 335
Leger, F. 151
Leigh, Conrad D. 344
Lenci 175
Lennon, John 373-375
Leopard Skin 27
Lesser Yellowlegs 162
Leydet, V. 338
Liberty 246
Liberty & Co. 82, 83, 246
Lifeboatman 156
Light Dragoons 45, 46
Lilly, J. 433
Lincoln, Joe 162
Lion 135
Lion Skin 26
Lionel 282
Lisica, S.A. 436
Little John in Trouble 325

Little Turk, A 325
Liverpool 68
Livingstone, David 33
Locherer, Alois 318
Locks 247
London 335
London Assurance 203
London Assurance Fire
   Office 202
London & Lancashire 202
London & Lancashire Fire
   Insurance Co. 201
London & N. W. Railway 360
Longton Hall 157, 158
Lor Three Legs! 325
Lorin, G. 345
Loupot, C. 346
Love on the Tiles 324
Low Life 325
Lucas 42, 43
Lucas, E. 105
Lucky Dream 128
Lucky Lesters Lone Hand 133
Ludwigsburg 412
Lyons Cakes 12, 13
Lyric 219

McAdam, John 47
McAlmon, Robert 71
McBean, Angus 319
MacDonald, George 107
Macfarlane Lang 66
Mackintosh, Charles R. 400
McPherson, Robert 314
Magic Catalogues 248-250
Magnet, The 134
Maillol, Aristide 75
Major, Ann 380
Malevich, K. 344
Mallard Duck 164
Man Ray 320
Manners, Katherine 34
Mansard 182
Mappin & Webb 365
Maps 251-255
Marathon 220
Marchese Ficino 32
Marinot 77
Marion 95
Marklin 279, 283
Marlborough 99
Marliave, F. de 338
Marque, A. 177
Marseille, Armand 176
Marsh, H.G.C. 106
Marshall, John 106
Martens, Friedrich Von 318
Martin Brothers 257
Martin, Vernis 199, 398
Martinware 257
Mary Gregory 258
Mary, Queen of Scots 34, 36,
   156
Masatami 304
Masks 256
Mason Decoy Co. 161, 165
Masons 103
Massachusetts 440
Match Box Labels 259-264
Match Cases 265
Match Strikers 266-269
Maurois, Andre 72
Mayer Bros. 348
Mayer, T. J. & J. 13
Meccano 168, 169
Medals 270-272
Medical 273
Meissen 59, 158, 411, 415
Mekuri Fuda 99
Mene, P. J. 80
Merganser Hen 163

445

Merganser Drake 163, 164
Meriton, Samuel 305
Merritt 429
Merryweather & Sons 43
Mickey Mouse 97 171-174
Middies, The 123
Midland Railway 360
Miller, H. 342
Millet, Jean-Francois 32
Millikin & Lawley's 250
Mills, Nathaniel 398, 432, 433
Milne, A. A. 104
Minerals 274
Minerva 97
Miniature Furniture 275
Miniatures 276-277
Minox 93
Minton 158, 416
Missus is Master 325
Mitchell, Madison 161
Mitchell, Mary 186
Model of Laxey, The 325
Model Planes 278
Model Ships 279-281
Model Trains 282, 283
Modesty 193
Moloch, B. 338
Money Banks 287-288
Monroe, Marilyn 145 315 327
Montreal Motorists League 43
Montrose Bank 50
Monzani & Co. 294-295
Moody Bros. 343
Moorcroft 289
Moore, T. Sturge 70
Moose Head 26
Mordan, Samuel & Co. 382, 403
Moreland & Sons Ltd., S. J. 260
Morning Prayer 194
Morrison, J. McW. 285
Morrison, W. 281
Morse's Distemper 13
Moscow School 230
Mosele, J. 419
Mother Goose 104-106
Mottel, H. 338
Mottoware 286
Movado 436, 439
Much Ado About Nothing 194
Mucha 339
Mucha, Alphonse M. 345
Mullen, Chris. 122
Mulls 296
Municipal Buildings 323
Munster, Sebastian 252
Muralt 277
Murray, R. C. & Co. 297
Music Hall Artists 119
Musical Boxes 291-293
Musical Instruments 294
Muso 303
Mustard Pots 296
Mutoscope 25
Myer Myers 83

Nagoya School 303, 304
Nailsea 96
Napier 103
Napoleon I 37, 158
Nash, Edward 276
National Bank 48, 49
National Bus Co. 87
National Insurance Co. of Ireland 201
Naturliches Zauber-Buch 69
Nautical Items 297
Navajo 17-21
Navy Cut 124

Nazi 52
Nazi Memorabilia 298, 299
Neilson, Kay 104
Nelson 30
Nelson Lee, The 133
Nesbit Brothers 85
Netsuke 300-304
New Alliance 123
Newcastle 392
Newman & Guardia 94, 95
Newport 130
Nicole Freres 291, 292
Nightwatchman, The 22
Nile Spinning & Doubling Co. Ltd. 12
Noke 185
North York Rifles 44
Nottingham Militia 46
Novra, Henry 250
Now They'll Blame Me For This 193
Nunn, P. 279
Nutcracker 122
Nutmeg Graters 305
Nymphenburg 399

Ocean Greyhounds 116
Oceanic Footwear 14
O, Do Leave Me A Drop 196
Ogdens 11
Old Squaw Drake 161
Omega 438
Optima 250
Organ Boy, The 193
Orphans, The 195
Orsini, Jeanne 176
Ortelius, Abraham 254
Otter 27
Our Best Wishes 193
Oysters, Sir? 193
Ozaki 227

Paisley Banking Co. 48
Pajot, Jean-Baptiste 294
Palekh School 229, 231
Pallard 333
Pall Mall De Luxe 129
Paperweights 306-308
Parian 309
Park Drive 14
Parker, Lloyd 163
Parnell, Charles Stewart 32
Passenger, Charles 167
Passenger Pigeon 65
Patch Boxes 310
Pautrot, F. 81
Peachey, Caroline 107
Pear, John 65
Peerless De Luxe 23
Pekin 396, 397
Pemberton, Samuel 310
Pepoli 32
Peppiatt, K. O. 47
Peppin, R. 296
Peregrine Falcon 65
Perille, J. H. 144
Perkins, Bacon & Petch 47
Perophone 218
Perth Banking Co. 50
Petrouchka 152
Phillips 359
Phoenix Fire Office 202
Photocards 99
Photographs 311-321
Pictorial China 322, 323
Pied-Billed Grebe 161
Pierpoint 437
Pilot, The 135
Pin Boxes 324, 325
Pin Cushions 331

Pins Madame? 324
Pintail Drake 161
Pintail Hen 161
Pin-Up Girls 115
Pin-Up Magazines 326-327
Pioneer, The 135
Piper 42
Pipes 328-330
Piquet, Audemars 438
Pisan Armour 29
Pissarro, Camille 32
Pistols 332, 333
Plates 334, 335
Playball 23
Player's Medium Navy Cut 127
Please Sir, 197
Plimer 277
Pluck 135
Pocahontas 79
Polar Bear 27
Polbor 344
Polyphones 336
Ponsam, Harald D. 338
Portal, Abraham 59
Postcards 337-342
Posters 343-346
Pot Lids 347, 348
Poultry 116
Powder Flasks 349
Powell 92
Powell & Hamner 43
Prams 350
Pratt, F. & R. & Co. 347
Prattware 351
Preiss, F. 238
Prestwich 95
Price, S. F. 283
Prout, John Skinner 71
Pub Signs 353
Puleston, Sir Richard 33
Pullars of Perth 13
Purcell Nobbs 414
Puritan Soap 14
Purses 354
Purvis, Tom 345
Pussy Shooter 23, 24

Queen Mary 116
Queen's Regt. 44
Queen's Royal 46
Quilts 355-357
Quycke, John 330

Rabery & Delphieu 178
Rackham, Arthur 104
Radio Fun 133
Radios 358, 359
Radio Times 12
Railwayana 362, 363
Railway Tickets 360, 361
Raleigh 370
Raschka, P. 340
Rathkeale Church 322
Rattles 364
Rawlings & Sumner 305
Razors 365
Reason Why, The 113
Rebus Cards 99
Record Watch Co. 437, 438
Red Ashay 97
Red Ditch 219
Regimental Standards 116
Reily, John 305
Rejlander, O. G. 317
Reliable Toy Co. 178
Remington-Rider 332
Returning At One O'Clock In The Morning 194
Reynolds, J. 34

Ricci, Nini 145, 147
Richards 93
Richmond, Thos. 276
Rich Uncle 124
Ridley, Humphrey 71
Rifle Brigade 44
Road Map of Scotland 117
Robbing The Male (Mail) 192
Roberts Navy Cut 123
Robertson's Golly Badges 366, 367
Robin 125
Robin Starch 12
Robins, John 305
Robinson, George 109
Robinson, Susan 109
Rockingham 187, 413
Rock 'n Roll 368-376
Roettier, Norbert 399
Rohmer 178
Rolex 437, 439
Rolex Prince 439
Rolls 437
Rolls Royce 97
Ronalds, Hugh 75
Rose 125
Rose, P. G. 282
Rouch, W. W. 92
Rowntrees 15
Roy, Campbell 33
Royal Automobile Club 42
Royal Bengal Fusiliers 45
Royal Daylight 15
Royal Dux 377
Royal Exchange 201
Royal Exchange Assurance 203
Royal Manchester Exchange 324
Royal West Kent 45
Royal Worcester 157
R.S.O. Records Inc. 369
Rudall Carte & Co. 295
Rudge Whitworth 63
Ruini, Carlo 74
Ruskin Pottery 378
Rutherston, Albert 151

Sabino 97
Sade, Donathien 37
Sakashi 427
Salamander Fire Office Soc. 202
Saltios 18
Samplers 379-381
Sanbourne, Linley 104
Sander, August 319
Sander & Crowhurst 95
Sandor, Baronne 152
Sandpiper 163
Saratoga Springs 319
Satsuma 187, 334, 413
Savery, Thomas 75
Scent Bottles 382, 383
Scheidt, George Anton 120
Schmidt, Bruno 176, 178
Schmidt, Ernst 349
Schoemau & Hoffmeister 41
Schoenhut, Albert 176
Schulze 43
Schutze, Eva Watson 318
Scott, Captain 118
Scott, W. H. 73
Screen Stars 23
Scrimshaw 384
Sea Eagle 65
Seals 385
Segalle, I. 153
Selo Film 13
Seq, Henry Le 318
Sert, Jose-Maria 152

Setright 84-89
Sevres 158, 413
Shakespeare's House 323
Shakudo 427
Shamming Sick 195
Shaw, Bernard 30
Shaw, John 433
Shells 386
Shepard Hardware Co. 288
Shepherd, Ernest 104
Sheringham, G. 150
Shibuichi 426
Shigemasa 304
Shigetsune 234
Shiomi Masanari 234
Ship Bank 49
Shoes 387
Shop Signs 388
Shourds, Harry 163
Shropshire Election 137
Shunko 304
Sibley, Richard 296
Siebe, Gorman & Co. 297
Signed Photographs 389-391
Silex Multiplier 204
Silvestre, Theophile 32
Simmons, Jane 380
Simon & Halbig 179
Sinclair Tropical 94
Sinclair, Una 95
Sioux 16-18, 20, 21
Slag Glass 392
Slingeland, Pieter Van 276
Smith, Edward 433
Smith, S. 42
Smith's Glasgow Mixture 15
Smook, Hendrik 43
Snooker Table 156
Snuff Bottles 393-397
Snuff Boxes 398, 399

Soakes, F. 419
Soho 92
Sohutamarko 314
Solo 218
Solomons Temple 155
Somerfield, Signor T. 249
Somerset & Dorset Joint
    Railway 360
Sommer, G. 312
Songster Bronze Pick-Up 217
Sonrel, Elizabeth 341
Soten 426
South Wales News 15
Sovereign Trutone 220
Sowerby, M. 339, 342
Speed 113
Speed, John 251, 253
Spillers 15
Spode 187
Spoons 400, 401
Sporting Memorabilia 402, 403
Sporting Personalities 118
Spratt's Dog Food 14
Spratt's Mixed Ovals 11
Squirrel 27
St. Bruno 13
St. Ives 243
St. Julien 11
St. Louis 307, 308
St. Mary's 322
St. Paul's 155
Staffordshire 189, 402, 403,
    412, 413
Staffordshire Figures 404, 405
Stag's Head 26, 97
Stanley Rule & Level Co. 419
Star of the World 125
Starley, James 62
Stars of Screen & Stage 118
States of Guernsey 47

Stechen, Edward 319
Steelcraft 421
Steiner 181
Steiner, Jules 177, 180
Steiner Patent 179, 181
Stereoscope 23, 25
Stevengraphs 406-409
Stevens, Thomas 406
Stevenson, Robert L. 109
Stewart, Alexander 36
Stop Your Tickling Jock 197
Strange Craft 114
Strange's Oil 12
Stuart, J. F. E. 33
Stubbs, George 73
Suffolk & General 203
Sun Fire Office 202, 203
Sunlight Soap 12
Superman 108
Surprise, The 135, 194
Sutton 92
Swans Electric Lighting
    Co. 188
Swansea 157
Swansea to Bristol 324
Swell, A. 197
Swift 63
Sylvatone 320

Tank 156
Tanner, Robert 78
Tanzbar 294
Tapley, John 187
Tatsuke Tagamasu 235
Taylor & Perry 432
Taylor, Joseph 401
Taylor, Wm. Howson 378
Tea Caddies 410, 411
Tea House at Glenariffe 323
Teapots 412, 413
Telephones 414
Television 23
Tenner 129
Tenniel 104
Tennis, Germany 365
Test Your Strength 24, 25
Thames Trout 27
That's Funny, Very Funny!
    193
The Companion 217
The Last In Bed To Put
    Out The Light 196
The Melba Needle 218
The Shoemaker In Love 196
The Tungstyle 218
Thimbles 415
Thirsk, K. B. 285
Thistle Bank 48
Thomson, J. 252
Thomson, James Hall 376
Thomson, John 321
Thornton Pickard 94
Three O'Clock In The
    Morning 197
Ticknell, Alexander 399
Tiffany & Co. 200
Tiles 416
Time & Money 114
Tissot, M. 370
Titus, Silius 36
Tlingit 18, 19
Tokyo School 300, 301
Tolkien, J. R. R. 32
Tomahawk 16
Tomomasa 302
Tomoyuki 302
Tonna 277
Toogood, Emma 379
Tools 418, 419
Toulouse-Lautrec, Henri
    De 346

Tower Bridge 156
Town Hall, Portsmouth 323
Toys 420-422
Trafalgar 138
Transport 423-424
Tree, Dolly 153
Treen 425
Tricks & Puzzles 118
Trilleau, G. 338
Tringham, W. 100
Trinquier-Trianon 339
Trotsky, Leon 31
Truly Any Form Is Not Evil
    197
Trumans 353
Trutone 219
Tsubas 426, 427
Tsuishu 235
Tuck, R. 339, 341
Tudric 246
Tunbridgeware 98, 428
Turf 128
Turkish Blend 123
Turner, Thomas 365
Twelve Months After
    Marriage 195
Types of the British Army 118
Typewriters 429
Tyrer, A. 283

Ultimate 86
Ultra 359
Union Bank 49
Union Jack, The 133
Unite, George 121
United Match Industries
    Ltd. 260
Universal, Geneve 437
Universal Juwel 94

Vacheron & Constantin 436, 439
Valentine Cards 430, 431
Vallotton, F. 338
Veale, P. 278
Vichy 39
Vicky 175
Victor, The 135
Vielmetier, Philip 421
Vienna 334
Vienna Du Paquier 157, 334
Vinaigrettes 432, 433
Visscher, Nicolaus 251
Voigtlander 93
Voloz, J. 341
Voodoo Kiss, The 321
Voyez, Jean 442
Vulcan 358
Vy Sarah You're Drunk 195

Wade 424
Waldegrave, Captain 30
Walker, John 265
Walker, Johnnie 142
Walking Sticks 434
Wallace, G. E. 164
Wallis, Thomas 91
Walpole, H. 30
Walter, A. 306
Ward Bros. 161, 162
Ward, David 162
Warwick, E. R. 280
Watches 436-439
Watchstands 435
Watcombe 286
Waterhouse 93
Waterloo Shako 46
Watkins, C. E. 321
Watson, W. 93
Watson & Son 93
Watts, Digby 32

Weatherly, George 104
Weathervanes 440
Wedgwood/Whieldon 412
Weegee 315, 316, 318, 320,
    321
Weiner Werkstatte 382
Weiss, John & Son 273
Wells 171
Wells, H. G. 75
West of Scotland Insurance
    Co. 203
Western Bank 50
Wet Reception 194
Wexford Hounds 26
What Is Home Without A
    Mother-in-Law 197
What Peace When The Old
    Girl Sleeps 195
Wheat, Saml. 91
When A Man's Married His
    Troubles Begin 194
Whieldon 412
Whistles 441
Whistler, James McN. 36
Whistler, John 315, 316
Whistler, Rex 152
Whitan Co. 421
White, Bob 162, 164
White, G. 160
White Horse 122
White May 11
Whittingham, John 160
Whittington, Dick 153
Whittuck, Saml. 77
Who Is Coming? 197
Wiers 144
Wiggin 346
Wild Flower 118
Wilkes Sprey Brand 204
Wilkinson Ltd. 130
Willebrews 84, 89
William IV 35
Williams 429
Williams, T. R. 315
Willingham, Ann R. 381
Willmore, Joseph 398
Willoughby, Hugh 153
Willis Good, J. 80
Wills 12
Wills, W. D. & H. O. 112
Winthorp, John 30
Wittop, Freddy 152
Wizard, The 133
Wolverine Supply & Mfg.
    Co. 422
Woman's Head 97
Women On War Work 118
Wonder Woman 109
Wonderful Century 113
Wood, Ralph 442
Woodlands 16, 17, 19-21
Woodworth, Elizabeth 379
Woolf, Virginia 37
Worcester 68, 158, 413
Worcester Fire Office 1790 202
World Fair 24
W. S. 433
Wucai 335

Yagerphone 219
Yapp & Woodward 433
York & Lancaster Regt. 46
Yosemite 321
Yoshitomo 238
You Dirty Boy 194
Young, Vernon 122

Zeiss 95
Zinkeisen, Doris 150
Zodia 23
Zonophone 222